Organising during the
Coronavirus Crisis

Mike Healy

Organising during the Coronavirus Crisis

The Contradictions of Our Digital Lives

Mike Healy
Chenon, France

ISBN 978-981-19-1941-1   ISBN 978-981-19-1942-8   (eBook)
https://doi.org/10.1007/978-981-19-1942-8

Cover illustration: Maram_shutterstock.com

This Palgrave Macmillan imprint is published by the registered company Springer Nature Singapore
Pte Ltd.
The registered company address is: 152 Beach Road, #21-01/04 Gateway East, Singapore 189721,
Singapore

This book is dedicated to Martine, Gilles, Claudine, Delphine, Tiffany, Sébastian, and Christine G, who helped me out in my moments of need. In memory of Dennis. He should have been here to see this.

Acknowledgements

COVID-19 is more than a virus. It is also a journey that has yet to be completed. I have had the privilege to share part of this journey with those who consented to be interviewed for this book and who agreed to share their thoughts and concerns with me and, by extension, the readers of this book. So, my first thanks must go to them. I hope I have preserved their presence in the following narrative as people rather than simply as subjects for study. I believe their voices speak to us all about our experience during the pandemic.

I would also like to thank Marion and Ananda at Palgrave Macmillan for all their patience and help in getting this book to fruition. Thanks, should also go to the peer reviewers for their positive and helpful feedback.

A short comment of process is required. I believe every researcher should clearly state their approach to their work. I am a naturalist materialist, who embraces Marxism as a social theory and who is a revolutionary socialist in practice.

Finally, I thank Joy, for her patience, encouragement, and criticism, and Shayniese. Their presence during the pandemic made lockdowns an interesting, but mostly, enjoyable, experience. Much love.

You can email me at mikehealy1917@gmail.com if you want to discuss the issues covered in this book.

Contents

Abbreviations

BKU	Bharatiya Kisan Union
BLM	Black Lives Matter
CCI	Cultural and Creative Industries
DTs	Digital Technologies
Ethernet	Hard-Wire Connection between Digital Machines
FIWON	Federation of Informal Workers Organisation of Nigeria
IFP	Indian Farmers' Protest
MSM	Mainstream Media
PPE	Personal Protection Equipment
SWP	Socialist Workers Party
UK	United Kingdom
US	United States of America
WHO	World Health Organisation
WTO	World Trade Organisation

1

COVID-19, Digital Technologies—A Challenging Time

Introduction

On 31 December 2019, the Chinese Wuhan Municipal Health Commission, issued a statement on cases of "viral pneumonia" in Wuhan. On 11 January 2020, China reported the first deaths from a new form of coronavirus. By April 2022, the World Health Organisation (WHO) reported 497 million confirmed cases of COVID-19 resulting in 6.2 million deaths (WHO, 2022). Even with vaccines, this illness, with all its variants, such as Omicron, will be with us for a long time. Almost every country has reported cases, every region has had deaths. COVID-19 has forced us to change the way we see our world, its relations, its possibilities, and its problems. It has made us confront and understand the complex relationship between economics, politics, the environment, and science, including digital technologies. It has revealed the frailties of our health systems and the weaknesses and priorities of those people and organisations whose primary responsibility should be to safeguard our safety and well-being.

Yet, while COVID-19 hangs like a toxic mist over our lives, life goes on. The additional problems the pandemic creates must be solved.

© The Author(s), under exclusive license to Springer Nature Singapore Pte Ltd. 2022
M. Healy, *Organising during the Coronavirus Crisis*,
https://doi.org/10.1007/978-981-19-1942-8_1

So, as we watched with horror at the mounting death tolls, and their consequential negative impact on economic and social activities, we also witnessed a starburst of creative energies as people sought to overcome the myriad of problems associated with the pandemic lockdowns. Who will ever forget the empty paper plates protest at the United Kingdom Government's denial of free school meals (Ng, 2020)?

Crucial to this process was the use of digital technologies (DTs) which, pre-COVID-19, have also had a negative impact, having been instrumental, for example, in undermining employment possibilities and working conditions for workers across the globe or increasing surveillance. COVID-19 spread through the globalised supply chain facilitated by DTs, technologies that have also facilitated and universalised the development of coping strategies and clinical innovation in the search for virus vaccines. This book explores the contradictory relationship between our response to COVID-19 and DTs by presenting the testimonies of those trying to organise in this moment of stress and in doing so it provides a unique study of the use of DTs within and outside COVID-19 lockdowns. It is international in its scope drawing upon a series of in-depth interviews across a spectrum of areas covering community activism, mental health, trade union organisation, the creative arts, and resistance movements.

This book does not claim to be the definitive work on this subject; indeed, how could it be since the COVID-19 story is a still unfolding drama. I hope more research of this nature is being or will be undertaken since a social history of the development, impact, and response of and to COVID-19 demands a multinational cooperative effort by international scholars from all disciplines. This book has a more modest ambition. It asks if concepts developed by Antonio Gramsci, an Italian communist, in a prison cell almost ninety years ago and contained within a series of handwritten notebooks (some 29 in all), together with Marx's theory of alienation, can be of value in researching and theorising the relationship between COVID-19, social movements and DTs. I believe the combination of these complementary concepts provides an effective range of tools for comprehending the impact of and the response to COVID-19. They encourage us to delve beneath the surface appearance of events, to excavate and reveal the underlying impulses driving those responses thereby enabling us to recognise the relationship between seemingly unrelated instances. They urge us to explore the primary relations involved in these events and to regard them as both problematic and transitionary, allowing us to see the total COVID-19 experience as a contradictory phenomenon; it is both a debilitating and facilitating condition. By engaging with the dialectical contradictions associated with technologies, inequality, and crises, the book examines the effectiveness of DTs in filling the voids created by the pandemic. Through a series of international qualitative in-depth interviews, it investigates the agencies, structures, and relations embodied in the use of DTs in this moment of uncertainty. I hope this book will vindicate the use of Gramsci and Marx in this context and encourage scholars to draw upon their works to inform their research in this area.

The research upon which this book is based was initially focused on writing a journal paper about the way trade union organisers were using DTs to facilitate ongoing union work during the lockdown. During discussions with trade union activists, I became acutely aware of a range of other issues that needed to be covered; trade union activists can also be poets or concerned with the relationship between words and dance, poets and theatre activists can be concerned with issues of mental health, those concerned with mental health can be campaigners for other issues and so forth. We are not one-dimensional beings. Then the *I can't breathe* and *Black Lives Matter* movements, protesting at police racism, brutality, and shootings, erupted onto the streets and across the digital space during Summer 2020. This was followed by the Indian farmers' protests, the largest protest movement the world has seen. How could these movements be ignored in any study concerned with COVID-19 and DTs? I needed to widen my focus to move beyond a one topic paper to encompass a range of seemingly disparate experiences which eventually shaped the structure of this book.

Any attempt seeking to extensively document people's experiences during COVID-19, inspired by the oral tradition (Hampton et al., 1995; Sitrin & Sembrar, 2020; Terkel, 2005) should be applauded, and encouraged. It may have been enough to record people's experiences during the pandemic but for their experiences to have an enduring legacy, I believe we need to theorise their voices. This is the ambition of this book and hopefully, the stories it contains will resonate far beyond those who participated in the research. This book shows people in motion during COVID-19, illuminating the contradiction where lockdown, self-isolation, and shielding created the conditions that fuelled an attempt to use DTs to overcome seclusion and to enhance social organisation. The stories reveal how the use of DTs flourished during the pandemic crisis, facilitating new ways to communicate yet they also throw into sharp relief the inadequacies of these technologies. They indicate that while form may change, content is rooted in the ongoing contradictory nature of people's experiences. It also argues that while the surge of creative endeavour based on the use of DTs sought to challenge and overcome the consequences of the pandemic, the prevailing economic and political priorities remained in place effectively corralling the potential of DTs.

COVID-19 does not simply denote an illness. The pandemic is an all-embracing phenomenon with physical, psychological, political, social, and economic ramifications. There is an interplay between all these aspects that determines the trajectory of the illness and its impact on our lives, and any consideration of COVID-19 has to be placed within an overarching frame determined by the prior and ongoing duel crises concerned with the global economy and environmental degradation. Appreciating these concerns highlights the necessity of addressing the relation between totality, mediation, and immediacy. The history of COVID-19 indicates that while it is a universal condition, our direct experience of the virus and how we respond are conditioned by time, place, immediate political priorities, and ongoing economic imperatives.

After outlining the trajectory of the pandemic and placing it within the overarching economic and environmental crises that existed going into 2020, this chapter moves on to consider the development of self-isolation, the impact of lockdown, the key features of the dominant narrative, and the developing critique of that narrative. The chapter will also outline the key concepts which provide the overarching analytical framework of the study. All the participants in the book were initially contacted by email, followed by an interview using Zoom. The interviews were transcribed using Otter.ai, edited, with the edited texts being sent back to the participants for their confirmation that the edited interviews were an accurate representation of their views. In many instances, a follow-up interview was possible. Finally, participants in each chapter were sent a draft of the relevant chapter enabling them to see how their contribution dovetailed with those of others and to allow for any last-minute changes.

The chapters are structured as follows. Chapter two covers DTs, the pandemic and organising labour and opens with an overview examining the impact of the pandemic on employment drawing upon a range of secondary research. It will focus on issues including the impact of pandemic on work, implications for Global South—for example, remittances, urban–rural migration, the implications for Global North, such as employment, unemployment, and safe-working. Included in this discussion will be reference to the impact neoliberalism has had on the work experience. It will also cover the response of governments, employers, management, organised labour, and the implications for precarious labour. The discussion will also reference the impact of COVID-19 on digital labour. This will be followed by a discussion based on a series of interviews with labour activists from: Australia, UK, Bangladesh, and the US.

Chapter 3 looks at DTs, the pandemic and mutual aid groups and covers issues such as the impact of the pandemic on community activity, coping with the pandemic in the local environment, the emergence of mutual aid groups, and the consequences for existing community networks. It places these developments within the overarching imposition of neoliberal strategies for community support (Bustad & Andrews, 2020). It will include reference to the response of policy makers, the consequences for community support practitioners, and the evolution of specific forms of community action as the pandemic spread. The discussion will then shift to focus of four case studies of mutual aid groups in the United Kingdom and United States.

Chapter 4 considers DTs, the pandemic, and mental health and opens with general introduction on the impact of the pandemic on mental health, using secondary research, within an overall context of the increasing privatisation of health services. This will include reference to the developing mental health crisis (Kovaceic, 2021). It will focus on issues including stress in isolation, the impact on outreach work, and stress at work and will outline the response of policy makers and mental health practitioners to mental health issues. The literature concerning COVID-19 and mental health was beginning to emerge in early 2020 (Rajkumar, 2020) and the chapter incorporates reference to most recent texts. It revolves around a series of interviews with community organisers concerned with mental health in the United Kingdom and the impact of DTs on organising around mental health projects.

Chapter 5 examines DTs, the pandemic and creative cultural activity by discussing artistic endeavour under the shadow of the pandemic. It includes reference to the response of governmental and non-governmental organisations to the crisis in the creative arts. This Chapter will also examine the imaginative ways practitioners in these areas reacted and adapted to the conditions posed by the lockdowns. The chapter develops to consider the experience of creative activists in England, Wales, the Netherlands, and Brazil.

Chapter 6 covers DTs, the pandemic and resistance. While initial mobilisations were focused on the ramifications of COVID-19 on health services and health workers, there were other manifestations of resistance many of which were directly connected to events occurring during the pandemic. Others were linked to ongoing struggles. The chapter covers both aspects by referencing the *I can't breathe* and *Black Lives Matter* movements that emerged during 2020, the Indian farmers' protest, the protests following the death of Sarah Everard, and the campaigns to preserve street markets in Nigeria. Chapter 7 is the conclusion, critique, and implications for future research related to that covered in this book. It draws together the dominant themes emerging from the discussions within the previous Chapters as they relate to DTs. It focuses on the experiences of the participants to examine whether concepts and theories referenced in this chapter clarify the use people made of DTs during the lockdown moments.

A comment on structure is required. There is a strong temptation to consider the impact of COVID-19 on the Global South and the Global North separately. However, COVID-19 is an international phenomenon that does not recognise our economic, social, political, or national categories and boundaries. For the virus, whatever our gender, wherever we live, whatever language we speak, whatever our skin pigmentation, or our sexual orientation, all of us are merely potential hosts. It is for this reason I have chosen to speak about COVID-19 from a global perspective while recognising that its actual expression is mediated through immediate circumstances. I believe the stories in this book will resonate with all communities seeking to cope with the pandemic. Of course, while the virus ignores national frontiers, access to appropriate medication and treatments does not. COVID-19 has made us aware that we all should be internationalists for the virus cannot be eradicated in one country unless it is done so in all countries. Yet dominant political and economic imperatives have hampered universal access to vaccines; perhaps there is another book to be written about people's experiences in trying to access vaccines.

This book covers an experience that is continually evolving and therefore subject to continuous research. While every effort has been made to incorporate references to recent pertinent texts, I am sure that readers will appreciate that it has not been possible to include references to other relevant research that may have been published between the time of submitting the manuscript in early 2022 and final publication. It has also not been possible to expand the discussion to include COVID-19 and the war in the Ukraine.

Development of the Pandemic

Each day WHO publishes the number of recorded cases and deaths (WHO, 2022):

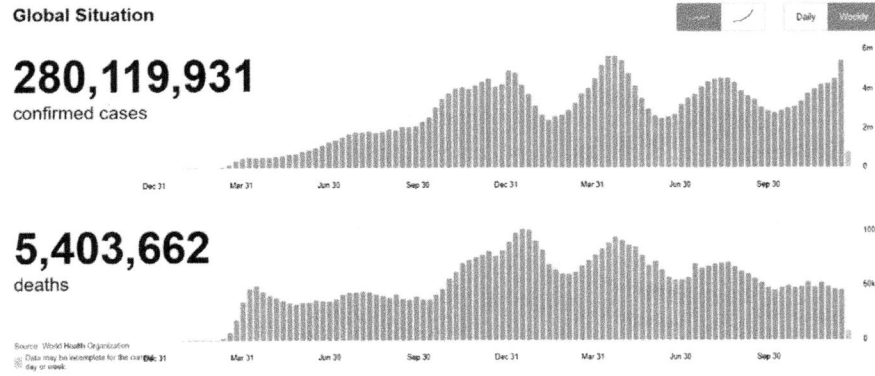

The statistics from the WHO show that as of April 2022, the pandemic had at least 5 waves, and while the Delta variant is the dominant form worldwide, the latest Omicron variant is the most transmissible. The numbers published by the WHO are staggering but for Joey Traywick, a nurse in Montana, USA, each case was personal, and he has held the hand of at least 23 people who have died because of COVID-19. At the start of the pandemic, he missed the death of one patient and thought

> I'm never going to let that happen again.... It snuck up on me, and it surprised me because it's so relentless. ... I (no longer) miss it. If I have to stay late after working, if it means doing it on my day off. They're not going to pass alone on my unit. Again. None of them. (Gutierrez & Gonzalez, 2020)

It is stories like Joey's that remind us that behind the statistics, the lives of millions of people have been and will continue to be, shattered by the virus. Equally, the stats alone do not show the wider context and impact of the pandemic.

The Economic Context

The Organisation for Economic Cooperation and Development (OECD) has presented a stark portrait of the pandemic's economic consequences. "The COVID-19 pandemic has triggered the deepest economic recession in nearly a century, threatening health, disrupting economic activity, and hurting well-being and jobs" (OECD, 2020). However, prior to the onset of the pandemic, the world economy was already in a fragile condition arising from the reverberations from the 2008 crash and the ongoing crisis of profitability (Carchedi & Roberts, 2018) leading to the International Monetary Fund (IMF) to record in February 2020 that "the global economy is far from solid ground. While some uncertainties have receded, new ones have emerged. The truth is that uncertainty is becoming the new normal" (Georgieva, 2020). By October 2020 the IMF was predicting a 4.4% decline in the global economy. Partial and total lockdowns, cuts in income, depressed international trade, meant reduced consumption and investment and while there was some economic pick-up in Summer 2020, the pandemic's subsequent waves re-enforced the negative economic consequences. The pandemic has also had a unique negative impact of economic activity. In previous depressions, manufacturing was hardest hit, but with COVID-19, it is the service sector. The IMF recorded that "the public health response needed to slow transmission, together with behavioural changes, has meant that service sectors...particularly wholesale and retail trade, hospitality, and arts and entertainment—have seen larger contractions" (IMF, 2020a). The advanced economies, and emerging markets and deverloping countries, were expected to experience a 5.8 and 3.3% cut in growth, respectively. There were of course variations both between and within different economic regions with India, Spain, Italy witnessing double digit cuts in growth closely followed by the United Kingdom, Mexico, South Africa, and France.

By the end of 2021, the OECD was making cautious predictions about slow but positive post-pandemic economic growth eventually achieving pre-pandemic levels but with greater indebtedness and subdued growth. Then the Omicron variant arrived leading economists to dramatically revise downwards future global economic growth with deep uncertainty about prospects through 2022. The Omicron economic shock will impact on incomes, expenditure, and consequently, on employment projections (Torry & Harrison, 2021). Each new wave or variant brings with it additional stresses on the world economy and therefore individual economies, further intensifying already established inequalities within the global financial system, hitting hardest those countries with low vaccination rates and poor healthcare infrastructures. The economic outlook is bleak with steep increases in debt, particularly in emerging markets and developing economies (World Bank, 2021). This situation is going to continue for the foreseeable future, with the world economy "expected to grow around 3.5-4.0% in real terms – a significant slowing compared to 2021 (down 25% on the rate). Moreover, the advanced capitalist economies are forecast to grow at less than 4% in 2022 and at less than 2.5% in 2023" (Roberts, 2022).

The Environmental Context

The dire economic situation was one half of the overall adverse condition when COVID-19 hit. The news during the Summer and Autumn of 2019 was dominated by wildfires in Australia and America burning out of control. Davis noted in reference to California, "A world set on fire by climate change has unleashed a dangerous transformation of plant ecology…A wet winter and early spring may mesmerise us with extravagant displays of flowering plants, but they also produce bumper crops of grasses and weeds that are then baked in our furnace summers to become fire starters when the devil winds return" (Davis, 2020). While some places burned, others flooded. In summer 2019, monsoon flooding and landslides in Nepal, India, and Bangladesh displaced more than 7 million people. Elsewhere, an unusually extensive dust storm from Africa's Saharan Desert has travelled across the Atlantic Ocean with NASA satellites showing the mantle of dust moving over the Gulf of Mexico, into Central America and over part of the eastern Pacific Ocean. NASA also records trends showing the "extremes in the frequency and magnitude of floods and droughts…[affecting]…everything from local weather to where crops can grow and have consequences that will ripple through communities" (Gray & Merzdorf, 2019).

Before the pandemic hit, the WHO had already anticipated that climate change would result in an additional 250,000 deaths per year between 2030 and 2050 from malnutrition, malaria, diarrhoea, and heat stress (WHO, 2018). Recent evidence suggests that the economic depression associated with COVID-19 led to a reduction in harmful emissions as industrial output fell and travel was curtailed (United Nations Environment Programme, 2021). However, such gains were significantly offset by ongoing environmental degradation which continues to fuel biodiversity loss that, together with intensive food systems, make zoonotic diseases more likely. As the floods in Britain and Brazil during February 2022 showed, the pandemic did not halt environmental degradation and unusual weather patterns. The pandemic lockdowns have also dramatically increased consumption of single-use plastics (European Environment Agency, 2021). There is a symbiotic relationship between climate change and the emergence of diseases such as COVID-19.

Artificial intelligence is championed as an effective tool for combatting climate change (Avelar, 2021). However, the big data processing centres used to compute climate data are part of a digital processing system that make a significant contribution to global warming because of power consumption (Andrae, 2017).

The Impact on Food and Poverty

In October 2020, the World Bank (WB) reported that "the current moment of crisis is extraordinary. No prior disease has become a global threat so quickly as COVID-19. Never have the world's poorest people resided so disproportionately in conflict-affected territories and countries. Changes in global weather patterns induced by human activity are unprecedented" (World Bank, 2021). The WB reports that COVID-19 has led to a reduction in domestic food production with consequent increases in prices resulting in an additional 130 million people facing acute food insecurity on top of the existing 125 million. The WB has estimated that COVID-19 will negatively impact on household incomes. For example, in June 2020, it estimated that COVID-19 would mean an increase of 71 million people in extreme poverty, which is identified with income of $1.90 a day. By October 2020, this figure had been revised upwards to between 88 and 115 million people but by December, the IMF reported that those living in extreme poverty had risen to 124 million with the possibility that it may increase to 150 million. These increases need to be added to the already existing figure of 689 million. An estimated four years have been lost in the effort to reduce global extreme poverty which has increased from 7.8% to 9.1% (Sanchez-Paramo et al., 2021). We are moving into a scenario where upwards of I billion people will be living in extreme poverty at a time when food resources are declining, the world economy is faltering, weather patterns are becoming extreme, COVID-19 variants are becoming more transmissible, and health systems are under extreme stress. Within this global picture there are regional variations with 83% of this increase being in South Asia and Africa.

These then are the key economic, environment, and social features comprising the overarching context within which the pandemic continues to develop. The next section outlines the conceptual tools I have used to undertake the research covered by this book.

Conceptual Tools

The approach taken for this book does not sit comfortably within the parameters of the dominant positivist research paradigm which sees "the world as being flat, undifferentiated and unchanging" (Bhaskar in Bhaskar & Callinicos 2003, p. 98), a criticism particularly pertinent to research within the field of DTs and COVID-19 since both, in terms of technology and the virus, as well as their relation to impact on our activity, are in a state of constant flux. Further, striving to create a closed system of experimentation in an effort to identify influential variables is problematic in a societal context because it denies the notion that any one particular (or set of particulars) is "modified and restricted in various ways because it's operating in relation to all sorts of other powers" (Bhaskar & Callinicos, 2003). Additionally, positivism cannot handle the dynamic interplay in the relation between agency and structure thereby casting serious concerns on its efficacy for researching the impact of and the response to COVID-19 since such research deals precisely with an aspect of the world that is constantly changing and mediated through specific contexts. From the critical perspective, the issues considered here are not intended to form part of the ongoing discussion concerning the nature of Gramsci's work and its place in the cannon of Marxist theory nor to do the same with Marx's theory of alienation. These aspects have been adequately covered elsewhere (Liguori, 2015). The next section opens by re-visiting Marx's theory of alienation.

Marx and Alienation

Marx first addressed the issue of alienation in the *1844 Economic and Philosophic Manuscripts* (Marx, 1970), a text that was not published, in German, until 1932 with the first translation in English appearing in 1959. While the concepts covered in the *Manuscripts* were presented in an abstract manner, Marx returned to the themes in his later works, notably the *Grundrisse* and in sections of *Capital*. He argues that our species being is rooted in our need to transform the world so we can thrive and the process of successful transformation requires a shared, collective effort to achieve this aim. In achieving this goal, we also change our social environment, a practical activity which loops back and transforms ourselves. By collectively changing our world, we see a reflection of ourselves and our relation to society. This is a dynamic interactive process requiring us to constantly re-evaluate and jettison those concepts or ideas which fail to provide satisfactory explanations of the material world and to develop new concepts and theories to fulfil this task. In this creative and innovative environment, ideas and our practical activity are intimately related meaning there is no one fixed *a*historical and *a*social human nature.

Marx argues that when we lose control over both the things we make and our own labour as well as the processes employed in their creation, crucial aspects of capitalist production, we become alienated and express this alienation in two ways. Rather than seeing others as part of a positive shared collective effort, they become competitors and are seen as a threat. The greater the number of people sucked into the production process, the greater the perceived threat. Consequently, we participate in alienating relations. Furthermore, this process entails self-alienation since we look to satisfy our lives in ways removed from the process of work and the products of our labour. Our labour, which should be life affirming, becomes an experience that "as soon as no physical or other compulsion exists, labor is shunned like the plague" (Marx, 1970, p. 111) Alienation is an objective reality that impacts on our practical activity but, because of mediation, it is expressed in specific events driven by material circumstances.

This process is amplified when our labour itself becomes a commodity to be bought and sold (Cox, 1998; Healy, 2020). For Marx, therefore, alienation is more than simply feelings of unease or dissatisfaction. It is the driving force that leads to manifestations of social and political unrest because it is imbedded in the irreconcilable conflictual relation between labour and capital. It is, as Harvey notes, a general oppressive condition shared by us all with its manifestations expressed, because of mediation, in specific contexts and ways (Harvey, 2018). Marx also argues alienation is a contradictory experience since it acted as a facilitator in the transition from previous economic forms to capitalism and creates the conditions enabling the transition from capitalism to a more equitable distribution of resources on a global basis. However, for the present, alienation can prevent the material development of society since it reinforces the imperatives of capital as opposed to the needs of people in general.

In addition, Marx argues that the conditions that create alienation are perpetuated by our own selves. While not having control over what commodities are made nor how they are made, nevertheless, it is workers who make commodities and undertake the work processes used in their production. We forge our own shackles. This is a weakness and a strength since while it is debilitating, it identifies the solution to alienation. If we are the creators of our alienation, then we are also the vehicle for its demise. In coping with the countless problems demanding practical solutions, people confront their alienation by recognising the need to work together in a collective rather than competitive environment.

While Marx's concept of alienation may seem difficult to operationalise in terms of a research agenda, it has been successfully used to theorise DTs and ICT professionals, academics and end-users (Healy, 2020), social work (Ferguson & Lavalette, 2004; Yuill, 2018) and dignity at work (Healy & Wilkowska, 2017). We can see Marx's concept of alienation illuminating the contradictory competitive yet collaborative environment in the search for a COVID-19 vaccine, with for example, the US, UK governments and the European Union forming internal partnerships with private companies to compete internationally with each other in the race for a vaccine. The search for a cure to a global pandemic was hindered as it was reduced to a market place squabble with countries engaging in "vaccine nationalism" (Katz, Weintraub, Bekker, & Brandt, 2021). Collaboration and competition are conflicting activities within capitalist production. The competitive environment also impacted on the digital track and trace technologies. Governments, allied with tech companies, competed with each other rather than co-operating to develop an effective, shared procedure. This resulted in the fiasco linked to the use of Excel spreadsheets for track and trace in the United Kingdom (Landler & Mueller, 2020). Alienation also impacts on the way we see and use DTs. Technologies offer the potential for developing new relationships, for enhancing our scientific understanding of our world, to design and create environmentally friendly machines. Yet they also act as levers of oppression, for increased surveillance, more rigorous control of our working lives, to facilitate egotistical space projects while millions starve, to act as conduits for oppressive and exploitative experiences such as online gambling. The stories in this book provide lived experiences of the alienated, contradictory way we have engaged with DTs during the pandemic.

Gramsci

If Marx's approach to alienation can help theorise the root cause of our experiences of DTs, Gramsci provides the tools that assist us in explaining how people sought to respond to the pandemic. Antonio Gramsci was an Italian Marxist active in the Italian socialist movement from 1917 to his imprisonment by Mussolini in 1926. Prison exacerbated his frail health and he eventually died in 1937. Gramsci did not have access to Marx's *Economic And Philosophic Manuscripts* but because of his active involvement in Italian working class struggles prior to emprisonment, he was well aware of alienation. In 1916 he favourably quoted the remarks of a fellow socialist who said "we must not forget that behind the worker there is still a man there, and we should not remove from him the possibility of broadening the horizons of his spirit, just so that we can enslave him right away; make him machine" (Gramsci, 1916). Towards the end of 1917 he wrote that the working class was "fully aware of its current state of misery….and [is] in a permanent state of turmoil and…chaos" (Gramsci, 1917). His discussion concerning the implemenation of the strict time management strategies of Fordism and Taylorism in the United States, indicates that he considered alienation to reach well beyond the workplace (Gramsci, 2000, p. 275).

Common-Sense and Good Sense

In his television address on 22 September 2020, Boris Johnson, UK Prime Minister said, that "the single greatest weapon can bring to this fight [against COVID-19] is the common-sense of the people themselves". He reiterated this message a month later during a televised address when he urged Britons to live "fearlessly but with common-sense" during the pandemic (Cameron-Chileshe & Payne, 2020). President Macron of France made a similar appeal during his broadcast on 14 October 2020. The US Missouri's Governor Mike Parson called for the use of common-sense to reopen businesses after the initial COVID-19 lockdown (McCarty, 2020). Kaushik Basu, a former chief economist of the World Bank, chief economic adviser to the Government of India and a Professor of Economics at Cornell University, argues that science should be "combined with common-sense to optimize our behavior" in tackling COVID-19 (Basu, 2020). These few examples are indicative of the numerous calls for the use of common-sense to resist the spread and impact of the virus. Yet, the notion of common-sense itself is left hanging in the air, the term simply becoming shorthand for some vague form of behaviour we all should instinctively know and practise. Invoking common-sense also shifts the responsibility for managing the pandemic from official institutions onto the individual. Essentially, the message is: if you get ill it is your fault.

Gramsci saw common-sense as the "beliefs and opinions supposedly shared by the mass of the population" (Crehan, 2016, p. 274). He was, however, was acutely aware of the myriad of forms common-sense can take because it comprises of ideas from the past allied to conceptions of the present rooted in specific contexts and is "the conception of the world which is uncritically absorbed by the various social and cultural environments" (Gramsci, 1971, p. 419). It springs from ideologies which encompass a range of themes and consists of an array of multiple distinct and contradictory notions which are fragmentary and in competition with each other. He argues that "common-sense is a chaotic aggregate of disparate conceptions" (Gramsci, 1971, p. 422) and does so because it derives from characteristics which reflect the people's contradictory alienated experiences of capitalism. The chaotic and disparate nature of common-sense prevents it from providing tools that can reveal the reality of a situation and is unable to provide a reliable guide to activity. Additionally, "common-sense is crudely neophobe and conservative" (Gramsci, 1971, p. 423) seeking to rest within the prevailing dominant set of ideas confirming the present and wanting to maintain the status quo thereby denying the possibility of change. Further, it is "a collective noun, like religion: there is not just one common-sense, for that too is a product of history and a part of the historical process" (Gramsci, 2000, p. 327). In many respects, Gramsci sees common-sense as an essentially romantic, idealist view of the past and an immobilising interpretation of the present.

However, he understands that the ideas framed within his view of common-sense do not simply fall from the sky or arrive by magic in a Twitter feed or Facebook post. They are rooted in the people's actual lived experience and are an attempt to comprehend that experience. We are surrounded by accomplished facts: capitalism and economic crises are real, states exist, national boundaries are in place, political systems exist, and COVID-19 kills people. We interact with economic, political, and social structures, such as hierarchies, which have a history and they can appear as part of the natural order of things. However, because these facts are mediated through specific contexts, they can also appear as being different and isolated from each other, feeding into the common-sense notion, for example, that peoples from diverse countries or cultures have fundamental differences between them. Further, the process of mediation, determined by actual lived experiences, creates that key characteristic of common-sense: it is comprised of contradictory and competing ideas. Therefore, while Gramsci's common-sense is universal, it is not *a*historical, and its universality is manifested in a varied manner. Further, since common-sense is an evolving and mutating condition, it can draw into itself, ideas that, in a previous period, may have been considered strange or critical or radical.

Previous common-sense ideas can be jettisoned to be replaced by those relating to more contemporary developments. The notion that the state should buttress social security and health systems is a common-sense view in many countries, yet these systems were introduced only relatively recently. It seems common-sense now that everyone should have access to DTs, but this too is a recent development. A further defining feature of common-sense is that it is not confined to any one social group. It can often appear that in talking about common-sense, Gramsci was focusing on the mass of the population, but he also talks of common-sense notions residing in, for example, an intellectual milieu. Several overarching key themes integrated into common-sense persist, including the role of the family, differences in intelligence, the function of the free market to distribute scarce resources, notions of hierarchy, the seemingly natural place of capitalist relations, the need for state structures and the competitive nature of social relations. All these are framed within the concept of common-sense.

Despite the varied, shifting, and contradictory nature of common-sense, it can seem to present an impenetrable block of ideas which are reluctant of embrace change and hold back social development. It becomes a composite of ideas that dominate political, economic, social, and cultural discourse which Gramsci conceptualises as a "moment of hegemony" (Gramsci, 2000, p. 195). However, it is a block in appearance only since the conflicting and competing sets of ideas within common-sense, create fissures and cracks undermining its intellectual authority. Our need to constantly grapple with serious difficult practical problems force us to continually evaluate how effective are our conceptions in explaining events and phenomena. Gramsci argues that by doing so, we come to recognise that common-sense is a speculative enquiry unable to fully explain the world. Confronting and seeking to overcome problems presented by material reality creates a process that demands a continual re-assessment of common-sense ideas.

Thus, we reach out beyond common-sense to seek a more plausible explanatory framework with which to understand our condition. It is this "necessity which gives a conscious direction to one's activity" (Gramsci, 2000, p. 329). Thus, a person can have two contradictory positions at the same time "one which is implicit in his [her] activity, and which in reality unites him with all his [her] fellow-workers in the practical transformation of the real world; and one, superficially explicit or verbal, which he [she] has inherited from the past and uncritically absorbed" (Gramsci, 2000, p. 343). Appreciating this clash of contradictions enables Gramsci to identify the process that can overcome the inadequacies of common-sense. The characteristics comprising common-sense provide the environment within which a reformulated common-sense, one that is not a composite of contradictory and competitive perceptions, can emerge providing viable concepts that can grasp material reality and which are "'historically true' to the extent that they become concretely -i.e. historically and socially -universal" (Gramsci, 2000, p. 347).

For Gramsci, good sense is an emergent concept which is "the healthy nucleus that exists in 'common-sense' … and which deserves to be made more unitary and coherent" (Gramsci, 2000, p. 329). It is a democratic and non-idealistic development as it arises from changes in, and rejects misleading perceptions of, people's actual experiences rather than being imported from without. This is an important formulation because it recognises that while common-sense and good sense are different, they are interdependent. Their relation is determined and manifested by specific contexts and from the confused chaotic strands that characterise common-sense, there can eventually emerge a single set of concepts bringing clarity to our material reality. This is a process where common-sense, good sense, and the development of abstract concepts pivot around and are influenced by material conditions. In effect, good sense is the critical analysis of common-sense and one which increasingly draws upon the existing critical concepts. "First of all, therefore, it must be a criticism of 'common-sense', basing itself initially, however, on common-sense in order to demonstrate that 'everyone' is a philosopher and that it is not a question of introducing from scratch a scientific form of thought into everyone's individual life, but of renovating and making 'critical' an already existing activity" (Gramsci, 2000, p. 332). This is an important perspective since it recognises that while there is a need to theorise activity, an understanding of that activity is simply not possible without people taking practical action in the first instance. Practical activity encourages questions about existing ideas, priorities, and structures.

However, the process through which an internally coherent set of ideas, designed to provide an understanding of society, emerges is neither spontaneous nor accidental. Gramsci argues that "everyone is a philosopher, though in his [her]own way, and unconsciously since even in the slightest manifestation of any intellectual activity....is contained a specific conception of the world" (Gramsci, 1971, p. 323) Unchallenged, this philosophy resides within the confused and contradictory realm of common-sense. Yet the problems that we face deriving from our material circumstances encourage us to develop a critical awareness of our existing conceptions and to take an active part in the way the world develops. As Gramsci argues "one's conception of the world is a response to certain specific problems posed by reality which are quite specific and 'original' in their immediate relevance" (Gramsci, 1971: 324). This impels people to look beyond their immediate knowledge base to acquire different concepts and skills. This is particularly true at times of crisis when common-sense ideas are put to the test and found futile for developing an effective plan of action. Under circumstances of stress, common-sense ideas fracture along a myriad of directions creating the space for more radical, critical perspectives to emerge. A good example of this process was the publication in April 2020 by *Policy Link* of their report *Principles for a Common-Sense, Street-Smart Recovery* (Policy Link, 2020). While common-sense handwashing was being proposed by the British Prime Minister, Boris Johnson, organisations like *Policy Link* were advocating radical measures such as hospitals and healthcare facilities clearly stating, in all languages, that immigration status will not be questioned and ensuring that immigration enforcement officials would be prevented from entering health facilities. The phrase "common-sense" has yet to be discarded but these proposed measures sprang from a developing "good sense".

The transition from common-sense to good sense creates a greater audience for formerly marginalised political perspectives or practices which were previously associated with relatively small currents. However, this operates on two levels. Firstly, there is the "contrast between thought and action, i.e., the co-existence of two conceptions of the world, one affirmed in words and the other displayed in effective action" (Gramsci, 2000, p. 328). The second, which derives from the first, is the developing conflict between existing common-sense and an emerging good sense. This outcome of this contested terrain cannot be confidently predicted. Gramsci's approach to the relationship between common-sense and good sense feeds into his discussion about hegemony.

Hegemony

For Gramsci, the concept of hegemony, is the idea that the economic interests of one class must reach beyond the economic frame to embrace "the sphere of political direction through a system of class alliances" (Forgacs in Gramsci, 2000, p. 423). Gramsci shows this in two ways. Firstly, by using specific historical moments to illustrate how one class develops a dominant position within a bloc formed with other classes. Taking the French Revolution of 1789 as an example, he argues that hegemony can initially be conceived as an alliance between oppressed classes in conflict with an existing ruling elite but with one class providing the political and organisational leadership. In this specific instance, "rural France accepted the hegemony of Paris; in other words, it understood that in order definitively to destroy the old regime it had to make a bloc with the most advanced elements of the Third Estate" and to accept its leadership (Gramsci, 1971, p. 79). The French revolution resulted in "the permanent hegemony of the bourgeoisie over the rest of the population" (Forgacs in Gramsci, 2000, p. 260). Secondly "it is qualitatively modified: hegemony comes to mean 'cultural, moral, and ideological' leadership over allied and subordinate groups" (Forgacs in Gramsci, 2000, 423). However, even in this latter sense, Gramsci emphasises the process is rooted in the economic interests of the dominant class with hegemony in the social and cultural spheres validating its priorities and imperatives. He also ties hegemony to the development and nature of the state. "The 'normal' exercise of hegemony in what became the classic terrain of the parliamentary regime is characterised by the "combination of force and consent variously balancing one another, without force exceeding consent too much. Indeed, one tries to make it appear that force is supported by the consent of the majority, expressed by the so-called organs of public opinion newspapers and associations - which are therefore, in certain situations, artificially increased in number" (Gramsci, 2000, p. 261). As with his approach to common-sense, Gramsci identifies hegemony as a contradictory process, it can be progressive and conservative. It is a process, rooted in historical contexts, which develops and is shaped, mediated, by the specific conditions of those moments. Gramsci argues that stresses on a given system create conditions resulting in the cracking of hegemonic structures. "A 'crisis of authority' is spoken of this is precisely the crisis of hegemony, or crisis of the state as a whole" (Gramsci, 2000, p. 218). Further, he argues that another consequence created during periods of crises and chaos is that people "become even more ordered in their thinking, they become ever more conscious of their power, of their ability to take on social responsibility and to become the judges of their own fate" (Gramsci, 1917). Once again, Gramsci is describing contested terrain resulting from the clash between old or vague concepts and a changing reality. It is in the context of common-sense, good sense, and hegemony that Gramsci considers the role of intellectuals as a social group.

Intellectuals

Gramsci is careful to argue that any discussion of the intellectuals cannot be *a*historical and must therefore take note of specific contexts. As Forgacs notes, Gramsci refused to "leave the terrain of concrete historical, social and cultural realities for abstraction and reductionist theoretical models" (Forgacs in Gramsci, 2000, p. 12). By drawing upon specific examples, Gramsci approaches the concept of the intellectual initially in two ways. The first sees the role of intellectuals as the buttress of conventional wisdom. Using the ecclesiastical and military hierarchies as concrete examples of this social group, Gramsci argues the importance of recognising that while both the composition of and general sets of ideas held by these groups are subject to change, since they are rooted in specific historical moments, the essential function of the intellectual core remains the same. As he notes "various categories of traditional intellectuals experience through an '*esprit de corps*' their uninterrupted historical continuity and their special qualification, they thus put themselves forward as autonomous and independent of the dominant social group" (Gramsci, 1971, p. 7). However, this perception is problematic since this social group while being the mechanism for delivering hegemony of existing, common-sense, ideas is also tasked with ushering in new concepts that can provide adequate explanations of a changing reality. Gramsci's formulation is helpful because it recognises that the traditional bloc of intellectual ideas can also be contradictory. However, Gramsci also maintains that no matter what the contradictions of this social group may be, ultimately it comprises the "political and cultural intermediaries... [whose function is] maintaining and reproducing a given economic and social order" (Gramsci, 2000, p. 300).

The second group of intellectuals are those that are associated with a movement that seeks to challenge existing political and social traditions, and who sharply articulate the critical argument against common-sense ideas. The composition of this group can be the development of a new strand of intellectuals together with those who have detached themselves from previous allegiances. This is the intellectual strata whose primary function is to provide an emergent class with its "homogeneity and an awareness of its own function not only in the economic but also in the social and political fields" (Gramsci, 1978, p. 5). More specifically, he argues that "In order for the working class to challenge that existing order and become hegemonic in its turn without becoming dependent on intellectuals from another class, it must create 'organic' intellectuals of its own" (Gramsci, 2000, p. 300). Here, Gramsci is highlighting the process where struggle from below both creates the need for and the process within which a new set of intellectuals, developing notions of good sense, can emerge.

He recognises however, that the formation and reformation of this intellectual strata is a contradictory process of continuity and change where once an emergent class has obtained economic, social, and political power, the function of intellectuals reverts to its role as conduit for dominant ideas. This is not a cynical or personal failing since Gramsci argues that the intrinsic nature of intellectuals is to be found "in the ensemble of the system of relations in which these activities (and therefore the intellectual groups who personify them) have their place within the general complex of social relations" (Gramsci, 1971, p. 9). In our time, intellectuals, as a social group, are shaped by and seek to perpetuate the ideas that justify exploitative hierarchical social and economic relations. However, Gramsci in recognising the contradictory nature of the intellectual social group, appreciates that within this group there exists space for argument, discord, and, occasionally, a sharp clash of ideas. This has been evident during the pandemic with, for example, the many disputes between politicians and scientists about the nature of COVID-19 and the measures required to contain it. The divergence between politicians and clinicians became particularly prominent from February 2022 onwards as the incidence of the Omicron strain sharply increased and governments talked of living with the virus.

His direct experience of the economic, political, and social traumas within Italy in the 1920s, made Gramsci appreciate that moments of crisis are inherently contradictory and thus temporary. The process of revealing the contradictory nature of common-sense ideas along with a fracturing of hegemonic structures and the emergence of confident and critical self-activity of movements from below that encourages the development of good sense, are part of the same progression. Each element is linked to and influences the others. It is a totality of actions. Further, Gramsci is assigning the pressure from below as the critical element in undermining hegemonic structures, including ideas, and he also argues that during "periods of crisis it is the weakest and most marginal sector which reacts first" (Gramsci, 1971, p. 93). It is here that he draws upon the concept of the philosophy of praxis.

The Philosophy of Praxis

For Gramsci, the philosophy of praxis is a code for Marxism but a Marxism within which there is a dialectical relationship between theory and practice. As Forgacs notes, Gramsci's "generalisations are invariably concerned with the investigation of the practical conditions for transforming the world by politics in the *specific* circumstances in which he wrote" (Forgacs in Gramsci, 2000, p. 12). However, the philosophy of praxis is not simply the preserve of already convinced Marxists, it "is the terrain on which determinate social groups become conscious of their own social being, their own strength, their own tasks, their own becoming" (Gramsci, 2000, p. 196) The word "becoming" is of significant importance for it implies a process, involving a growing awareness by people of the contradictions in common-sense ideas along with a critique of hegemonic structures, and a developing recognition that the possibilities of challenging both lies within their own activity. Further, Gramsci argues that movements from below necessarily involve developing a criticism of existing ideologies and structures, including self-criticism because they "have an interest in knowing all truths, even unpleasant ones, and in avoiding deceptions…by the ruling class and even more by themselves" (Gramsci, 2000, p. 197).

While initially reacting to specific events, successful grassroots movements increasingly examine the structures supporting hegemonic perspectives. This can be seen in the development within the *Black Lives Matter Movement* from outrage at police shootings to examining the role of police forces in general and demanding the defunding of police forces in the specific. Similarly, criticism of the official response to COVID-19 evolves into a criticism of political priorities, social structure, and economic imperatives. As Gramsci argues, it is "on the terrain of ideologies that men become conscious of conflicts in the world of the economy" (Gramsci, 2000, p. 213) and recognise that such conflicts are not simply "psychological or moralistic in character, but structural and epistemological" (Gramsci, 2000, p. 215). Gramsci is not talking simply about economics, but the character of an economic system which would include reference to issues such as the environmental crisis.

The concepts Gramsci was exploring, like those encompassing Marx's approach to alienation, cannot be detached from each other. Together, they provide an overarching framework that, when used to examine a given moment, make it possible to prise apart the contradictions of material life and offer a guide of action to resolve those contradictions. In several instances, Gramsci's discussion on common-sense reprises many of the themes found in *The German Ideology* (Marx & Engels, 1970). The concepts discussed above may be termed concrete abstractions in that they that seek to express, as near as possible, the key dominant features of practical reality. They facilitate the comprehension of the driving forces buttressing those features. However, because these abstractions are derived from and find their expression in, and are thus mediated through, our actual lived immediate experience, their manifestions will be expressed in different forms in different contexts. The application of these concrete abstractions sensitises us to the underlying commonalities of apparently differentiated events.

Having outlined the conceptual tools used in this study, the discussion now shifts to look at the response to the severe problems posed by COVID-19. Three broadly defined responses are considered: governmental policies, the reaction of health practitioners and organisations, and the response from grassroots organisations and movements.

COVID-19 and the State

The state is generally recognised as the guarantor of a nation's well-being, with, for example, the 1789 French statement on the Rights of Man, the Constitution of the United States, and the United Nations Declaration of Human Rights all referencing notions of safety. The WHO identifies public health systems as the key mechanism enabling people to maintain and improve their health and well-being or prevent the deterioration of their health. A major focus of public health should be the eradication of diseases and the provision of vaccinations. It is not surprising therefore that over 150 countries implemented a range of fiscal measures and social policies, both within and outside lockdowns, in response to the pandemic, including curtailing movement, closing schools, shutting non-essential commercial activity, and encouraging social distancing (IMF, 2020b).

Governments in the United States (under Trump) and Brazil opted for a non-interventionist approach even as the death tolls in those countries continued to increase to 939,202 and 645,735 in February 2022, respectively (WHO, 2022). The dominant official narrative within these two countries was that COVID-19 was a virus that would eventually disappear and attempts to apply government directives would undermine the economy and individual freedoms, and that statistics showing cases and deaths were being manipulated by the media. Research undertaken by Cornell University concluded that President Trump of the United States, was most likely the largest driver of the COVID-19 misinformation infodemic with the Trump administration being responsible for at least 38% of content (Evanega et al., 2020). Between January and August 2020, Bolsonaro, President of Brazil, was estimated to have made over 640 fake or distorted statements on COVID-19 (Statista Research Department, 2020).

A much more interventionist approach, such as that of New Zealand, resulted in a comparatively reduced death per million population ratios with just 56 deaths. However, while the response of each individual country lies along a spectrum defined by these two poles, a review of the national COVID-19 policies outlined by the IMF shows that a constant theme evident throughout the pandemic was the conflict between a "market logic" of protecting the economy, and a "public health logic" of protecting lives. This was illustrated in March 2020, when Boris Johnson, United Kingdom Prime Minister, said; "I want to stress that for the vast majority of the people of this country, we should be going about our business as usual" (Johnson, 2020), a position which became increasingly untenable as the virus spread. The French government's proposals for the second lockdown in early November 2020 reflected this contradiction and while the election of US President Biden, in November 2020, marked a dramatic shift of emphasis on policies concerning COVID-19, as number of cases and deaths continued to rise America, it was also framed within a narrative concerned with market logic.

While the reaction of politicians varied, the responses to COVID-19 from clinicians were increasingly informed by science to reach a consensus on the management of the pandemic. From the onset of the pandemic, international organisations focused on global health, such as WHO and the United Nations, were relatively unified in their devastating impact assessment of COVID-19 and the extensive range of urgent measures requiring implementation. At a national level however, health professionals debated both the extent of, and the action needed to tackle the pandemic. The use of face masks, the extent of possible immunity, and even the number of cases were areas of dispute as late as August 2020 (The Conversation, 2020). The running dispute between Didier Raoult, a microbiologist with over a million YouTube viewers, and other French clinicians and the French government over the use of anti-malarial chloroquine, and its related compound hydroxychloroquine, was a continuing feature within France during 2020 (Braun, 2020).

Issues such as the transparency of information, scientists' lack of adherence to their own advice, the relationship between scientific advisers and politicians, the speed and extent of response to the pandemic, and the bias of scientific advisory groups, were all issues of concern throughout all waves of the pandemic including the Omicron variant.

Other issues, such as the lack of personal protection equipment for hospital staff and carers in general, the initial lack, and the cost of face masks, the failure of track and trace procedures, an insufficient number of testing kits, were also matters of concern as the pandemic progressed. This overarching context included the rapid growth in COVID-19 cases and deaths, the initial sanguine governmental approach, the confused, sometimes contradictory political, and scientific messages, the lack of appropriate material to manage the pandemic, the conflict over political, economic, and health priorities, and the flawed tendering processes involved with awarding contracts for PPE. These issues became so pronounced that a section of the British medical establishment, in the form of an editorial in the British Medical Journal, argued

> Science is being suppressed for political and financial gain. Covid-19 has unleashed state corruption on a grand scale, and it is harmful to public health. Politicians and industry are responsible for this opportunistic embezzlement. So too are scientists and health experts. The pandemic has revealed how the medical-political complex can be manipulated in an emergency—a time when it is even more important to safeguard science. (BMJ, 2020)

The core reason for these arguments was the conflict between economic demands and public health priorities with economic imperatives being seen as paramount. As the pandemic widened and deepened, and two years after the virus was first identified, attempts were made at the international level to blur the distinction between pandemic health policy and economic policy and to shift the narrative from the need to provide emergency pandemic aid to one in which substantial sums in health investment should be seen as "a strategic investment that benefits every nation" (International Monetary Fund, 2021). The situation was so critical that the IMF, a body renowned for championing structural adjustments programmes that undermine public services, argued that "our collective failure to heed scientific advice and invest in pandemic prevention and preparedness has inflicted a catastrophic toll" (International Monetary Fund 2021). In making this argument the IMF called for $15 billion investment per year to buttress international collaboration for future pandemics. Implicit in this approach was a recognition that official government responses during COVID-19 have been a failure, that future pandemics are likely, and that cooperation, not competition, is needed to combat pandemics.

The Response from Below

While the reaction from organisations like the WHO to the news in late 2019/early 2020 to the emerging pandemic was almost immediate and urgent, governmental responses were mixed and this was reflected in the attitude of people in general. However, as cases and deaths began to mount and lockdowns or imposed self-isolation were implemented, it was possible to discern three interrelated developments. The inaction of official structures to respond appropriately to the needs of those negatively impacted by the lockdowns created a vacuum that was partially filled by the flowering of thousands of mutual aid and other groups (MAGs). It is impossible to fully determine how many mutual aid and other groups were established during the pandemic. However, three examples show the extent of this activity. Within the United Kingdom, the London School of Economics and Political Science estimates that during the pandemic, "10 million people have volunteered to help in their communities and thousands of mutual aid groups have been created across the UK" (London School of Economics & Political Science, 2020). In Nantes, France, *Entraide Nantes* was established and "only two days after the start of the lockdown, 800 people had volunteered. Some 1400 families were reached with aid, and 3326 packages were distributed during the initial period March-May" (WHO, 2020). Similarly, in other areas impacted by lockdowns and restrictions, such as the creative arts and the mental health sector, there were attempts to devise and implement strategies for coping during the pandemic. Protest movements also continued and adapted, or were a response, to the lockdowns during the pandemic.

A challenge to governments' "common-sense" narrative was an integral part of this process. The flourishing of MAGs, reflecting the need to act locally, fed the emergent criticism of official policies. As will be discussed in later chapters, implicit in the practical action required to resolve very real and immediate problems in many instances, was a rejection of sanguine official policies. It was also a recognition of the increasing distrust of governmental narratives. In effect, the IMF's argument in late 2021 was merely an official catch-up analysis of a situation that grassroots activists had recognised and responded to 20 months previously.

The process also saw the development of what Gramsci called good sense, a recognition that an alternative set of ideas was needed to understand the events and guide action. Cooperation, not competition, was necessary. Solidarity by supporting strangers, not social atomisation, was required. New ways of seeing localities surfaced as seemingly tranquil appearances were stripped away to reveal deep inequalities and loneliness. DTs were seen as a critical component of coping strategies during the pandemic but, as will be shown in later chapters, experience in their practical use exposed their shortcomings.

The emergence and widespread dissemination of fake news stories through digital media about the origin and extent of the pandemic was also indicative of the increasing disconnect between official and unofficial approaches towards COVID-19. A further response, which is not covered in this book, was the emergence of a wide range of conspiracy theories about COVID-19 extending from outright rejection that the pandemic existed through to the dissemination of fake news (Romer & Jamieson, 2020). While this trend was most pronounced within the United States, adherents to conspiracy theories and/or fake news were to be found in many countries with, for example, 25% and 59% of British and Nigerian people respectively believing that COVID-19 death rates are false (Henley & McIntyre, 2020).

Before moving on to consider the specific case studies covered in the following chapters, some reference must be made to the validity and analysis of the data used. Qualitative work of this nature is often criticised for lacking objective, impartial measures to drive data collection and appropriate metrics to validate analysis. However, the multiple settings approach enabled a sharp focus on resonance through "transferability and naturalistic generalisations" rather than the generation of statistical information (Tracy, 2010). Naturalistic generalisation is realised when we reflect on how the experiences within in this book touch a cord with us, connect with our own experiences, and enable us to see the value of concepts developed by Marx and Gramsci. In doing so, it helps us identify and clarify the causes and expressions of our own condition and to reframe grassroots activity to see it more than simply an ad hoc reaction by some clever and dedicated people to unfavourable circumstances. A multi-group approach also enabled triangulation which employs the use of multiple comparison groups and refers to the within-method which "essentially involves cross-checking for internal consistency reliability" and the between-method "which tests for the degree of external validity" (Flick, 2018, p. 603).

One final point. Researching and writing this book has made me mindful of Gramsci's words about seeing "how plans construed too rigidly and schematically go bang, wrecking themselves against the hard reality" (Gramsci, 1928). Problems: personal, technical, and social were all encountered in the journey to complete this book. But then Odysseus faced obstacles, and he made it home…eventually. He thought his journey was worth it, that is how I feel about mine.

The following chapters focus on the relationship between COVID-19, DTs, and the need to respond under the shadow of the pandemic.

References

Andrae, A. (2017). Total consumer power consumption forecast. *Conference: Nordic Digital Business Summit*. Retrieved January 14, 2021, from https://www.researchgate.net/publication/320225452_Total_Consumer_Power_Consumption_Forecast

Avelar, L. (2021, July 21). *How can technology help combat climate change.* Retrieved January 12, 2022, from World Economic Forum: https://www.weforum.org/agenda/2021/07/fight-climate-change-with-technology/

Basu, K. (2020). *COVID and common sense*. Retrieved October 22, 2020, from China Global Television Network: https://news.cgtn.com/news/2020-08-05/COVID-and-common-sense-SGzOohGlBS/index.html

Bhaskar, R., & Callinicos, A. (2003). Marxism and critical realism. *Journal of Critical Realism, 1*(2), 89–114.

BMJ. (2020, November). Covid-19: politicisation, "corruption," and suppression of science. *British Medical Journal*. Retrieved November 18, 2020, from https://www.bmj.com/content/371/bmj.m4425

Braun, E. (2020). *In France, controversial doctor stirs coronavirus debate*. Retrieved November 10, 2020, from https://www.politico.eu/article/how-a-french-doctor-is-turning-into-a-pr-headache-for-macron/

Bustad, J. J., & Andrews, D. L. (2020). Remaking recreation: Neoliberal urbanism and public recreation in Baltimore. *Cities, 103*. https://doi.org/10.1016/j.cities.2020.102757

Cameron-Chileshe, J., & Payne, S. (2020). *Johnson tells UK to live 'fearlessly but with common sense'*. Retrieved October 22, 2020, from Fiancial es: https://www.ft.com/content/df14c89b-6cab-464b-ad15-fe9c45fb0f42

Carchedi, G., & Roberts, M. (2018). *World in crisis: A global analysis of Marx's law of profitability*. Haymarket Books.

Cox, J. (1998). An introduction to Marx's theory of alienation. *International Socialism, 2*(79). Retrieved May 20, 2020, from https://www.marxists.org/history/etol/newspape/isj2/1998/isj2-079/cox.htm

Crehan, K. (2016). *Gramsci's common sense inequality and Its narratives*. Duke University Press.

Davis, M. (2020). *California's apocalyptic 'second nature'*. Retrieved October 17, 2020, from https://rosaluxnycblog.org/california-fires/

European Environment Agency. (2021). *COVID-19 and Europe's environment: Impacts of a global pandemic*. European Environment Agency. Retrieved December 28, 2021, from https://www.eea.europa.eu/publications/covid-19-and-europe-s/covid-19-and-europes-environment

Evanega, S., Lynas, M., Adams, J., & Smolenyak, K. (2020). *Coronavirus misinformation: Quantifying sources and themes in the COVID-19 'infodemic'*. Cornell University. Cornell Alliance for Science. Retrieved November 28, 2020, from https://allianceforscience.cornell.edu/wp-content/uploads/2020/09/Evanega-et-al-Coronavirus-misinformationFINAL.pdf

Ferguson, I., & Lavalette, M. (2004). Beyond power discourse: Alienation and social work. *British Journal of Social Work, 34*(3), 297–312. Retrieved from https://doi.org/10.1093/bjsw/bch039

Flick, U. (2018). *An introduction to qualitative research*. Sage.

Georgieva, K. (2020). *Finding solid footing for the global economy*. Retrieved October 27, 2020, from IMF: https://blogs.imf.org/2020/02/19/finding-solid-footing-for-the-global-economy/?utm_medium=email&utm_sou rce=govdelivery&fbclid=IwAR3LnpvE_ZkejPqIyRTbbsxuHWhQDXjLeo UVGOG-omddY0AoMPNX_yZ48UQ

Gramsci, A. (1917). *The revolution against 'capital'*. Retrieved September 13, 2020, from marxist.org: https://www.marxists.org/archive/gramsci/1917/12/revolution-against-capital.htm

Gramsci, A. (1928). *Letter to Tania Schucht*. Retrieved April 17, 2021, from https://www.marxists.org/: https://www.marxists.org/archive/gramsci/1928/new-year-letter.htm

Gramsci, A. (1971). *Selections from the prison notebooks* (1978 ed.) (Q. Hoare & G. N. Smith, Eds., & Q. Hoare, & G. N. Smith, Trans.). International.

Gramsci, A. (2000). *The Antonio Gramsci reader: Selected writings 1916–1935* (Forgacs, Ed.). New York University Press.

Gray, E., & Merzdorf, J. (2019). *Earth's freshwater future: Extremes of flood and drought*. Retrieved October 28, 2020, from NASA Global Climate Change: https://climate.nasa.gov/news/2881/earths-freshwater-fut ure-extremes-of-flood-and-drought/

Gutierrez, G., & Gonzalez, C. (2020). *'We are broken': Montana health care workers battle growing Covid outbreak*. Retrieved November 3, 2020, from NBC news: https://www.nbcnews.com/news/us-news/we-are-broken-montana-health-care-workers-battle-growing-covid-n1245526

Hampton, H., Fayer, S., & Flynn, S. (1995). *Voices of freedom: An oral history of the civil rights movement from the 1950s through to the 1980s*. Vintage.

Harvey, D. (2018). Universal alienation. *Journal for Cultural Research, 22*(2), 137–150.

Healy, M. (2020). *Marx and digital machines: Alienation, technology, capitalism*. University of Westminster Press.

Healy, M., & Wilkowska, I. (2017). In M. Pirson & M. Kostera (Eds.), *Dignity and the organization* (pp. 99–124). Palgrave Macmillan.

Henley, J., & McIntyre, N. (2020, October 26). Survey uncovers widespread belief in 'dangerous' Covid conspiracy theories. *The Guardian*. Retrieved November 18, 2020, from *The Guardian*: https://www.theguardian.com/world/2020/oct/26/survey-uncovers-widespread-belief-dangerous-covid-con spiracy-theories

IMF. (2020b). *Policy responses to Covid-19*. Retrieved November 4, 2020, from International Monetary Fund: https://www.imf.org/en/Topics/imf-and-cov id19/Policy-Responses-to-COVID-19

International Monetary Fund. (2021, December). *Safeguarding the world's health and wellbeing.* Retrieved December 31, 2021, from https://www.imf.org/external/pubs/ft/fandd/2021/12/pdf/fd1221.pdf

Johnson, B. (2020). *Prime Minister's statement on coronavirus (COVID-19).* Gov. UK. Retrieved November 04, 2020, from https://www.gov.uk/government/speeches/pm-statement-at-coronavirus-press-conference-3-march-2020

Katz, I., Weintraub, R., Bekker, L.-G., & Brandt, A. M. (2021, April 8). From vaccine nationalism to vaccine equity—Finding a path forward. *New England Journal of Medicine, 384*(14), 1281–1283. Retrieved December 29, 2021, from https://www.nejm.org/doi/full/10.1056/NEJMp2103614

Kovaceic, R. (2021, February 21). *World Bank Blog: Mental health: Lessons learned in 2020 for 2021 and forward.* Retrieved March 29, 2021, from https://blogs.worldbank.org/health/mental-health-lessons-learned-2020-2021-and-forward

Landler, M., & Mueller, B. (2020, October 6). In U.K.'s test and trace: Now you See 'em, now you don't. *The New York Times.* Retrieved October 12, 2020, from https://www.nytimes.com/2020/10/05/world/europe/uk-testing-johnson-hancock.html

Liguori, G. (2015). *Gramsci's pathways* (D. Broder, Trans.) Haymarket Books.

London School of Economics and Political Science. (2020). *Mutual aid groups and community responses to COVID-19.* Retrieved November 11, 2020, from Centre for Analysis of Social Exclusion: https://sticerd.lse.ac.uk/lsehousing/research/Mutual-Aid-Groups/

Marx, K. (1970). *Economic and philosophic manuscripts of 1844* (D. J. Struik, Ed., & M. Milligan, Trans.). Lawrence and Wishart.

Marx, K., & Engels, F. (1970). *The German ideology* (C. J. Arthur, Ed.). Lawrence and Wishart.

McCarty, R. (2020). *Opinion: Common sense best medicine against COVID-19.* Retrieved October 22, 2020, from The Missouri Times.

Ng, K. (2020, October 26). Queues of people wait to leave empty plates in office garden of Tory MP who voted against free school meals. *Independent.* Retrieved November 24, 2020, from https://www.independent.co.uk/news/uk/politics/free-school-meals-conservative-mp-david-amess-empty-plates-protest-b1338075.html

OECD. (2020). *Covid-19 focus on the economy.* Retrieved October 27, 2020, from OECD.org: https://www.oecd.org/coronavirus/en/themes/global-economy

Policy Link. (2020, April). *COVID-19 & race: Principles for a common-sense, street-smart recovery.* Retrieved December 10, 2021, from https://www.policylink.org/sites/default/files/Covid-19-race-compilation_final.pdf

Rajkumar, R. P. (2020, August). COVID-19 and mental health: A review of the existing literature. *Asian Journal of Psychiatry, 52.* https://doi.org/10.1016/j.ajp.2020.102066

Roberts, M. (2022, January 1). *Michael Roberts' blog: Forecast for 2022.* Retrieved January 2, 2022, from https://thenextrecession.wordpress.com/2022/01/01/forecast-for-2022/

Romer, D., & Jamieson, K. (2020). Conspiracy theories as barriers to controlling the spread of COVID-19 in the US. *Social Science & Medicine, 263,* 113356. Retrieved November 18, 2020, from https://doi.org/10.1016/j.socscimed.2020.113356

Sanchez-Paramo, C., Hill, R., Mahler, D. G., Narayan, A., & Yonzan, N. (2021, October 7). *COVID-19 leaves a legacy of rising poverty and widening inequality.* Retrieved December 29, 2021, from World Bank Blogs: https://blogs.worldbank.org/developmenttalk/covid-19-leaves-legacy-rising-poverty-and-widening-inequality

Sitrin, M., & Sembrar, C. (Eds.). (2020). *Pandemic solidarity.* Pluto Press.

Statista Research Department. (2020, September 14). *Number of fake or distorted statements on COVID-19 made by Brazilian president Jair Bolsonaro from January to August 2020, by month.* Retrieved November 19, 2020, from https://www.statista.com/statistics/1118867/bolsonaro-fake-statements-coronavirus/

Terkel, S. (2005). *Hard times: An oral history of the great depression.* New Press.

The Conversation. (2020). *Three major scientific controversies about coronavirus.* Retrieved November 10, 2020, from https://theconversation.com/three-major-scientific-controversies-about-coronavirus-144021

Torry, H., & Harrison, D. (2021, December 27). *Omicron variant is expected to dent global economy in early 2022.* Retrieved December 28, 2021, from *The Wall Street Journal*: https://www.wsj.com/articles/omicron-variant-is-expected-to-dent-global-economy-in-early-2022-11640631554

Tracy, S. J. (2010). Qualitative quality: Eight "big-tent" criteria for excellent qualitative research. *Qualitative Enquiry, 16*(10), 837–851.

United Nations Environment Programme. (2021). *Greening the Blue Report 2021 The UN system's environmental footprint and efforts to reduce it.* UNEP. Retrieved December 28, 2021, from https://www.greeningtheblue.org/reports/greening-blue-report-2021

WHO. (2018). *Climate change and health*. Retrieved October 28, 2020, from World Health Organisation: https://www.who.int/news-room/fact-she ets/detail/climate-change-and-health

WHO. (2020). *Nantes Entraide—Citizen mutual aid project*. Retrieved November 11, 2020, from https://www.who.int/news-room/feature-stories/ detail/nantes-entraide-citizen-mutual-aid-project

WHO. (2022). *World Health Organisation Global*. Retrieved January 14, 2022, from https://covid19.who.int/region/amro/country/us

World Bank. (2021). *The World Bank group's response to the COVID-19 (coronavirus) pandemic*. Retrieved December 29, 2021, from https://www.worldb ank.org/en/who-we-are/news/coronavirus-covid19

Yuill, C. (2018). Social workers and alienation: The compassionate self and the disappointed juggler. *Critical and Radical Social Work, 6*(3), 275–289.

2

COVID-19, Digital Technologies, and Labour Organisation

Introduction

The conflict between labour and capital did not cease during the pandemic so nor did trade union organising, but the virus created new problems and issues within the context of disputed priorities between labour and employers. It demanded a greater use of digital technologies to overcome organisational difficulties to cope with issues such as unemployment, safe-working, social distancing, remote working, and precarious employment during a period of extended lockdowns. The chapter opens by describing the general contours evident during the pandemic that determined the work of trade unionists and is followed by a series of interviews with labour activists from, Australia, UK, Bangladesh, and the US. The Chapter concludes by using Gramscian concepts to theorise the experiences of union activists organising under the shadow of Covid.

As Chapter 1 has already covered the response of governments to the pandemic, the following discussion will focus on the response of employers and specific instances are cited as illustrations of general over-arching trends. The International Labour Organisation estimates that

© The Author(s), under exclusive license to Springer Nature
Singapore Pte Ltd. 2022
M. Healy, *Organising during the Coronavirus Crisis*,
https://doi.org/10.1007/978-981-19-1942-8_2

Covid has impacted on 98% of the globe's working population leading to the loss of 225 million full-time equivalent jobs (ILO Monitor, 2021). Of course, the loss of jobs was not uniform across all sectors and demographics with women and young people being disproportionally affected. During the first Covid wave, only a small minority of UK businesses (25%) were prepared to let vulnerable workers homework unconditionally, while 29% would not consider letting any of these workers remain at home. In the third wave, only 13% offered employees access to occupational health schemes (Department of Work & Pensions, 2021).

Militant workplace action declined during the pandemic and its associated recession. During 2020–2021 the US Bureau of Labor Statistics (BLS) recorded just 8 major workplace strikes, the third lowest since 1947. The BLS figures do not, however, include a multitude of smaller stoppages covering workplaces of less than 1000 and lasting less than one shift. Other sources have identified over 1200 strikes during the same period (Leon & Elk, 2021). The EU experienced similar trends (Kinnunen & Gustafsson, 2021). Compared to 2019, working days lost because of industrial action in Spain diminished by 47% during 2020. Ongoing issues confronting union organisers included self-isolation, testing, the provision of safety equipment such as masks, homeworking, and health and safety, and mental health. Where industrial action was undertaken during the pandemic it primarily concerned issues associated with Covid health and safety such as the DVLA dispute in the United Kingdom (Public and Commercial Services Union, 2021).

As vaccines became available, US employers urged their workers to return to work yet only in a minority of instances did employers actively encourage employees to be vaccinated or to organise vaccine screening with 76% indicating they were lifting or relaxing Covid protocols (Iley & Bickley, 2021). There was not any legal obligation in the UK, US, EU, and Australia requiring employers to test employees for Covid although there are general regulations mandating employers to provide a safe working environment. Workplace Covid passports did become compulsory in Italy from October 2021, but while employers had no responsibility to have their employees tested and vaccinated, they were required to enforce Covid passport checks with workers being financially penalised and subject to disciplinary action for not having one

(Pavone, 2021). A trade union in Canada lost a challenge to the right of employers to introduce compulsory testing and isolating because it penalised its members. While time for testing and recuperation was sometimes compensated, workers were laid off, without pay, after a positive test result (Levy et al., 2021).

As vaccination programmes expanded, labour issues held in abeyance during the pandemic, such as renumeration and redundancies, re-emerged, in tandem with serious concerns associated with protocols for returning to work, homeworking, and hybrid working. This was the changing and challenging environment confronting trade union activists and, as the following stories show, digital technologies play a crucial, but sometimes, contradictory role in their work. The next section opens with Chris Smalls' story concerning his ongoing and ultimately successful struggle to unionise an Amazon warehouse. It will be followed by Pete's experience as a union organiser in Australia.

Unionising Amazon Workers

I first spoke to Chris in April 2020 when he worked in the non-unionised Staten Island Amazon warehouse employing 5000 workers from New York. When Covid broke, warehouse employees were classified as essential frontline staff, required to work even when workplace Covid cases were confirmed. He described how concerns over COVID-19 began to appear in the warehouse.

> In late Winter 2020, managers from Staten Island returned from Seattle which was then the pandemic epicentre for America. One of them left early because she wasn't feeling well. I made a mental note of that. Be clear, I am not saying she was patient zero, but I was in tune with the pandemic's development because, every night, I followed the news, monitoring its progress, and taking precautions because I was worried.

Chris described how events developed in his workplace. *I noticed that a domino effect with my colleagues, they began to fall ill, some of them were dizzy, some of them fatigued and others were vomiting at their workstations. Many had flu like symptoms and were leaving work early. It was very alarming.* This was the initial period of the pandemic when cases and deaths in the United States, while rising, were still quite small. By mid-March the nature of the pandemic was becoming clear. Within the United States, there were 51,914 cases and 402 deaths with the daily rates of change being 24.38 and 34.83%. New York was now becoming the pandemic's epicentre and six Amazon warehouses across the United States reporting cases of Covid. Chris outlined the response of the local management.

> We weren't protected. We didn't have face masks, proper latex gloves, no social distancing guidelines, or temperature checking. I asked the Human Resources department to close the building and introduce a quarantine, to be proactive instead of reactive, to make sure that everybody was safe. It was to avoid spreading the virus into my co-workers' homes and families. Managers were nonchalant because there weren't any confirmed cases in our building. It was with business as usual, no need to panic. They said they were following guidelines.

Chris refused to accept the conflicting priorities between public health and continued economic activity. His analysis drove him to act, taking days off to protect himself and his family, and challenging the then official common-sense position of the Amazon management.

> I didn't want to get sick myself and sent emails to the health department, the CDC (Centre for Disease Control), the State Department of New York, and others, trying to bring attention to these safety concerns.

However, by early Spring, New York public health bodies were under extreme stress.

> All the departments I contacted were overwhelmed, which is understand-able, so I continued to try other ways to get that building closed. I sent out numerous emails to major media outlets. At the time these didn't respond, they had bigger stories.

The failure of his efforts to externally publicise the situation prompted Chris to go back to work. He recounted:

> I returned to work March 24 and saw a colleague at 9am. She had blood-shot red eyes, a rosy, puffy, face and fatigued. She was sick and although she didn't have a fever but was very sluggish. She'd been tested the night before. I strongly suggested she went home because she's my friend and we work together as supervisors engaging with employees face to face. Two hours later at the daily manager meeting we learned about the first positive case in our building on March 11. A week earlier, in Queens, New York, an Amazon warehouse had one case and managers closed and sanitised the building sending everyone home with pay for the day. I expected Staten Island, to do the same thing. I asked management if they would do the same thing. They said no, "Don't tell the employees. We don't want to cause a panic. We're going to see individuals."

Chris recognised this was not a strategy for dealing with coronavirus within the warehouse and felt his own appeals to management were having no effect. He decided on a different course of action.

> I wanted everybody to know the truth. I left the building an hour later at noon. We decided to take our stand right there and no longer return as employees. I did go back into the warehouse, sitting in their main cafeteria for three days for eight hours a day, off the clock, telling employees the truth because my colleague had texted me saying she's tested positive. Employees been exposed to somebody who tested positive, and I wanted to make sure that everybody in the building was aware of what was happening and what management was hiding.

However, Chris realised that this approach could only have a limited impact and decided more direct action was required.

> At 9am for three days, I brought groups of 10 into the general manager's office, interrupting management meetings, asking the building to be closed and sanitised professionally, we were pleading but got nowhere except excuses about implementing safety guidelines and following rules.

While no action was taken to control the virus within the warehouse, the manager did have time to act against Chris.

> On Saturday, March 28, when I came back to the building, he decided to quarantine me but not the other 90 employees who'd been exposed to my colleague for 10 hours over multiple days. They didn't even quarantine the person I ride to work with every single day. The quarantine was about silencing me and stopping me from organising protests or mobilisations.

It was during this week that the *New York Post* reported the story and a journalist phoned Chris for an update.

> I said I was organising a protest walkout on March 30 to demand better protection and the building to be closed and sanitised. I created a private social media group with some employees who were still working, and they passed notes around, photocopying material, putting them in the restrooms in the building and spreading the word. Outside a team helped me by using social media platforms to publicise the walkout. Everything came together at the right time. Sixty or so people walked out March 30 12:30pm in the afternoon and were joined by supporters. The protesters told the truth to the media about what's happening. There were other voices there, normally unheard, like people with underlying health conditions, like bronchitis, severe asthma, lupus, senior citizens standing in solidarity with us. It was a successful walk out.

Digital technologies were critical in mobilising the protest. Posters and signs were coordinated through the web since people in different buildings were in quarantine. This walkout was a peaceful protest to highlight serious health and safety concerns. Yet within a matter of hours, Chris was sacked by Amazon. Dismissal seemed to be the default position for Amazon as it subsequently sacked several other employees for acting over health and safety concerns. Chris' determined action and continued publicity, including interviews with MSNBC, may have contributed to Amazon texting all its employees about COVID-19.

> They published regular texts showing the total number of cases but soon stopped when they realised how many cases there were. Instead, they just

put additional cases in these text messages. Every time somebody tests positive, employees in the warehouse are sent a text message but there is no official total. There's an unofficial team working in all the warehouses across North America trying to tally the numbers. We have estimates and it's astonishing how there are.

Chris, and other Amazon employees, spent 2020 seeking an accurate picture of COVID-19 cases and deaths within the company's US warehouses. A full array of digital technology was used in this process. Chris mainly used Instagram and Facebook with some work on Twitter. For others it was private email messages, Facebook groups, Twitter, Reddit, and checking reports online. This fact checking had an impact. On 1 October 2020, Amazon announced that 20,000 COVID-19 cases had been recorded in warehouses.

Chris used Zoom and Telegram to help coordinate further, international, action.

I'm on Zoom conference calls every week. I talked to about 75 warehouses internationally and we're organising an international walkout on May Day, which is May 1st. The Zoom calls have between 50 to 75 people dependent on people's schedules because some people are still employed.

Employees from other online outlets such as Instacart and Target began to get involved.

Chris made extensive use of social media during this period because there was no other option and they facilitated mass communications with multiple recipients. He was keen to get the Amazon workforce unionised, but he wanted to ensure this would benefit Amazon employees rather than any union. His experience of previous unions has made Chris cautious.

I've been on both sides of the spectrum having been in a union three years prior to Amazon. So, I know the pros and cons of unionisation and having worked for Amazon for almost five years. I know the company and can relate better to the workforce than an outsider. I want to make sure that the union would be supportive of me, instead of me being supportive of it.

His experience has shown Chris the value of digital technologies in organising workers.

> Union organisers use Facebook Live with weekly question and answer sessions as well as weekly podcasts. They're adapting to the social media times but at the same time with Amazon is a little different because the workforce is about 65 to 70% minorities. For Staten Island the figure is more like 80%. people of colour.

Chris sees digital technologies as useful in achieving goals.

> Technology is just a tool to communicate and stay connected. Once you learn how to use it, and you practise using it, you get better at it. I didn't know how to do anything at first. But life changed in 24 hours. I had to learn. I think the technology has improved and we can easily communicate internationally. I love it because we can talk like this.

During this period Chris had only a mobile phone to undertake his work. In an act of solidarity, I was able to raise over $800 from trade unionists and socialists to help buy Chris a computer.

For several reasons it was not possible to complete a follow-up interview with Chris. However, his enduring story has been covered in numerous publications and while Chris continues to use DTs, he set up a blue tent at a public bus stop opposite the Amazon warehouse, so his team is highly visible to the workforce. They use the tent to distribute union material and to talk directly to workers (Press, 2021). The campaign to unionise the Amazon Staten Island warehouse was successful and the campaign organisers are now reaching out to other warehouses. The work continues to be difficult, but the approach that links DTs with direct contact may be one that will eventually spread to other areas.

Working as a Full-Time Official

Pete is a full-time union organiser for a union with 57,000 members working in Australian manufacturing covering automotive, metal manufacturing, white collar laboratories, technical planning, food manufacturing, and the printing industries. He is responsible for coordinating campaigns across naval and commercial shipbuilding, aviation, and construction. His union employs about 250 people including elected officials, industrial officers, and administrative support who are all connected via a mainframe computer utilising Microsoft 365 and cloud computing. During the first lockdown, the union's offices were closed with staff working remotely.

> We're two weeks into operating remotely but can still engage directly with our members using technology. But in many instances, our field organisers still have access workplaces but obviously implementing extremely strict health measures. Our government's lockdown guidelines mean social distancing and we can't go out for shopping, except for shopping emergency trips.

However, in some respects, the lockdown did not negatively impact on some of his work because he already used digital technologies.

> I use technology for my work more than other people in my organisation because I do significant international work with unions in the UK, USA, Europe and across the global south. So, I've always used this technology. The lock-down means changes to way I connect with local unions reps.

> I've been urging people to use technology more and the pandemic has forced people to operate differently. We've much more video conferencing with delegates in the workplaces. I have probably done more coordinating now verbally online than I did before and connect with people more than previously. We have more conversations.

He went on to amplify the point.

> I connect with several teams such as education and skills trades. I talk to my teams during video weekly meetings. I used to talk to our office admin on an ad hoc basis. But now, because people are working in isolation, I'm talking to them a couple of times a week via video to make sure they're ok.

Pete was conscious that working in isolation meant an absence of physical daily interaction and recognised the need to compensate by scheduling more online connections. Previously, if he required the admin to do something, he used the centralised email pool. Before the lockdown, the admin support staff would have talked more to each other than to him. Now he has a lot more personal contact with them and a greater under-standing of the possibility of adverse physical and mental effects on his staff from the lockdown.

> Before, we had an appreciation, from an organisational perspective, about a duty of care for our staff. Working in isolation has been challenging and has required the organisation to ensure our staff remain connected and engaged. In my job I travel a lot and often work in isolation. But working from home can be traumatic for someone used to an office. We are conscious of their wellbeing and focus attention on mental health issues.

This sensitivity towards negative aspects of isolated home working, expected from a union, was not replicated across several industries. Australian trade unions energetically campaigned for wage subsidies, which the government rejected. Ironically, the Conservative government in the United Kingdom moved rather swiftly to deal with the wage subsidy.

> The Australian government tried to use the pandemic to amend the Workplaces Relations Act to deal with several issues around special arrangements on workers leave. Our opposition resulted in a consensus which means unions can still take disputes in relation to Covid to the Fair Work Commission, an industrial tribunal. Without safeguards, unscrupulous employers can take advantage of the situation.

A wage subsidy, paid directly to employers, was eventually imple-mented for workers still employed and Pete's union negotiated with good employers for payments for workers who tested positive for COVID-19 and self-isolated. There were also cases where employers, such as one airline, refused to provide a safety package for those with the virus.

Apart from difficulties encountered concerning provision of adequate sick leave payments, some anti-union employers tried to use the pandemic to prevent union organising.

> There are employers who don't like unions or unions organising their workforce. They have used social distancing regulations to prevent union reps talking to workers at the workplace or holding meetings. But we've adapted, conducting meetings in smaller rather than big groups with meetings outside rather than inside the workplace.

> One branch uses Zoom to invite the delegates across the states and territories to online meetings resulting in 130 workplace delegates attending. It enables effective sharing of information. We're also looking at townhall meeting webinars inviting a broader group of members. We're planning one across shipbuilding and anticipate high participation rates.

Pete believes the technology has opened the possibility of much greater attendance and participation at online union meetings because union members are "are hungry for information that they feel comfortable and trust". Digital technology is crucial in this process and has been remarkably effective.

> We've 35 union delegates across many sectors and previously some engaged when something interested them, others didn't. Now we're having weekly Microsoft team catch ups with them and this morning there was 18 participating. We discuss issues at a national level and percolate the results across Australia using closed messenger groups. There's one closed Facebook forum that's got about 430 people. We encourage members to check their closed Facebook group and in one week, we had an extra 70 join.

Pete contrasted the effectiveness of the union approach to those of employers.

> We've really stepped up our communication because many of our members are part of the hundreds of thousands of workers furloughed. Employers generally use intranets to communicate to managers and while

useful at the top, they fail at local level. Because of our quick response, many of our members know what is happening within a company before local managers. In one case, managers got information which we'd already filtered down to local reps.

In these uncertain and quickly changing times, union members have multiple questions and concerns and so require more sophisticated and expansive use of technology to enhance communication. Digital technology allowed for horizontal and vertical information flows within the union. Pete explains,

> A convener in Sydney administers and regularly updates a closed Facebook group. The national coordination and a closed messenger groups play an important role in ensuring delegates share information. In addition, national offices coordinate weekly video conferences enabling delegates to give feedback upwards allowing for a quick turnaround of information.

The technology also enables union members to liaise with workers internationally. Pete cites the shipbuilding industry, where digital technologies allow regular, instantaneous discussions between workers in Glasgow and Australia despite time-zone difficulties. The pandemic has created the need for the widespread adoption of DTs with the likelihood they will continue in a post-lockdown world with other sectors replicating his Section's experience. He undertook all his video conferencing from home.

> I'm home working and try to stick to normal hours but international work, across time zones, makes this difficult. I sit on several union committees each with frequent video meetings online, three this week using Zoom or Teams. Often many board members need help because they're unfamiliar with the technology, but my colleagues are becoming increasingly positive, recognising that digital technologies can make them more effective; there'll be a culture of using these technologies when people return to a conventional working environment.

Pete was considered a digital innovator and was asked to help develop digital networks in other parts of the union. It opened space for those keen to adopt the technologies, but also revealed a poor level of computer literacy.

> I've discovered that some people who I considered IT literate were not and was surprised to find many were amazed at the possibility of simple actions like cut and paste. I also found that problems with low bandwidth Internet speeds fed negative attitudes towards digital technologies.

For full-time union officials like Pete, digital technologies have played a critical role in continuing with effective union activities during COVID-19. They have also encouraged organising at a grassroots level. The next section opens with an interview with Patricia in New York and is followed by the experience of Nazma in Bangladesh.

Organising Migrant Labour in New York

Patricia Campos-Medina is the Executive Director, The Worker Institute, School of Industrial and Labor Relations at Cornell University. She explained the motivation for her work.

> I am an immigrant to the United States, and I believe the only way workers can achieve power, to be able to improve their working conditions and their economic power right is to organise into unions. I was a labour activist and union organizer before becoming an academic. We conduct applied research and help union activists and labour advocates develop best strategies by providing training, policy support, and to improve workers' rights on the job. My work is about advancing collective bargaining and workers' rights. I have a real experience of organizing low wage workers as I worked for several low wage worker unions in the US before joining academia; unions such as SEIU, UNITEHERE and UNITE.
>
> We undertake applied research; drawing upon qualitative methods like worker interviews and surveys for any industry we are studying, trying to

identify their working conditions, from their own experience. My work involves qualitative, experiential research which provides the best analysis of since it's based on workers' own lived experience.

I concentrate on low wage blue collar workers, which tend to be African American or Latino immigrants, working in distribution centres, the service industry, as nannies or healthcare home workers, or the food supply industry in airports or schools.

Before COVID-19, Patricia also advised a coalition of community, religious, environmental, and union groups in New York concerned about the deteriorating wages and conditions for warehouse workers.

These large distribution centres, built often on former contaminated properties/ground, often supported by public funds, use low wage and often immigrant labour. They generate hubs of poverty, pollution, and social need without any commitment to creating well paid jobs or enabling workers to organise. Previously trade unions had been concentrated in traditional textiles and existing warehouse and they had been able obtain union contracts 11 years ago with some labels who used to be union labels like Taharu, DonnaKaran or Liz Taylor. The new warehouse giants like Amazon and Walmart warehouses are anti-union and pose major obstacles for unionisation, a process further complicated by the existence of several unions representing workers in the sector.

The confluence of large-scale employment centres, environmental degradation, increasing social need, and attempts to unionise, motivated social, religious, unions, and environmental groups to work together.

After California, the New York-New Jersey region is the biggest market for logistics and distribution-centre workers in America. But there's a dramatic 40% wage differential between the two regions favoring the West Coast even though the cost of living is about the same. We publicized this stark reality during the workers campaign to organise Target and Amazon and to improve their wages and working conditions. Governments were funnelling tax dollars to encourage this industry without demanding any improvement in wages and working conditions.

Two years research involving meetings, discussions, focus groups, and personal interviews with workers about working conditions in different workplaces, produced a report with recommendations for improving warehouse employment. Social distancing and other safety measures added further complications to Patricia's activity advising workers. Digital technologies began to play a critical role in her work.

> Zoom, WhatsApp and Google Hangouts enabled us to stay on top of what's going on. Some community groups had identified problems at New York and New Jersey warehouses (Barnes & Nobles) where workers used WhatsApp and Facebook to organise and communicate about who was feeling sick, who stayed home. Workers even talked about who needed to stay home because their kids were home from school after schools shut down. Because we were hearing similar complaints all over social media, union organisers were invited to join the Facebook Live meetings so workers could ask questions about their rights to demand health and safety protections, or their rights to some paid sick leave.

> Social media made it easier to provide some advice to workers on their legal rights, to make suggestions for organising actions on the warehouse floors, and technical help about publishing notices about their rights under CDC rules. We also helped them draft press statements and press releases, and in some cases gave them advice on how to file complaints about unsafe working conditions. Immigrant community leaders used this social technology to organise mutual aid work which was used as a tactic to create camaraderie in the workplace because everyone was looking out for each other. It was a mixed of union organizing enhanced by community mutual aid work. Technology was a conduit for bringing community and workplace issues together

Patricia's team works with Athena,[1] a community organisation for Amazon workers concerned about their working conditions or have worries about COVID-19 in their workplaces and taking the illness back to their families.

---

[1] https://athenaforall.org.

Before Covid, workers were reluctant to talk to unions or community groups but it's different now. They know if they don't fight, they can get sick and die. And what will happen to their families? They get sick at work; they bring it home to their families. The pandemic allied with the technology has facilitated organising at a faster pace with, this is true even for immigrant women who find it easier to attend a union meeting via WhatsApp or Zoom at night than to attend a meeting at a union hall. It would've taken longer before requiring more resources including sending an organiser to a workplace or someone's home to find workers to talk to.

Now, communication with one worker via WhatsApp, Zoom or Facebook live, can be easily expanded to 10 or 20 more; we reach more people with one text message or a Facebook connection. It's an organic way to connect more easily, and we can upscale the level of contacts. There's still many one-on-one discussions required with leaders to agitate and turn "anger over something" into a drive to make something different happen. But with the accessibility of technology, leaders can use less time to identify potential leaders and agitate them into action.

The word "organic" implies that technologies, often seen as creating problematic relationships, are considered natural and critical in facilitating more intimate personal relationships that may have developed from handing out flyers when workers change shift. The coupling of COVID-19 and DTs encourages personal conversations about work to percolate into normally private conversational spaces with the lines dividing public and intimate discourse becoming necessarily blurred and stretched.

Technology makes sharing your experience easier and sharing reveals commonality of experiences, helping turn shared experiences into common knowledge. With social media, people openly share what's happening in their lives. This encourages action, political action, or action against your employer. There's still some intervention needed from the union, community organisations or labour activists to say what's happening shouldn't happen and this is what you can do about. You must agitate. You must educate. And you still must train them.

Social media is, however, a double-edged sword. It makes it easier to organise, to share information, to have multiple conversations in real time, but, as Patricia notes, it can have consequences.

> Chris Smalls is a good example. He organised rallies against Amazon and was active on social media. When Amazon saw it, they fired him. There're consequences but workers make a cost benefit analysis: I speak out or I might get sick or worse. Because of Covid, they're more willing to act because not speaking out is a greater than the risk of staying silent. There's a sense of false security thinking Facebook or Instagram will respect privacy. But people feel more confident with WhatsApp to organise actions. They're still communicating but using WhatsApp because it doesn't share as much personal information, it's a texting app. In moving from sharing to action, people change how they communicate.

Workplace action is critical to advancing workers' rights, but Patricia appreciates the value of taking online actions to sustain activity.

> Using Facebook or Twitter, we designate a time in which everybody sends messages to a company, to an elected official like a Governor or a Senators. We have online petitions which we urge people to sign. And we have online press conferences where workers can speak from their cell phones.

Migrant workers, particularly those who are undocumented, are extremely sensitive to issues of security and confidentiality online. They know they can be tracked so they use the technologies to minimise the risks. Patricia recalls:

> I recently interviewed undocumented Haitian workers unwilling to give me their phone numbers, but they were all communicating through WhatsApp. They knew how to make WhatsApp video calls so they told me here's my code name, look me up. They're very resourceful and we shouldn't make assumptions about their technical understanding or skill levels.

Patricia believes it is easier to communicate across different language groups and to organise online providing there are leaders providing a point of contact or who can translate simultaneously.

> Sometimes we do actions in multiple languages such as Spanish, Creole, or Portuguese with different organisers speaking different languages. If we hold a press event where workers tell their own experiences using their own language, we allow for translation time. Real-time actions to energise workers, may involve multiple languages and we make sure we have a worker that can translate. Sometimes some of these meetings can take three hours because people must hear things in several languages.

> Language inclusion is part of building unity, the idea that workers are all in it together. A three-hour meeting can be long especially for those with caring responsibilities, but many are committed to that kind of organising. And this accessibility has increased the number of women who have become leaders because in the past it was hard for a mother to leave their kids after dinner to go to a union meeting. Now they just call in through WhatsApp and they are in the meeting. In this way, we have seen an increase of women participation in union activity. So, in many ways, it was democratised participation for women low wage workers.

Patricia went on to discuss the role of women in this process:

> The times and length of meetings means making a conscious effort to give spaces for women's participation. Sometimes it is not possible with other times being more conducive for their involvement. But it doesn't always work. For example, there's an organising group meeting at 9pm and a woman that said we shouldn't meet then because it's her kids' bedtime. Yet, everybody else can meet at 9pm and they end up with mostly men on the call. The fix was to make the call at 9:30pm and more women were able to join.

> Including women as leaders always require greater effort, and it varies depending on the type of workers you are organising. But it is absolutely a fact that most often than not, if there is a mobilisation action in warehouses, it's the women who have the bigger networks, that pull more people to a rally or an action.

Patricia notes that technology can facilitate the participation of women.

> We must be responsive to group dynamics. Recently, we noticed there were no women in one of my Coalition's Calls and so we tried to hold it at 9pm. On other occasions we can have break out calls at different times or choose smaller committees for enable greater participation. Technology can help with this.

Patricia highlighted the emergence of Internet-based radio stations that talk directly to immigrant communities.

> The National Day Laborer Organising Network[2] uses an online radio station to communicate with immigrant workers on the streets. Their night-time show gives the location where workers can get labour rights information. Many immigrant groups have online radio stations for news and communication. It is a tool that marginalized communities use to keep their communities involved. It's another area where technology helps. Internet radio stations existed prior to the pandemic, but their value to their communities has increased. People are increasing relying on them for information and updates because mainstream media doesn't focus on these communities. These radio stations are educating people about their rights and events in their community.

While appreciating that shopping online can make life easier, Patricia knows technology puts a distance between the shopper and the distribution worker.

> Most consumers don't consider what happens when placing an order. Who picks it? How do Amazon warehouses and distribution centres work? Twenty years ago, we broke hard ground talking about exploited workers and adverse impacts on local businesses when we campaigned against Walmart. Amazon is the second wave; they have used technology to separate the shopper from the interaction from the worker who processes the order. But COVID-19 made the faces of those workers real--it made consumers realise that while some could stay at home ordering from their laptops, millions of workers had to get up every day, expose

---

[2] https://ndlon.org.

their lives to Covid so they could get their orders at their doorstep. That consciousness is there from consumers now. As organisers we need to tap into it and turn it into a demand for better working conditions for those who put their lives on the line to keep some of us safe.

Patricia argues that labour organisers and activists must sustain the level of long-term commitment after the pandemic ends and believes things have changed.

The pandemic crisis has changed expectations about workers or what society in general should expect from our government and for corporations. I hope there's a higher level of civic responsibility meaning that people are becoming more conscious about who's responsible for the safety of entire communities, that it's more than individual responsibility. There's a lot of work to do to.

Offline activity lies at the heart of Patricia's work and the value of DTs is measured by how effective they can be in enabling her to build trade union solidarity and to, for example, facilitate the greater participation of women in decision making. The next section covers union organisation in Bangladesh during the pandemic.

Garment Workers' Union in Bangladesh

Nazma is a leading member of a trade union with over 100,000 members in the readymade garment sector in Bangladesh. She focuses on building the union and achieving decent pay and working conditions. The legal minimum monthly wage for garment workers in the country is 8,000 taka (£73.85, US$ 94.31, and €78.53). The digital context within which Nazma works is fragile and unreliable. In 2021, 34% of the population did not have Internet, the rest mostly used mobile connections. Rural areas are poorly serviced by providers and Internet speeds are the region's slowest because of lack of frequency spectrum and poor infrastructure. The system also frequently experiences outage problems. Nazma described her work.

Our union tries to organise workers and educate them and provide legal and healthcare support. There are many different areas of work and activities in our organisation. Covid means social distancing, and this affected our activities. We've stopped face to face work. Sometimes we go out, but most of the time we work online.

Apart from making it difficult to carry on with her work with garment workers, the pandemic has created more work that was not directly related to her core activities.

Journalists, our working partners, and people from different organisations have sent hundreds of emails asking what's happening to garment workers during Covid. While they want to know about the consequences of the pandemic, they're not interested in our real work. We're busier with outside people than dealing with our members. There's a time difference as well. We're 4 hours ahead of the EU and 10 hours ahead of the US meaning in many cases we get called middle of the night. That's a problem because it affects our sleeping and daily life; everything is affected. Last night I went to bed at 01h30 in the morning. This was not happening before the pandemic.

Multinational retail fashion brands and other multinationals have cancelled orders leading to thousands of workers losing their jobs and factories closing. They are also demanding cuts in prices, reductions in orders, and increasing late payments (Naimul, 2020),

This is a disaster and it's not about our usual priorities concerning pay and conditions or organising the union. We've over 100,000 members working in over 2000 factories, and we would normally negotiate collective bargaining agreements. Now, we fighting to keep jobs with local suppliers, multinationals, or brand retailers. USA, European and Australian companies, our biggest markets, have cancelled orders. It's the challenge we face, and it is very hard time. This is not our regular work; we are now struggling and fighting for our survival.

Social distancing makes our work difficult, but we urge members to social distance because they're more worried more about survival rather than precautions against covid.

Nazma spoke of her use of digital technologies.

> I use WhatsApp, LinkedIn, Teams Twitter, Skype and Zoom. Most of our members use IMO or Messenger, WhatsApp to speak to each other and some use Facebook or WhatsApp, to talk to us or share using Twitter. We can communicate with most but not all our members, and we use programs such as Excel to keep their data.

> Most members have smartphones using the Internet and they watch television for the news. Mainly they're using Facebook Messenger to talk to their friends, families, and others in the countryside. Some have husbands or wives working in the Middle East or elsewhere. Our main incomes are remittances from migrant workers overseas and the garment industry. When jobs are lost in the Middle East, Malaysia, Europe, and America it hits the remittances.

This situation is a double blow for Bangladesh. Reduced international markets for manufactured garment goods means increased unemployment and a fall in income from overseas remittances. In addition, overseas migrant workers who have lost their jobs come back to Bangladesh further increasing the levels of unemployment. In these conditions, getting access to information is crucial and digital technologies play a vital role in this process because they enable workers to communicate.

COVID-19 is likely to have a dramatic impact on Bangladesh's development strategies. Nazma believes that the pandemic could have a lasting impact on people's livelihoods doubting if it will be possible for Bangladesh to become a mid-income country.

> Women are especially vulnerable because of increased domestic violence. When there's no money, they will be hungry which affects children. Women do use technology to talk to each other and we are concerned with domestic violence, workplace violence and sexual harassment. These are key concerns for the union's leadership. When a worker has a domestic problem, they call our phone, use Messenger, or IMO.

Nazma and her staff now mostly work from home but must cope with a poor Internet infrastructure. Sometimes the sound is poor making it difficult to get voice messages. While the poor Internet infrastructure is a legacy issue and not a result of the pandemic, measures like social distancing means having to rely more on the technology further exposing the digital problems facing Bangladesh. Nazma has a range of views about digital technologies.

> The technology is good, making it easy to communicate, like this; you in France and me in Dhaka. But sometimes people get upset with the technology, with Facebook, WhatsApp, Messenger, or they spend time gossiping online. Maybe my co-workers seem working when they're chatting or playing a game using the technology. But this happens everywhere.

> Digital technology can become addictive leading to loss of sleep. Many workers, talk with the family, chatting all night, or watching YouTube, which is popular. By morning they are irritated when coming to work.

> When I was young, my mum fed us early in the morning, so we got up early. Now I see children study at night and sleep during the day. This effects people's lives. Young people are affected with many not wanting to read or write. They search online and cut, copy, and paste. This can mean that very real, important information is discarded with online information misleading people into think fake news is authentic. Digitalisation becomes very complicated.

This is not simply a complaint about the technology but a real problem for Nazma because the Bangladesh Bureau of Statistics (BBS) reported in 2020, the literacy rate stood at 74.70% last year, which was 73.91% in 2018. However, the pandemic has meant the closure of adult education centres in Bangladesh and the literacy rate increase slowed to just 0.8% during 2020. Nazma was also concerned to talk about anonymous posting of social media.

> Digital crime is also a problem. Misrepresentation or anonymous harassment online happens especially to domestic women. She's a woman, she's a mother, but she's victimised and society has not accepted this can be happening also, especially a poor country.

Nazma is describing a situation where digital machines have become an indispensable component in the fabric of daily life in Bangladesh but where they create a contradictory experience for their users. A further problem arises because the Internet service is not free and so workers on reduced income because of the pandemic have to pay for the service. At the outset of the pandemic, problems of communication arose with members because of lack of experience using digital technologies. However, appropriate training and the introduction of online banking has enabled union staff and some members to become more proficient with technologies by mid-2021.

> The Internet is not very expensive, and workers can use a pay as you go mobile service. It's possible to buy small amounts of data depending on the sim card but for people who are struggling to buy food, the Internet and social media are not priorities. Their families are also affected too. They use the Internet to talk but how can people buy data when they have no food? Digital technology makes it easy to access things. But there are also a lot of challenges and struggles.

Nazma's story is indicative of the experience during the pandemic of low-income countries relying cheap exports and remittances. The ongoing problems with Internet access in Bangladesh and the obstacles these create for trade union activists reminds us that, in many instances, DTs operate within a fragile infrastructure. The next section covers the experience of a rank-and-file trade unionist with extensive access to DTs running in a reliable environment.

Organising Local Government Workers in England

David is a Branch committee member of a Branch with over 12,000 members mostly employed by local government but with over 3000 members working in the private sector. It covers workers in housing, schools, refuse collection and street cleansing, child welfare, social work, Council residential homes, private nurseries, private residential homes, and private care agencies. There are many union activists, a Branch office, and 30 people with union facility time. It is a large operation. David splits his working week into two days on facility time and two days working directly for the council. As the pandemic broke, the union became clear about how serious it would be.

> A week before the Government lockdown, we decided to close our branch office moving those on facility time to homework. We had about 25 union smartphones, four or five laptops, with another eight iPads but this equipment was in the main office. We had to consider how to keep people connected while not being physically in the same building? Our traditional ways of working were not possible at a time when members were raising loads of issues. Trade unions are based on their collective experience, members meet to discuss and debate, and if you're socially distant this is not possible. Giving advice to individual members is also a problem.

Normally, David's Branch has an officers' group, consisting of five senior elected officers meeting weekly at the branch office, a Branch Executive with 30 senior stewards and a Branch Committee of 100 stewards. Covid meant the weekly meeting became a twice weekly Zoom online session with the Branch's two admin staff home working taking members' calls.

> The meetings we've held online have been vibrant and with some better than normal meetings. The pandemic crisis is the focus of discussion leading to increased participation and everybody speaks at every meeting, which is unusual. Members have adapted quickly to teleconferencing or Zoom, becoming familiar with speaking on camera. The Branch Committee has 100 stewards and we've 50% attendance which is better or about equal to previous meetings.

There are different sectors of the branch with two full-time caseworkers covering the private sector and the key phone numbers of all our activists were publicised to private sector members because significant problems had been anticipated.

We implemented a weekly open Q&A session using Zoom with over 30 members at each one. Main concerns are the lack of PPE, problems associated with shielding for members with on-going health issues, such as diabetes and asthma. We urged our employer to move beyond government guidelines and stop insisting people should go to work. Many questions focused on employers re-defining roles leading to untrained people working in potentially dangerous situations. While the Zoom sessions are small compared to the size of the Branch, we also encouraged members to submit questions by email, which were then re-routed to the appropriate union rep, but we only have email address for 7000 members. Our Facebook page is a further means of communication. Zoom meetings have attracted members not previously involved and we've tried using survey gizmo to reach more people. You try what you can because it's about opening multiple channels of communication to members.

In talking about Zoom meetings, David said,

Some people have felt negative about Zoom because of publicised security breaches. I've arranged some Zoom meetings for my workplace team but only a minority participated but that is fine. I finally got my work laptop five weeks into the lockdown because I was low on the list of priorities. Now my workplace colleagues have work laptops we may try Microsoft Teams.

At this point in the lockdown, David was not aware of how digital technologies were being used by Union shop stewards.

Because I've not heard of any initiatives in this area, it doesn't mean that they're not happening. Some workplaces have established union WhatsApp groups, others have Microsoft Teams. It's patchy. Right now, we're focused on the macro level of the branch and mindful that members employed in street cleaning, parks, maintenance etc, are still at work and we need to talk to them. Union communication is so important, and I have been critical about our Branch's communications to members in the past.

We convinced one of the Union's six Assistant General Secretaries to participate in an activists' meeting using his home equipment and he was quite well received by the stewards. It was easier to arrange online than a physical meeting. He's an Afro-Caribbean guy who'd been based in Birmingham, so he talked about covid's impact on black and minority ethnic communities. We also discussed the pandemic's effect on activists including their mental health because we've had members of our branch die from Covid. There's been several issues concerning social distancing and restrictions at funerals with members being unable to see dying relatives or talk to hospital social workers. Our meetings cover these issues including what care we can give.

PPE frequently appeared as an urgent matter because members who are home carers were not allowed to use PPE unless they're dealt with someone who's been diagnosed with or displaying symptoms of COVID-19. This clearly caused concern because someone could be asymptomatic, and carers were moving between homes without an adequate tracking system. This led to arguments with management, and elected counsellors because Public Health England's guidance was inadequate. All these issues create greater stress for union reps. David went on to explain how members direct experience informed the view of the Branch.

We've got nearly 100% trade union membership in the home care sector because over the past two years because of an ongoing industrial dispute involving over 80 days of strike action. One of the best organised areas of the Branch covers the most vulnerable workers. and they were contacting the Branch Secretary, day and night, letting her know their fears. Refuse collection is another area with lots of issues. These members have good reps and were using WhatsApp and emails to organise. This pressure from below prompted our demands on regional and national union officials to be more proactive about the risk to members from Covid.

We disagreed with advice in the early stages from our local full-time non-elected officials and argued the Branch had been abandoned by the Union nationally which maintained that Public Health England advice was fair, reasonable, and should be followed. We then approached our national officers via telephone, letters and emails saying we're unhappy with the union's stance.

However, these discussions occurred at a time when regional and national union meetings were suspended.

> I'm elected to the leadership body of the Union's local government section and the Union immediately moved to suspend all section, regional and national meetings without replacing them with alternatives using technology. There was a Zoom ban within the Union which I think is being run by full time paid officials with no real live input from members. If I say this to my regional official, he says it's problems with the hardware and software and finding suitable technology. Right at the beginning of the crisis, trade unions were not critical of the government's approach and were more interested in getting government invites to discussions over big issues.
>
> They didn't want us criticising government policy or advice and things like that. We had a senior regional official reprimanding us for questioning scientific advice, telling us we're not scientists and criticising us for using our Facebook page to demand PPE. I'm not an expert scientist but I know about protecting members, what the issues are, and the official advice didn't square with what members were telling us.

Trade unions did begin to pressurise the UK government on these issues and launched an online petition calling for more PPE. David went on to describe the ways in which rank-and-file activists began to organise in the absence of normal trade union activity.

> We helped establish Coronavirus Action groups for health and care workers which are open to anyone. We've held Zoom meetings, sometimes inviting local Labour Party members of Parliament, MPs and other speakers. Videos of these meetings were posted on Facebook. This initiative involved elected members of Union's National Executive and many other people. These groups created a sort of parallel rank and file structure to the official channels allowed within the union.
>
> The carers group involves a mixture of frontline care workers providing useful information which is channelled back to our union. The Northwest region of the union is very strong in the residential care sector, and they too are Zooming. Union officials had to tread carefully when it came to

being negative about the Covid action groups because these are seen as a civic response to a severe crisis.

The union hierarchy took a very different stance to other, informal online activities.

> A group of left activists tried to set up a Zoom meeting and they were threatened with disciplinary action by the Union which argued this was an attempt to undermine the union structure. Normally Branches channel communications through the union's hierarchy which is not keen on direct branch to branch communication.

David was describing a situation where the union full-time officials effectively attempted to censor the use of digital technologies by rank-and-file members during a moment when normal communication channels had been suspended.

> Email makes it easier to communicate laterally and the online meetings organised by a left caucus discussed problems of union organising during the Coronavirus crisis. That initiative immediately provoked a letter from the Union's HQ threatening them for organising the meeting and saying the mere criticism of the Union was not allowed. But the Union's bureaucracy is not a monolith, so our local officials were less inclined to pursue this line enabling us to have a least some leeway.

David also explained how the technology also assisted in helping his union Branch to become involved in local actions concerned with COVID-19.

> There's a local Coronavirus Action Group with many people from different unions meeting weekly on Zoom with 30/40 participants. We mobilised for the clap nights, broadcast live on Facebook, at our local hospital and workers from different trade unions, including firefighters and ambulance staff, came. There were between 4 and 5 hundred people at these events which have encouraged cross-union and community group collaboration.

We also organised the first online Branch International Workers Memorial Day advertised using email and Facebook which we called a tea-break meeting which ran from10h40 to 11h00. Someone sang a song, followed someone else reading letter about a union member who had died. After a poem, there was one minute's silence at 11h00. Over 40 Branch members participated which is quite good for the first attempt that needed more time to prepare. It was Zoomed which caused a few problems because of syncing and time delays.

Speaking a year later, David said the national union had wholeheartedly embraced webinars and Zoom teams and was planning to have an online National Conference. This meant greater central control over the Conference which could be problematic for rank-and-file activists. His local Council had partially reopened its offices and were trying to introduce new ways of working covering office-based, home-based, and hybrid methods.

There's a divided view amongst union members with some thinking it will mean reduced commuting time and more flexible work patterns. These changes will need to be negotiated and will require good broadband and training. Others will miss the workplace environments. There is also a question of environmental resources concerning the energy efficiency of multiple individual offices verses one office centre.

The Union nationally is preparing for major industrial action concerning pay.

Our member consultation used email addresses linked to survey Gizmo to ballot the members on the offer. We sent hard copy to 8% or so members who didn't have email and held physical workplace meetings. Interestingly, the Gizmo and paper ballots resulted in 20% return with 90% rejecting the offer whereas the meeting return was 100% with 100% voting to reject the offer. Clearly workplace meetings are the best, most democratic from to hold ballots.

If the pay dispute does mean industrial action, home working could provide an easy route for strike breaking. Technology doesn't solve these problems for trade unions.

For the Branch organisation, David is convinced DTs cannot replace physical collective organisation and solidarity, which can help undermine the sense of isolation associated with home working.

The UK University Sector

A similar set of problems were experienced by trade unionists working in higher education. At the start of the first UK lockdown in March 2020, university administrators used emails to deliver information to staff but these instructions lacked clarity. Tina, a lecturer employed on short-term contracts at an English university, said "we received an email saying that we can start moving…to the first week of transition to online teaching. And the second week it will be online teaching [but], it was very confusing at the beginning because the information that was provided by the university was not clear. It was not directly saying we are closing the campus" (Interview with Tina, temporary language lecturer worker, 04 April 2020). The lecturers' union, University and College Union (UCU) while acknowledging the serious nature of the situation and calling for a shutdown of face-to-face teaching, believed "some university and college infrastructure should stay open, including student accommodation and, where agreed with staff, medical research units" the emphasis was an appeal for "much more urgency from the government and university leaders in shutting down as much as possible to reduce unnecessary contact on campuses and to protect the health of students and staff" (Cressey, 2020). The Union was asking Johnson's government, which had prevaricated over the seriousness of the pandemic, to take things more seriously. This was in effect giving pre-eminence to faulty official government advice derived from conflicting priorities and thereby underpinned the common-sense narrative Johnson was so eager to pursue.

Not surprisingly, this approach was re-echoed by university managements. Tina recalls that at the start of the first lockdown, her line manager told her by email that she would have reduced hours at the start of the new academic year in September 2020. He "just said we are trying to move things forward as quickly as possible in these unprecedented circumstances and we can only ask for your patience and understanding...basically he mentioned that they are trying to identify the essential features...[and] that they need to cover the staff on full-time contracts before offering me any work" (Tina interview). Tina's experience was replicated across the sector so for lecturers on temporary/short-term contracts, Covid intensified precarious employment. This approach by UCU was replicated later in its advice to members at the start of the Autumn term in September 2020.

Russ is a paid union administrator for a trade union branch covering lecturers and researchers in UK Higher education. Before the pandemic, Russ' Branch had been involved with strike action concerning cuts in pension entitlements.

> 200+ members participated on the picket lines across 14 days of strike action, an excellent response. We used WhatsApp groups to organise picketing. Of course, the action's been thrown into disarray, and we'll be coming back in a completely different environment. After we generated much enthusiasm for the strikes, with the Branch on a high, the lockdown took the steam out of things. We've the Internet for basic communications but from my perspective, Zoom sessions can't replace face-to-face meetings, Knocking on someone's door and have a chat in their office. Meeting three or four people to make plans is invaluable.

> I use email for routine daily work but our Branch committee, with 20 members, uses Zoom for meetings. We've grasped the technology and the chair does a pretty fine job now. We're all kept on mute, using the hand icon to indicate to speak.

Russ described the problems of information overload.

> I try to take minutes of Zoom meetings but there can be multiple messages appearing on the screen. So, I'm responding to these messages while writing at the same time and seeing more messages shooting across the screen in the bottom. People referring to documents can mean falling behind in the conversation. Sometimes I do feel there is too much information coming at me and I can't keep up.

This problem is compounded when there are many WhatsApp groups seeking committee member participation thus creating a deluge of messages.

> People feel they must join or follow the groups they've been invited to and find themselves following conversations not directly related to them. Someone can be a health and safety officer and a Branch committee member, and then end up trying to follow threads concerning other unions which may be interesting but not directly relevant. Social media can have the effect making a person feel they've got to respond to everything. Information overload is a real problem for union activists.

> We also use Loomio, an open source collaboration tool, used for organising the Branch Committee. There could be different threads on WhatsApp, on Loomio, on emails, Zoom, Twitter, Facebook, and our blog site. There are multiple points of information which does lead to overlap. I've probably spent most time catching up with WhatsApp messages or going through the Loomio and email threads.

Before the pandemic Russ' Branch mainly used social media to organise the strike but during the pandemic, technology appears to have evolved into an information overload machine. Russ believes that even without the pandemic, this would have happened eventually.

> We would've continued using WhatsApp for the dispute because we were getting good feedback concerning votes for action and it helped motivate and organise members for strike action. Of course, if the action had stopped, we would've discontinued use the WhatsApp groups.

> We've a Loomio subsection for 50/60 UCU Branch organisers from different parts of the uni which is another area for discussion. Some of Branch Committee discussions spill into that and it's a mechanism for formulating, for example, petitions or motions.

Speaking 14 months later, Russ commented that union members *"seem more comfortable with technology, particularly those engaged with the union and our use of digital technologies hasn't changed since the pandemic, all our meetings are online*". He also said the problem of information over-load had been partially resolved by a more "disciplined" approach to participation in various online forums.

Russ explained why the union does not use the University's official Internet and Intranet facilities.

> We had used the University's email system but stopped three years ago over concerns about the University accessing our communications. A disciplinary case revealed the University's management had authorised the weekend removal of the member's computer hard disk from their office replacing it with a copy. They were looking for evidence to justify disciplining them. If they're prepared to go to those lengths, they could be monitoring a member's communications with their caseworker to gain advantage. The Branch stopped using the University's server, any university email addresses, and to ceased using our website hosted by the university. We use private emails for all our confidential committee work, the health and safety officers, and caseworkers. We pay for Loomio, our branch email domain and our blog site. Of course, there are always people who will inform the management of our general emails to members, but we're more secure now.

While Russ believes their system has greater protection from management, it does have some technical problems.

> We have several minor network problems such as the occasional 15 second freeze when someone is talking or connection issues, but these tend to be temporary difficulties. We haven't any major concerns about users' technical competence. The main issue is information overload for Branch activists such as Branch committee members since there's expecta-tions, they'll join all communication channels and want to be included in many other, inter-union groups as acts of solidarity. Previously there was an inter-union committee comprising of key activists from the unions at the University plus reps from the Student Union.

> During the industrial action more activists joined the strike WhatsApp group and at the end of the strike, we voted to allow all the people on the WhatsApp group to join the Loomio threads. This increased the end points of the information flow.

Russ also discussed the issues concerning the University's management use of digital technology during the pandemic.

> There are issues particularly with staff on part-time contracts not being able to retrieve payslips because they don't have security clearance to access on-line payslips which is a real problem at a time when deductions are being made, people want to see what was happening to their pay. The University management wouldn't provide hard copies of payslips. Their Facebook group page is heavily moderated, censored in fact and when some Branch Committee members wanted to ask questions about payslips, their posts were rejected. Management welcomes posts about how wonderful it is to work at university etc. It's a propaganda page.

> Management has also not agreed on extensions for PhDs and master's theses. They say research isn't affected so the work must finish by the set date. On the other hand, for degree students the University is bending over backwards, sideways, north, and south to make sure they graduate. For self-funded postgrads it's hard luck. That adds to pressure particularly for postgrads who also teach.

> The exams have been cancelled but academic related staff will be pressured to work during Summer because technology will allow that. Management ignores other pressures. For example, one member told their line manager they had caring responsibilities because their partner is working 12-hour shifts, several nights a week and on those days, they must look after their 15 month old baby. The response was that on certain days, weekends, and when the baby is asleep, the member should be able to work. Staff from overseas are also impacted.

Speaking in September 2021, Russ noted that the University's managers were reluctant to introduce online teaching.

> Despite the extensive online teaching last year, the work hasn't been done to do the same this year and it appears managers want everybody back on campus, even if home working is possible to create a 'vibrant campus' and enhance the student experience reducing covid precautions and possibly creating a spike in cases. There's a record number of students this year and management probably believe online teaching may leave students

wondering why they're paying £9000 in fees or for accommodation while they're sitting at home. Universities need to protect their accommodation income stream and also have significant influence in the cities and towns where they're based because they generate income for local economies. If there's no students, that influence will diminish

Managers say teaching rooms are no longer considered crowded spaces even though they're going to be twice the capacity than previously since social distancing has gone. They're mimicking the government line and causing problems by posting confusing messages such as contradictory risk assessments. One risk assessment said masks are required for teaching rooms, but this has been dropped, they're repeating the Government line.

We fear managers want everybody back on campus, possibly creating a spike in cases, and the Union's position is to avoid staff being on campus. Using technology, we're polling members on levels of concern because we've already had emails and WhatsApp messages. Many who either have or care for people with underlying health conditions, are concerned about transmitting the virus to their families. The results will guide our advice to our members.

Most academics feel face-to-face teaching is a better experience than the online environment particularly for large groups. It may work with smaller groups, but student engagement is an issue online. There's some academics like online working because it reduces travelling to campus, particularly for staff who don't live in the University's immediate vicinity. Perhaps some form of hybrid teaching will emerge.

National Executive Committee meetings, and section meetings have been well attended. There were over 1000 participants in a recent Zoom meeting with Joe Grady, the general secretary, about pensions.

Russ indicated in September 2021 that the campaign against pension cuts will continue.

To build the campaign against pension cuts, we're coordinating our door knocking and displaying posters around the campus. We're fine tuning our communications by updating our database. It's going to be interesting to see whether we can perfect our digital communications and improve democracy by using the e-voting app. The introduction of hybrid working could mean academics spending more time at home which may have a significant negative impact on our organising abilities since union solidarity depends on face-to-face discussions.

On the picket lines in winter 2020, many said that, despite the cold, they really enjoyed being there and talking to colleagues. It really boosted collegiality and developed solidarity. That could be undercut if academics are further dispersed and isolated through digital technology. Conversely, adapting and using technology creatively may well be crucial in overcoming this problem.

Conclusion

This chapter has drawn upon the experiences of labour activists working across a range of differing contexts, each of which can appear to be unique. However, general trends are revealed by delving deeper into each context. The first is that employers were initially reluctant to address the severe health and safety concerns associated with COVID-19. Even during enforced lockdowns, employers sought to minimise concerns by not taking seriously social distancing or the lack of PPE. Further, whether, for example, in building trades in Australia, higher education in the United Kingdom, or migrant workers in the United States, employers sought to use the pandemic to assert their priorities. Amazon declared its warehouse workers essential staff, despite the spread of the virus. For garment workers in Bangladesh, it firstly meant unemployment because factories closed as multinational firms cancelled orders, followed by attempts to drive down the prices when orders recommenced. Employers embraced the common-sense language of governments, echoed loudly by the MSM, seeing it as a mechanism for shifting the duty of care onto the individual. COVID-19 laid bare the alienated labour–capital relation described by Marx by showing that even in hazardous circumstances, workers must work, for they have nothing else but their labour to sell, even if it puts their lives in jeopardy. The virus illuminated the precarious nature of all work and in doing so provided a damming criticism of those proclaiming that labour in 2021 is a more positive experience compared to that of the nineteenth and twentieth centuries.

However, the stories also show that across different continents, workers refused to accept the role of victim and based on their direct experience, developed their own notions of good sense: the virus is deadly, and health and safety issues are not optional extras. They needed to build pressure from below. The stories show how a critique of the dominant common-sense went in tandem with a change in practice, and will resonate across multiple workplaces where workers are, or want to be, organised. They show how workers took hold of technologies previously seen as tangential to their activity turning them into effective organising tools for asserting workers' priorities. From the migrant online radio stations to the widespread use of Zoom, labour activists saw the potential of DTs to organise, and recognised the need to develop greater communication skills. This was real, practical activity responding directly to a perceived threat and flowing from a rejection of the common-sense ideas propounded by governments and employers.

The experience of the union activists also shows that while DTs can be valuable tools, they cannot compensate for the lack physical offline communications. The migrant online radio stations provide information about street meetings, the UK council workers look towards workplace balloting for strike action, and unionising Amazon requires direct action and putting leaflets in workers' hands. The pandemic has shown the benefits of DTs for organising workers, but it has also shown that, ultimately, direct contact and patient arguments with and between workers is the only way to build solidarity.

References

Cressey, D. (2020). UK universities left in limbo as schools and colleges told to close. *Research Professional News*. Retrieved April, 2022, from https://www.researchprofessionalnews.com/rr-news-uk-universities-2020-3-uk-universities-left-in-limbo-as-schools-and-colleges-told-to-close

Department of Work and Pensions. (2021). *DWP COVID-19 employer pulse survey: Interim report*. DWP. Retrieved September 12, 2021, from https://assets.publishing.service.gov.uk/government/uploads/system/uploads/attachment_data/file/1003633/covid-19-employer-pulse-survey-interim-report-final.pdf

Iley, B. T., & Bickley, S. L. (2021). *Looking to the post-pandemic landscape*. BlankRome. Retrieved September 20, 2021, from https://www.blankrome.com/siteFiles/COVID-19-Employer-Workplace-Survey-Summer-2021.pdf

ILO Monitor. (2021). *Covid and the world of work: Seventh edition*. International Labour Organisaton (ILO). Retrieved September 16, 2021, from https://www.ilo.org/wcmsp5/groups/public/---dgreports/---dcomm/documents/briefingnote/wcms_767028.pdf

Kinnunen, A., & Gustafsson, A.-K. (2021, April 6). *Relative calm on the industrial action front in 2020*. Eurofound. Retrieved September 18, 2021, from https://www.eurofound.europa.eu/publications/article/2021/relative-calm-on-the-industrial-action-front-in-2020

Leon, C. A., & Elk, M. (2021, July 13). *The Bureau of Labor Statistics counted only eight strikes in 2020, payday report counted 1,200*. Institute for New Economic Thinking. Retrieved September 21, 2021, from https://www.ineteconomics.org/perspectives/blog/the-bureau-of-labor-statistics-counted-only-eight-strikes-in-2020-payday-report-counted-1-200

Levy, R. B., Kuretzky, B., & Vassos, G. (2021, July 14). *Ontario, Canada arbitrator upholds employer's compulsory rapid COVID-19 testing policy*. Littler. Retrieved September 12, 2021, from https://www.littler.com/publication-press/publication/ontario-canada-arbitrator-upholds-employers-compulsory-rapid-covid-19

Naimul, K. (2020, October 16). *Fashion brands accused of exploiting workers at risk of layoffs*. Reuters. Retrieved October 10, 2021, from https://www.reuters.com/article/us-bangladesh-workers-rights-trfn-idUSKBN27100B

Pavone, A. (2021, September 24). *Italy makes Green Pass mandatory for all workers*. Global Workplace Insider. Retrieved October 10, 2021, from https://www.globalworkplaceinsider.com/2021/09/italy-makes-green-pass-mandatory-for-all-workers/

Press, A. N. (2021, December 7). Amazon and Jeff Bezos's worst enemy is Chris smalls. *Jacobin*. Retrieved December 12, 2021, from https://www.jacobinmag.com/2021/07/amazon-staten-island-jfk8-chris-smalls-jeff-bezos-union-organizing-working-class

Public and Commercial Services Union. (2021, August 3). *Strong support for DVLA strike as month-long action underway*. Retrieved September 21, 2021, from https://www.pcs.org.uk/news-events/news/strong-support-dvla-strike-month-long-action-underway

3

COVID-19, Digital Technologies, and Mutual Aid

Introduction

COVID-19 set millions of people in motion working to provide practical solidarity and support to vulnerable or isolated people in local communities. We can only guess at the number of non-profit mutual aid groups (MAGs) created in response to COVID-19 and the numbers of people involved. Estimates in the United Kingdom range from a minimum of 4000 MAGs formed involving over 3 million people to hundreds of thousands involving 10 million volunteers, working with people they had never met before. These are additional to the 750,000 people who responded to the United Kingdom's NHS call for volunteers and the work of local authorities (Legal and General, 2020; Mao et al., 2021). This picture was replicated internationally in Australia, France, Canada, Ireland, Brazil, India, and the US to name a few other countries. The stories in this Chapter illustrate the problems confronting MAGs at the start of the pandemic and how organisers sought to employ digital technologies to resolve the challenges they faced. They show how

© The Author(s), under exclusive license to Springer Nature
Singapore Pte Ltd. 2022
M. Healy, *Organising during the Coronavirus Crisis*,
https://doi.org/10.1007/978-981-19-1942-8_3

MAG organisers stepped into the massive void created by the lack of official public action and show that millions of people who, by their actions, rejected common-sense ideologies that champion the individual over society. They understood that the only way to overcome the disastrous social consequences of the pandemic was through shared, collective activity.

While governments focused on measures targeted at individuals, MAGs embraced a philosophy that recognised collective social responsibility and drew upon the deep well of solidarity that is hidden from view in normal times. The MAGs could not have operated if not supported by further millions who responded to their call. COVID-19 demanded a retreat from normal social activity into enforced isolation, but it also enabled us to express our unity of purpose and to reach out to help millions survive the lockdowns. The following discussion opens with Paige in Oakland, California and then moves on to cover George in Britain.

Mutual Aid in Oakland, USA

Paige, an internet marketing strategist, was instrumental in establishing *Oakland at Risk* (OAR) MAG during the initial outbreak of COVID-19 in Oakland in 2020. She was already involved with Mercy Brown Bag, a MAG providing groceries to low-income seniors, and saw that food distribution sites were closing with numbers seeking groceries suddenly declining by 35–40%. While seniors were fearful of going out, the need for food had not diminished.

> We saw this crisis looming and knew there would be many high-risk people, particularly elders of low income, needing assistance, because they couldn't safely get out. OAR launched as completely digital, which helped us quickly gather volunteers - but provided a challenge when we tried to reach elders using a digital platform.

> A friend of mine, Krista, messaged on Facebook saying someone in Louisville had organised a neighbour helping neighbours' activity and she

suggested we could do something like that. A third friend quickly created a website on Wix, that feeds into Google Sheets, where people could sign up to be a volunteer or sign up for help. The next day, because I'm the marketer, I blasted it out through every possible social channel, including the Nextdoor, a local neighbourhood app.

OAR sought to pair healthy low risk adults under 60 with someone having high risk factors and/or quarantining after exposure or diagnosis. After matching, OAR coordinated the delivery of essential supplies such as food and prescriptions and created a check-in schedule by phone or other electronic methods. Some matches involved food bank pick-ups for low-income residents.

Within the first 48 hours of only doing social blasts, we had 600 people sign up to help. Enthused by this response, I also tweeted a local journalist, and a couple of other well-known activists. The journalist interviewed me and my colleague, Krista and after a few weeks, we had about 1200 volunteers.

Linking SM with MSM prompted an excellent response from volunteers. Paige described the website design as "an ugly workhorse" but the results show it worked. The skilled website developer was able to link the site directly to Google Sheets. Subsequently, Paige was approached by two MIT students, who had found out about OAR at a UC Berkeley Hackathon and were really interested in helping with the organisation. They wrote an algorithm that sought to match 6 to 8 local people on language because, as Paige recounts, there are 146 different languages spoken in Oakland. Unfortunately, the algorithm failed because of complications on Google Sheets concerning linking verbatims and predetermined buttons for location and language. Ultimately 1500 people volunteered and over 700 households were matched with a volunteer.

However, the successful call for volunteers generated problems linked to tracking all the data and putting stress on the system and on Krista and Paige. Two Google Sheets were used to hold data on volunteers and those in need and tracking matches became problematic.

We tracked who was matched with whom for lots of reasons, including liability. Tracking had to cover those who had not yet been matched but been contacted, and those had been matched and didn't need matching again. This was hard because we both have jobs, and we were trying to do this at the end of a long day or throughout the day. Originally, we thought we could match people by zip [post] code, but zip codes can cover five miles which could mean 25 minutes from one household to another depending on the zip code.

We had to look up a street name, and then go to Google maps to search for volunteers in that locality. It was an arduous process. In the beginning, we were doing 10 to 12 of these a day which is a lot when it's your side hustle. Also, data required updating because people were returning to work, or they were leaving the area, or they were sick. We would also have to email or text or call people to find out if they were still healthy and available. So, it was a lot of work. I also refer 10 or 15 people to Mercy Brown Bag because they're in need of groceries but who are not isolated.

The creative use of DTs to develop OAR quickly generated significant increases in manual work requiring more people to run the organisation. An extra volunteer helped Paige and they worked in shifts because of the high anxiety levels of those seeking help. The team tried to match people within 24 to 48 h of first contact. For example, an 81-year-old isolated senior who normally was unable to go out and grocery shop without fear, would now be in hyper isolation. Paige was trying to connect with such people as soon as possible.

OAR's use of technology revealed a further problem linked to the level of technical skills.

Many users are not tech savvy and that's a challenge. We get many referrals from clients of social or medical workers (some 20%) and as well as other sources. We then send an introductory email, copied to the client and the volunteer, confirming the match to protect everyone's privacy. But sometimes people don't realise they've gotten an email, so don't know the person we've matched them with or don't realise they have already received the email address. We solved this problem with a hybrid approach. We ring those who have a memory issue or are not tech savvy, saying they have been matched and a vetted volunteer will be calling.

The resolution of this problem though fed into another challenge for OAR.

We don't know all the people signing up and don't have the money to do individual record checks. So, when I am not matching people who literally live across the street from each other, some form of check is needed to protect the vulnerable. Volunteers must provide first and last names and from that I can find their digital footprint. I use LinkedIn, Facebook, etc. and check any publicly available records to see if we have someone in common. I don't know what we would do if I didn't have that digital option. I would also usually call them if the client were particularly vulnerable.

While DTs allowed for some basic background checks, the task itself generated additional work. There was a constant churn of volunteers with some unable to continue, others joining the group, and some having forgotten they had joined. The student algorithm was initially seen as the solution to the problem of constant updating by highlighting the most recent volunteers.

Over time, fewer clients were signing up, but we then had to sift through 5 and 10 people before matching a volunteer. This also became more labour intensive. I want to ask the MIT students to do expand the algorithm to include a type of weekly, quick yes, no, online survey, on a mobile, that asks if a volunteer is still healthy and available. And then up-date the database.

Paige described the positive support networks, like the Sikh food pantry, Free Meals.org and the restaurants donating free meals, that had arisen in her area and who used Google Sheets. People, especially the older and low-income groups without access to a smartphone, could ring a general resource number, to get information on OAK.

While DTs were important in facilitating the work of local mutual aid groups, they also enabled a nationwide discussion between groups about strategies, plans, progress, and problems.

> There are a lot of COVID aid or MAGs that have popped up. There's a Facebook group that includes people like me who have started up these neighbourhood organisations and one of the people on there is the woman in Louisville, who sparked all this. There is a Zoom meeting today for eight organisers from all over the country to share our experience. It's an online mutual aid summit.

Paige described the way DTs facilitate a shared, informal learning experience generated from the grassroots. The pandemic drove the need for practical activity and, at the same time, the need to share the problems and positives arising from that activity. It required discussion with others doing, or wanting to do, the same thing and to discuss the best way to take the movement forward.

> In the first month, I probably did 15 calls, Zoom, or otherwise, with people all over the country, who saw what we were doing and wanted to learn from it. Every single day, I learned something new about what was and wasn't working. The things we needed to add to the site, new ways we needed to do outreach, how we were doing our matches. And, it was great, because after those discussions, people acted in places like Manhattan Beach in Flint, Michigan or in Connecticut. I talked to a group of seniors who wanted to do the same thing, but they were very tech challenged. That's why our site then had a page showing how it was built. People could see how easy it was to design and publish a Wix site linked to Google Sheets, and do it themselves.

Despite the valuable communications channels available through DTs, Paige recognised the need to also employ more traditional forms of media, especially when faced with 146 different languages and low levels of technical skill.

> High school groups contacted us asking what they could do to help. We created an online flyer that could be downloaded, printed, and posted

in mailboxes. We then asked high school students, for example, to drop the flyers in their older neighbours' mailboxes. There are lots of high-rise buildings that cater specifically to seniors, so we wanted to post in the lobbies. When some feared the flyers could transmit COVID, we asked the students to tape them, facing in, to windows. Basic, but it helped to get the word out.

We also actively pursued the press, and I always did an interview when asked because seniors still read newspapers, watch the news, and listen to the radio. We used the local public radio which resulted in a spike in signups from seniors. The journalist who did the first piece did a follow-up article a month later. And again, we saw a spike in seniors signing up. That's been really helpful.

Clearly, traditional old school media, newspapers, television, radio, played an important part in reaching seniors. Paige explained that initially there were problems contacting some vulnerable people in different minority groups for several reasons.

We have a lot of undocumented people in one neighbourhood who are fearful of putting any of their information into anything. Many Spanish speakers signed-up as volunteers. Our biggest need was Cantonese speaking volunteers because there is a huge Asian population here, with, for elders, Cantonese being the dominant language among 50 Asian languages. We were able to do a couple of things.

I paid for Facebook ads asking for Cantonese speaking volunteers, even if all they could do was the phone work. We hooked up with the Mayor's outreach programme for isolated seniors which gave us a dedicated Cantonese speaking volunteer, who is employed as a librarian. She sends me 8 to 10 people daily who speak only Cantonese, who are primarily low income, and need groceries. We either signed them up for Mercy Brown Bags, so they don't have to make another call or referred them to Asian House. We also ask our Cantonese speaking volunteers if they can either take on another senior or if they can ask somebody else in their family or community to help. It's been challenging but because the Cantonese culture emphasises care of elders, it's been a little easier to get them to take on more than one. For Tigrinya, spoken by the Eritrean community, we use an Eritrean social worker as a translator.

This was a complicated activity encompassing local officials, vulnerable groups covering several languages, high school students as well as many volunteers. Basic email was the scaffold technology enabling the work to proceed. Paige talked about the community service projects high school students undertake and how that helped OAR.

> I am contacted every couple of weeks by somebody representing a high school group or by someone who is otherwise unable to be a volunteer because we're not going to send teenagers out. Sometimes people in their 60s want to volunteer but they can't for liability reasons. I ask them and the students to download a flyer, print, and distribute it. Occasionally that has been problematic because some people don't know how to download a PDF and print it.

The system developed by Paige appeared to work effectively for those in isolation.

> People will email, text, or phone their shopping lists to their volunteers. But there also people who have no money for food, so a volunteer can't really help them. With people in this crisis, because of the delay in agencies being able to step up and provide them with food, we've been using Instacart which is a portal enabling shopping at a variety of stores. There is a picker, someone who will go and do the shopping and deliver it. There's a small fee for that and I add a big tip because they're the ones assuming the risk. We've delivered many bags of groceries to people who are in desperate need, using Instacart for delivery without ever speaking to the picker.

On the surface this approach seemed to answer one set of problems. However, Paige said

> Instacart was completely overwhelmed, cancelling orders left and right during the first month of the crisis, because everyone was trying to use it. Same thing happened with Amazon Fresh. The whole system became inundated leading to a total technology fail. People were placing orders

only to find many items missing from the checkout basket or there was no shopping slot for three weeks. That was a disaster. We began tapping into food banks at schools and other satellite locations to avoid the hours-long lines at the main food bank.

Paige made several interesting points concerning the relationship between gender, demographics, and technology.

> I often find women tend to be more tech savvy than the men. When it comes to the recipients we support, it's the men who seem to be very overawed with the idea of having to do a sign up online and following up on an email. I know a lot of elders who are women who have a smartphone, and they figured out how to use PayPal or Venmo (digital wallets) to reimburse their shopper. Men tend not to be able to do that as easily.

> I think the biggest impact on the use of technology is income. Affluent seniors will have access to and be able to use digital technologies. The lower the income, the less likely they are to have any type of digital device or desktop. They're reliant on phones. A lower level of income and a higher age adversely impacts on ownership and use of smart phones. I was working with a guy in his late seventies, he has a flip phone. I talked to a woman living in a senior residence and she's got a smartphone. She knows how to use it but she's also more affluent, and probably had access to technology for longer and access to something like a smartphone, which is not cheap.

Paige sees this digital divide in another area of her voluntary work, such as a coach for a group called Soccer without Borders, concerned with kids from low-income immigrant and refugee families.

> These kids live in the same areas as many of the seniors we're trying to serve. But because of the pandemic, they are out of school and none of them have computers at home. They have no way to access online classes. Laptops were bought (by Jack Dorset, Twitter CEO) for every kid in the school district, they will be able to learn from home as we go into fall, when we're mostly going to have online classes. That's easy, because it's a

purchase, I hand this to the kid, who figures it out, because they're used to the technology.

With this entire elder base, it's not as simple as just providing them with a laptop or a smartphone because then they need tutorials and Wi-Fi, which for many, on a fixed income, is beyond their budget. These people are half-way below the poverty level. I'm not sure how to resolve it.

My experience has shown that the safety net we're supposed to have for elders, and for low income, is just full of holes. And when pandemic goes away, this crisis will still exist. These people will still need help and food. There are so many homebound seniors with no money. I've been trying to figure out, you know, how we can do more outreach? I think the problem cannot be solved digitally.

The inequities are incredible and there is a dearth of cohesive services. I've advocated on the part of many elders with their service providers, a social worker or with a county agency, to try get assistance. These agencies put information online and simply say go to our website. Accessing this information isn't always possible.

It would be great to make local Wi-Fi available city-wide, like a lot of cities in Mexico and some in the US have done, but it has only happened in a few corridors or areas. But I think that could make a huge difference. I also think there should be more computer literacy instruction for low income and the elderly.

The OAR experience is indicative of the MAGs that flourished during the initial phases of the pandemic as people drew upon their knowledge of DTs to create community support systems required to fill the void left by official structures. Yet, their use of DTs also created a range of challenges that could not be resolved by technology alone. Phone calls and hard copy fliers were crucial in reaching into those groups who were either unfamiliar with or unable to use DTs. It also illuminated to deep running digital divide that continues to exist.

Mutual Aid in Hackney, Northeast London, UK

George has a long history of activism in the British labour movement and for over eight years, had been the secretary of a trade union branch with 3000 members. Although retired, he is the Chairperson of a trade union committee in London. He is also active in the British Labour Party. He was familiar with DTs including Facebook, Twitter, and Telegram, before helping to set up the Hackney COVID-19 collective in northeast London. This collective had developed out of mutual aid groups that emerged in March 2020.

> The collective is focused on union and workplace issues and has been involved in organising protests at construction sites that remained open during the lockdown. It has also coordinated a protest outside the Hackney Learning Trust, the body responsible for education in the borough. It was a symbolic protest to show opposition to the premature reopening of schools which is part of the Tory Government's plan to reopen the economy.
>
> The collective holds a weekly Zoom meeting which attracts about 50 participants, including several local Labour elected officials. The core group is made up of people who are Labour Party members, members of the Socialist Workers Party and some nonaligned, long-standing activists, mainly from trade union backgrounds. One driving force has been Reel News, an activist video collective. There is also a regular presence from the London Renters' union.
>
> The COVID-19 collective has organized five socially distanced protests at construction sites. One was at a large site, publicly funded by Hackney Council. It had been shut briefly, apparently because of health and safety concerns linked to COVID. The local mayor seems incredibly determined to keep the site open.

George explained how the COVID-19 mutual aid group was initially created by a local LGBT+ network using Facebook and reacting to the lockdown and recognising the need to have an umbrella group to help coordinate action. The LGBT + QueerCare network was crucial in forming the mutual aid group.

> QueerCare was already providing aid to people identified as immunocompromised, perhaps because of HIV, and they had existing risk assessment procedures in place for dealing with individuals who are immunocompromised. That was the key building block locally. It was QueerCare that initially set up the Facebook group. Many with pre-existing conditions were instructed to shield or self-isolate. We organised food drops around what people needed, what food was available, how that food was going to be collected, and how it was going to be distributed.

> We also wanted to use our existing links with local trade unionists, particularly with our local hospital where there were concerns about the provision of personal protection equipment (PPE). Several of us had already been involved in campaigns concerning the London living wage, around occupational sick pay, moving towards parity of conditions with direct NHS employees, and eventually bringing back in-house a workforce of 300 people that had been outsourced to a private company [Danish-based multinational ISS]}.

Several local politicians were also involved from the start and there has been a positive relationship between the mutual aid groups and local council. George described the valuable role the local council performed in this moment.

> It has been especially useful, in fact, they have been particularly good at identifying unmet needs and vulnerable people that hadn't previously been addressed by central government. Central government food parcels gave no consideration to dietary requirements. Vegetarians and vegans were getting red meat in the form of spam. No attention was being paid to needs of the Muslim and Orthodox Jewish communities. The Council has done a reasonably good job in addressing that. Although it was controversial, they've done a particularly good job in trying to keep parks and green spaces open because the borough has many people living in accommodation without a garden or any other outside space. Yet, the decision to continue with work on the construction sites remained as issue.

The involvement of a former trade union branch secretary at the hospital also gave the mutual aid group a direct link with the hospital workers. This meant the group could support action by hospital staff over issues such as PPE and, from the outset, the group saw its role as being more than organising deliveries of food and other support.

The Hackney COVID-19 collective involved a core group of between 6–8 people on an email list. George considered this a small self-appointed group and was concerned about possible accountability issues. George described the response to a call for support.

> While there were some small businesses wanting self-promotion, there has been an outpouring of goodwill by a lot of small catering outfits and restaurants, maybe because they have stock that will otherwise go to waste. But I also think there's been a genuine wish to assist people.

George went on to describe the experience of one small catering company.

> A friend owns a cafe but is now running a new food bank/soup kitchen from an old working men's club on Newington Green. While her staff are on furlough with 80% of their usual wages, she, for historical reasons, couldn't qualify for the self-employed scheme. She's waiting for Universal Credit social benefits. Thankfully, she has some savings, and she has siblings who are in full-time paid employment. She's been central to developing the food bank that's running two or three days a week. That aid work is separate from the social media platforms. She's someone who is not normally politically engaged.

George talked about the importance of digital technologies for the work of the group.

> I think we were the first people who met via Zoom to discuss union workplace issues and the pandemic. We worked on statements to the press concerning the protests about the construction sites. We also produced an open letter/petition. The Zoom meetings are scheduled for Wednesday, early evening. It's a relatively small number of people who are participating. It would be good to have more people but that poses problems

especially when the meetings last 90 minutes. Beyond that time, it is difficult to maintain concentration. Often people drop out of large meetings.

George described how different platforms were being used including Facebook, and the Slack app, which became increasingly important, at least in some of the mutual aid groups, because it enables more targeted discussions around specific areas. George thought Slack to be more effective than WhatsApp. With a Facebook group, there can be many rather peculiar individual requests and comments.

George believes the pandemic crisis has created the need for people to work together.

> I think it has forged some links between people who may not have worked together before even if they were previously active and it has reached out to others. Activities such as some of the neighbourhood-based things like food, medicine collections, and deliveries have engaged new people who perhaps haven't previously had any experience of community organising.

> While the mutual aid work continued, so did the protests outside the Education Trust, mentioned earlier. We also organised an event on International Workers Memorial Day 28 April 2020 outside the Homerton hospital. We had a minute's silence, but we also had some speeches including from one of the outsourced ISS employees. I read Michel Rosen's poem: *These are the hands*. The Branch Secretary from the Unison local government branch also spoke. There were about 15 of us with homemade signs along with the Hackney Unison and Hackney North Labour party banners.

George recognises there will always be tension within groups and people who come from different perspectives yet see the need to work together. It was most notable when the group held an international Zoom call.

> This call was organized by Reel News with speakers from Spain, Italy, and Switzerland and also from Pakistan. We also found that people in Britain but outside Hackney took part. I think that although a lot of interesting information was shared, we lost focus in that meeting. This is one of the

challenges of Zoom, and probably of other video conferencing platforms. They require a lot more intense concentration than a face-to-face meeting and can easily go off topic, especially when interpreting is required. The meeting was problematic because we were terribly busy in the run up to Mayday and we didn't have much input into the scope and structure of the meeting. But we did hear about the situation in other countries. But it was a bit of a fait accompli, you know.

George thought leaving an online meeting is easy and can go un-noticed thereby diluting tension. However, it is also doubled edged.

People who are alienated can leave but those who are determined to stay may become increasingly frustrated at the inability to give voice to their objections to the way a meeting is going ahead. Obviously, it's possible for the host to mute anyone and the chair may have greater control than perhaps in a live meeting where people might start heckling or speaking over the chair.

He was also aware that digital technologies helped reduce spatial constraints and encouraged more borough-wide involvement in the work of the group. They also helped to sustain pressure on locally elected Council members around issues such as schools reopening after the lockdowns. The process also encouraged others to organise their own activities. Here, George cites the response of parents to school reopening.

Some parents arranged a Zoom meeting last night to discuss a parental boycott at the school reopening. I don't know how many took part in the call and while there were parents already involved in mutual aid work etc., there were some who were nonaligned, and I hadn't met before.

The pandemic has created space where technologies like Zoom have made it easier for people to work together. There've been differences in emphasis but those cut across traditional party-political affiliations. Locally, the teaching unions are strong, and it seems schools will be in the front line in terms of reopening the economy. So, last Wednesday's meeting, with 50+ people, focused on schools and the education sector, it took up three quarters or more of the meeting. And I think everyone was agreed that it was the right thing to do.

The response to the pandemic also led to united action involving a wide range of minorities.

> Well, what has impressed me is the role played by QueerCare, and the presence of black people, black British, African, and Caribbean. They have been represented in our Zoom calls. Three of the four counsellors who took part were black as well as some black trade unionists. This was a positive aspect.

George believes it is possible to side-step the normal constraints imposed by the rules and conventions deciding how meetings should be run. Online discussions can be flexible. He also considered email an important tool for facilitating the group's work by circulating documents, and provisionally agreeing to agendas for meetings. He considered the email exchanges to be "quite comradely".

> There were some tensions after the international meeting, but we managed to smooth things over relatively quickly with a couple of individual phone calls as well as emails. The next meeting was unproblematic. I think people realised that mistakes arose from imposing the format for that international zoom meeting with so little notice. And there was a shared desire to overcome petty squabbles to respond to the critical situation.

During a later conversation, George noted how significant traditional forms of communication, such as door-to door-leafleting, had been in building local support networks inclusive of those with limited knowledge of or access to digital social networks. He also mentioned the importance of crowd funding and local support to help keep the soup kitchen going. A further important development was the formalising of MAG activity by third sector organisations, i.e. those that are neither private nor public, funded by local councils.

Mutual Aid in San Mateo County

Nora Grossman, and co-worker and CEO Brian Jaffe, had been active in VOCA, a self-funded DT platform created in 2017 to strengthen and simplify local level civic participation enabling a greater voice for people. Using SMS text-based communication formats, VOCA aimed to inform people about local issues and to send feedback to elected officials. Initially based in San Mateo County, California, it expanded to both local and regional state-wide levels. The platform, in operation until 2021, grew to over 60,000 participants generating thousands of opinions each week. The participants in VOCA, while skewed slightly to seniors, generally include those from a broad demographic population. Then the pandemic lockdown hit.

> It was a wake-up call. What can we do to help the situation? We were aware of the high engagement rate amongst people who cared about what was going on in their local community. We wanted to use our technology to build local support. We were inspired by the work of our neighbours who were already checking on other neighbours, particularly seniors, who didn't feel comfortable going out to the grocery store. We wondered if we could create a network for people who don't have those connections already? Because VOCA participants responded well to the idea, we expanded beyond VOCA into the community to see if there were others we could reach. Although SMS was the primary form of communication, we were leveraging social media and anything else we could use.

Covid Assist, with about 1300 volunteers and over 100 recipients of aid, effectively became a side project of VOCA, with VOCA paying for the servers and other costs meaning minimal development work was required. However, Nora's group, Covid Assist, faced a problem common to others building support networks. Those in greatest need of support, particularly seniors, may not always be familiar with online social networking. The local government agreed to put a link to Covid Assist on its website and to post flyers at senior centres. They also put some ads on Facebook specifically targeting seniors and sought to get media coverage from local news sources. This activity generated many contacts for the MAG. Pulling data from the SMS source did not present any major difficulties.

> We had already created our own custom software through VOCA to process text messages, respond and aggregate feedback. We cloned that technology, tweaked it a little, modified our content management system to enable our organisers and volunteers have access to the text messages. We were able to automate some features such as an automatic response when people sign-up. We got more volunteer signups than people requesting aid. But that was good, because for any one person who was looking for help, you might have to sift several potential volunteers to find someone suitable.

Initially the support focused on errand running, such as picking up groceries or medications but, inspired by other groups, Nora's group expanded to offer things like a friend to talk to on the phone, to check in with people quarantined and isolated at home. These actions could be done remotely yet give people a sense of connection. The success of the group locally encouraged Nora's team to develop a wider presence.

> We had an algorithm that would match volunteers with recipients based on their geographic location and we didn't have to physically match since that could be done programmatically. Place ceased to be an issue and so we asked, why limit to the Bay Area and San Mateo County? At that point, we started putting ads on Facebook, not just to the Bay Area but throughout other states looking for people to sign up throughout the country.

Nora was pleasantly surprised to have quite a few signups from across the country although she thinks this may have been primarily through word of mouth. However, social media was crucial later in the process.

> People in the Bay Area who saw the ad or signed-up, encouraged family members in other states to volunteer or ask for aid. That's how it spread throughout the country. The challenge we then faced was helping those in need in an area where we didn't have any volunteers. That's where social media came in strongly. One of the most effective ways to find

volunteers was to look for location specific social media and put out a targeted specific appeal using a sub-Reddit for a town where someone who is sheltered at home and needs assistance. Usually, we got multiple local volunteer signups.

The group's success generated more work than they could manage, and they began recruiting volunteers to help with the admin.

There are many more volunteers than recipients, so in one of our update emails, we asked if anyone wanted to become more involved by coming on our team. Our team is now between 10-15 people at various levels. It's really been kind of amazing; the community we've created, a small group of volunteers that responded when we asked for help with admin.

While most of her admin volunteers were concentrated in the Bay Area, the team had helpers in North Carolina and Texas. Nora found that while the people requesting aid tended to be older, she was also contacted by those with a disability or who were immunocompromised and anxious about going out. The volunteers also spanned the age range and those unable to run errands helped in other capacities. The team did not hold any specific demographic data about either volunteers or recipients of assistance. Language was not a barrier to the operation, since Nora spoke reasonable Spanish and two volunteers, one of whom was based in Texas, helped translate the site and respond to requests in Spanish.

For Nora, the pandemic was a contradictory process. It meant lockdowns but also facilitated the development of wider networks needed for mutual aid, thus opening the possibility of extending personal relationships.

It is ironic and funny. We moved to Redwood City from San Francisco a couple of years ago, and we hadn't really met that many people who live here. But just in the last few months, we've met three or four times more people who are interested in the same things that we are because of the process of trying to do something to help the community during Covid. And that's been fantastic, honestly, very unexpected. It's been an incredible experience.

Nora also appreciated that some people in need may not be able to use her platform, echoing the problem identified earlier by Paige. There will be some who, for various reasons, cannot access the online information, while others who may see an online advert, may not be able to sign up online. Nora explained the steps they had taken to minimise this problem.

> We've set up a Google Voice phone number for people who either don't feel comfortable signing-up online or would rather have a phone number to call. We have had several signups that way. But even with that, there's still there's been challenges in reaching out to people who are not in our immediate networks. While the pandemic has shown that many people are not comfortable with the technology, they are now more open to using it than before because other options are limited. Before you could just go out and talk to someone in person.

From the start of Covid Assist, Nora was mindful of the data privacy and other security problems associated with volunteers and those asking for support.

> In these unique circumstances, people need much greater assistance than normal. But using Google spreadsheets etc doesn't give control over who's seeing the information. We wanted our system to offer at least one step up from that. This was one of our goals since we can aggregate information. It's not perfect, but it's slightly more secure. Doing things like running background checks is costly, requires a lot of setup and we can't do that digitally. But we've learnt from other mutual aid groups. We have a process of verifying someone's address, talking to them on the phone. We're trying to find that balance between taking care of our recipients and our volunteers but also making it easy to participate readily and quickly.

Nora had several interesting things to say about working with other groups.

> From the beginning we wanted to connect with other MAGs and in this unique moment there's no competition because we're not trying to make

money or trying to edge others. There's no sense of that. We're all working towards the same goal, and we know that we can't do it all alone.

We started looking for local and national partnerships because while our system was effective in finding volunteers in places we knew, it couldn't provide the same depth of experience for someone say, in Massachusetts. MAGS are springing up all over the country, most of them are volunteer led using simple Google's sheets a lot of the time to sign-up people. We started finding partnerships and we built these into our website sign up. This meant if someone signed-up in an area where we have a partner, we will let them know about the local group. This encourages volunteers to connect to their nearest group.

Finding other MAGs required basic research and culling together information about activity elsewhere and then reaching out to establish contact. This resulted in a network of partnerships with other MAGs. She found most groups were using basic technology.

While most groups were using Google Sheets, we also met groups that were far beyond us in terms of technical setup. They did have help from other companies with financial support, so they have more resources and were able to dedicate time and infrastructure to make things happen.

COVID Assist was keen to see its work develop.

After matching volunteer and recipient, we really leave it to them to coordinate but we've heard from many recipients that they don't want this stop once the pandemic is over, that they've made friends even. They've made connections with people they might not have connected with otherwise. And that I think is something that pandemic or no pandemic people are craving. So that's an aspect I would like to see that carry on. Particularly when it comes to groups, like seniors, who may not have wide connections in their communities. I am focused on this aspect now.

I think we should leverage the technology to make it easier for us to orchestrate this work so those who are participating get what they need from the system without lots of monitoring of every activity. That may mean many more people will be involved.

Nora's experience was showing that the pandemic had foregrounded a pre-existing problem normally hidden from view. The isolation that many people felt before COVID-19 was amplified by the pandemic. Nora spoke of the desire for groups to come together to discuss and resolve technical and operational problems.

> We hosted a virtual summit with the organisers of some 10 mutual aid programmes to the possibilities of working together particularly for the people who had already invested a lot of time and energy in other technical solutions. As I said before, it's not a competitive environment. It's about how can we share the tools and strategies we've created to make something better for everybody. We're still figuring this out but our goal moving forward is to work with other groups and share what we've built. Hopefully by sharing we will have a product that will last beyond the pandemic.

> The meeting was fantastic. We had an intimate conversation about the challenges in running mutual aid programmes, particularly on a volunteer basis. Almost everyone has a day job they're trying to do as well. It was a good discussion about what strategies groups have found useful. These included managing volunteer verifications and how to meet the need for a service we're not able to provide. These are some of the difficult things that each group has been figuring out on their own. We're hoping to have another online meeting.

The desire to cooperate arose from the need to solve several practical problems linked to making mutual aid more effective.

> Our initial conversations were about avoiding a situation where volunteers were signing-up with multiple groups. We also know there can be small but important differences between the work of groups. For example, our model is primarily about matching volunteer to recipient. Other groups with more technically advanced solutions are leaning towards an Uber or Doordash approach style where a one-off request is picked-up and covered. It is like a free, fast Instacart service. You don't have to wait to find a medium-term volunteer because it can connect immediately with someone who may already be shopping at that moment. While effective, there's not the sense of developing a relationship between the

volunteer and recipient. While I think there's room for both, I like the idea of creating ongoing relationships.

The desire to share technologies was there but Nora recognised that the trajectory of the pandemic would be a factor.

Honestly, I would love for it to happen quickly and having a summit was to start that conversation. While the pandemic is far from over, I think it feels that we're moving into a new phase with a reduction in the numbers requesting assistance and volunteers. It's not that anything has gone away, but that maybe people are adjusting and so the MAGs we've spoken to are also adjusting. We're aligning our long-term vision, but we must have more of a strategy and a timeline that's not imposed upon us. At the beginning, there was just this huge sense of urgency. And while the conditions are no less dire than they were, I think the sense of urgency has diminished a bit.

Nora discussed the role open-source software could play in sharing process.

We've talked about the possibilities to open source our software. At least two other MAGs I've been in contact with already use open-source software. That is fantastic. We're in a unique situation because we basically cloned our proprietary software for reuse with COVID Assists and we've been trying to figure out what steps would it take for us to open source it because that's a desire that we have. We're all working towards the same goal here and we want to contribute to the work already done. I would love to see us open-source part of our software or work with an existing open-source project to contribute some of our features to it. I do think that that is a fantastic way to make this technology available to more people.

Zoom was created, in part, with to make money while with MAGs, making money was never the motivation and the idea of open sourcing seems really second nature. Whether the pandemic will shift how people think about that, I don't know. But it speaks to the kind of uniqueness of the situation that we're in right now and the uniqueness of the mindset that people have. It would be a fantastic experience if all these tech companies, who are normally so competitive, decided that they wanted to work together to create one great product that everyone could share. That won't happen because that's not their motivation. I hope this spirit of collaboration will continue because we're really all on the same side here. I would love to see that continue.

COVID-19 has changed people. This is true for me. We are so much more inclined to help and to volunteer to do something outside of the norm. Because these are unprecedented times, at least in our lifetime. Suddenly, people who maybe they thought about profit, because that's what we have been taught to think about, are now thinking about how can we use technology for good even if we don't profit from it?

The pressures linked to maintaining the activity led to Covid Assist merging its team and recipient list with another MAG, Helping Hands Community. Nonetheless, Nora's comments provide several insights concerning the use of DTs, MAGS, and COVID-19. Her reference to the non-competitive environment is indicative of the feelings of many MAGS linked to the pandemic and shows that shared problems and solutions were needed for the work to be effectively undertaken. Something deeper also occurred. Practical action was needed to address the real practical challenges facing people during the pandemic. In undertaking this activity, Nora's experience reveals that it changed both those who delivered assistance and those who received it, and that new and ongoing relationships were established. The next section looks at the work of a MAG based in Northwest England.

Football fans supporting foodbanks.

Dave is an active trade unionist, socialist, and an ardent life-long supporter of Everton football (soccer) club. He explained how the mutual aid group, Fans Supporting Foodbanks (https://twitter.com/SFoodbanks), started.

In October 2015 we had a meeting with the UK football Premier League management over exorbitant ticket prices. We had launched the 2020 campaign to bring down ticket prices. At that meeting, the chief executive of the Premier League went to great lengths to explain that the Premier League was an incredibly charitable organisation, and, while he didn't say it, he was implying that fans were being greedy for wanting a price cap. What would probably surprise yourself and people like you, is that the Premier League has a slush fund that gives out solidarity payments of about £17 million a year to the Professional Footballers Association or the League Association which receives £3 million. The only ones who get nothing are the fans.

We argued they've got an extremely valuable commodity, sold on the global market, and one of the main reasons it's got such value is because of the noise, the colour, the excitement and vibrancy fans bring to the game. It's ironic that players get paid for image rights so do big companies but nothing, no royalties for paying fans. We are not asking for payment, just a price cap on tickets. The extremely valuable commodity will lose value appeal if the fans sit there quietly and say and do nothing.

During the pandemic, this has happened with no fans in the stadia and television companies running crowd noise tapes during games. Dave explained that in 2015 tickets for away supporters could cost between £58–60 but now they are that now are capped at £30. This policy has been extended until 2022. This was a huge success for Dave's campaign. There was an additional spin-off. The campaign undercut the notion that football fans could not work closely together while being fervent supporters of their own clubs. Dave described how fans from rival clubs met on a regular basis during the campaign and so became good friends and "comrades".

One of the things that was always said to Everton and Liverpool[1] fans when they went down to the campaign meetings was that scousers always stick together.[2] On the way back to Liverpool after one of the meetings we discussed what was unique about the fans' culture from Liverpool compared to other clubs. With the greatest respect, I don't think fans from Manchester United or Manchester City or the London clubs could do things collectively. We also talked about doing something to show the positive side of football fans.

---

[1] Liverpool and Everton football clubs are in the same city,
[2] Scouser is a slang term to describe people who come from the city of Liverpool.

The Liverpool and Everton football clubs are also in the same parliamentary constituency and six of the wards[3] in the constituency are often placed in the 20 most socially and economically deprived wards in the country. This proximity encourages strong ties between the rival fans. The day following one of the London ticket campaign meetings, Dave, as part of his trade union activity, visited a community centre to meet some construction workers.

> I saw a queue of about 20 people at the Centre and asked what was happening. The chairman of the Community Association explained it was a queue for a food bank and went on to say the food bank was just about to run out of food. He took us into their stockroom and there was very little, or nothing left, only an extremely large bag of pasta and a couple of tins of tuna which were being divided into smaller and smaller parcels to make sure that everybody got something.

It was this meeting that motivated members of the supporters' groups, Liverpool's Spirit of Shankly and Everton's Blue Union, to come together to act.

> We decided to use our expertise and organisational skills we had from bringing trade unions and workers together, to approach football fans. We were determined that no matter what we set up we weren't gonna compete with something that was already in existence. We decided that we would use our contacts in football to support food banks. The following week Everton played Manchester United and we turned up outside the stadium with a wheelie bin and collected empty crisp packets, empty beer cans but also about eight bags of food, which we were immensely proud of. From that day in October 2015, we've collected food at every single game at Anfield.[4] It has been so successful that 30% of all the food collected for the food Bank is collected outside Anfield and Goodison Park.[5] This is about a ton of food each game. We now use a sprinter van to collect the food.

---

[3] Electoral sub-division.

[4] Home ground of Liverpool football club.

[5] Home ground of Everton football club.

Now there are approximately 35 other football clubs with food bank collections outside stadiums. We've got Manchester United and Manchester City supporters working together collectively.

Whenever Everton or Liverpool play away to teams that also collect food, we make sure we have food to donate as an act of solidarity. When those teams come to play us, their supporters bring food for our food bank. It's all about fans putting aside tribal differences and giving to the community. Look, our enemy isn't someone with a different local accent, such as Cockney or Scouse or Brummie[6] or Mancunian.[7] It's those who have forced austerity on us.

In doing this, the team were creating a movement within football that has the fans thinking and planning before a game: I've got the ticket, got the scarf, now do I have my food donation? Going to a match involves thinking about an act of solidarity.

To be honest with you, it's a really simple process. There can be 40,000-50,000 fans at a game. If every single fan donated one single tin when they came to a match, we would have 50,000 tins of beans or soup or tuna; we could eradicate hunger on Merseyside.

The group makes good use of social media to organise food collection. It has over 13,000 followers on Twitter with an estimated 4000 followers on Facebook.

Most of our social media posts go via Twitter. We can get anything up to half a million likes when we put something out on Twitter and get hundreds if not thousands of retweets. We've also appeared on the Russell Howard show (available at Vimeo.com/384491623). Bill Shankly was probably the epitome of football and socialism and Fans for Food banks have won awards from football fans. The Big Issue newspaper named us in the 100 of its game changer list. We have been able to promote the work we do rather than the individuals involved.

---

[6] Term for someone who lives in Birmingham, UK.
[7] Term for someone lives in Manchester, UK.

In talking about digital technologies, Dave recalled,

> We didn't use Zoom before because prior to the lockdown, given we would probably be covering two games a week, we'd meet regularly. And it wasn't just match day collections we were doing. We'd started doing trade union branches, Labour Party meetings and constituencies, we started speaking on events. One of the things that we've done right from day one was to target minority groups. We've worked a lot with the Muslim community such as collecting for the food bank. Football fans knocking on the doors of the local mosque and asking for help is totally unexpected. It helps change the perspective on who football fans are.

> Now the four main mosques in Liverpool are involved with collecting for and supporting the foodbanks with regular work. And you talk about it's also about using technology, well during 2018 world cup, I could guarantee that if we'd have walked into the Abdullah Quilliam Mosque in Liverpool, which is the first place of Islamic worship opened in Britain, the vast majority people in there, they would've asked us the same question. Can you get tickets for the matches? Now unfortunately, the answer is always No. However, we decided that we would take football to the mosque and so during the world cup we'd done live screenings of world cup games into the mosque on a big screen using technology.

> We beamed the Russia vs Egypt game to the mosque and invited about 300 people from the local community. That was a deliberate attempt to build bridges, not walls to get communities working together. That worked well and got a lot of publicity. There was some Islamophobic abuse at one of the Liverpool players when Liverpool played West Ham in London. So, we invited the West Ham supporters' group to Liverpool and took them to the Mosque. Then we introduced them to the Iman at the mosque who did his Friday talk wearing a West Ham scarf. He was accepting the hand of friendship. That's the direction we are going in with our movement.

No football matches were played during the first UK pandemic lockdown which stopped the work of the group causing a major problem for the group because it was not possible to collect food. To overcome this difficulty, the group helped set up a donations page on the JustGiving crowdfunding website linked to Donor Box. During the first month of the lockdown the group collected over £100,000. The team chooses this method for a specific reason.

> We're not a charity and we wish to remain political. Excuse my choice of language! I'm going to use the F word, ok? Fans for Food Banks is like a franchise, though that's something I'm not comfortable with saying. It's an incredibly strong brand. The food we collect locally goes to the North Liverpool Food Bank which is a charity, and it was better for them to setup the Donate box, using their charity number but our brand name and logo. That's how we managed to collect over £100,000 and that money was ring-fenced so couldn't be spent on anything other than food. That helped fill the void created by not being able to do match day collections. The big advantage with the Donate box is the lower rate of commission.

This was an imaginative use of internet-driven crowd funding platforms enabling a local charity to benefit during the first lockdown period. However, the use of the technologies went beyond facilitating funding. One of the Fans for Food supporters in Liverpool was furloughed and began to use his 3D printer at home to print pandemic masks. Dave explained how their contacts in the Northwest Ambulance Service were saying they did not have any personal protection equipment (PPE).

> We came up with the idea of printing masks and spoke to several people including an architectural designer who had been recently furloughed. We appealed to anyone with the necessary skills or equipment to get on board and we did some fundraising. Very quickly, we got several individuals and groups together. Yesterday, we produced over 600 face visors. And we are now making scrubs. Its developed into something of a cottage industry with over 20 people involved.

However, as Dave outlined, this was only one side of their work during this period.

> Liverpool City Council gave us the Anfield Sports Centre, which was available because the council had closed all its leisure facilities. We were

able to turn the Centre into a food production hub. So, we've got people in the Centre putting food parcels together to send out to people who are shielding or self-isolating and who have no access to food. We are getting food parcels to single people families. Workers from British Gas are distributing these parcels throughout the North end of the city. So logistically, there are a lot of people involved here. There is upwards of 20 schools, colleges, or universities, where we're using their IT design departments and their expertise to produce PPE. There's a lot of people with relevant educational backgrounds involved. The Wavertree Technology Park has also become a part of the effort.

All this work was generated from the grassroots using the network established by Fans for Food Banks. It was at this point in the interview that Dave said he had been socially isolating because of his underlying health problems but he was quick to comment that being in isolation because of the pandemic did not mean someone had to be isolated. The role of social media technologies was crucial here.

I mainly use Zoom and social media running on my mobile phone. I'll give you an example. Last week I was contacted by a support group in Glasgow who had been raising money for PPE and they wanted to order 5000 face visors. They wanted a price for these. I was quite surprised by this since we give everything away. We don't charge for anything we do or design. We also needed to be aware of charging for something that doesn't have the British kite mark, which hasn't been accredited. We always say we will help and assist, and hope for a small donation. That way we avoid any liability.

We must purchase the material we use to make the PPE. Last week, one of our supporters went down to Brighton to get the raw material. So, we are using the Internet, social media, contacts to get the materials we need. Because you're in self-isolation doesn't mean that you're isolated. Far from it. I'm busier now than I have ever been.

Dave went on to say that in some ways digital technologies have allowed for a busier period. Online Zoom meetings cut down the time usually occurring between physical offline meetings meaning he could fit in more online discussions.

I can work anywhere between Crewe and Carlisle which covers a vast geographical spread. So, I could be in a car for two or three hours travelling. Now because of COVID-19, I'm not travelling and as soon as I've had a bit of breakfast, I'm working without any problem, without any travelling. I'm probably far more productive than I normally am because I'm not travelling such long distances.

However, he thought that online meetings undermine other, important aspects of human interaction, such as visual cues, body language, how people move, whether they got a question that can be clarified. Signals that can be missed in the online environment.

I am a socialist and incredibly social as well. I like to see the whites of people's eyes, to see what they're thinking and how they're reacting to me. This is particularly important when you're trying to organise something. You lose that personal interaction via Zoom, or Skype or whatever it is. It's a poor substitute, dare I say, for the interaction I want to have.

To be honest, I don't know if I will continue to use the technology after the pandemic. I've got mixed feelings about that. My job involves a lot of organising people on greenfield sites where there's no trade union recognition and there's no trade union members. And a lot of that is done by bringing people together. Getting them to mix. Instead of someone being that fellow over there on the opposite side of the factory, I try to get them to interact with each other. The trade union movement is built on camaraderie. Can you get that camaraderie on a Zoom call? I suspect you won't. Online meetings have many, many, many benefits. But will never get over that sort of thing.

There is also another problem. I took part in a Zoom call on Friday with 18 of my colleagues on the screen and I think there were several of them paying little or no attention to what was going on. They were just going through the motions. It's about interaction, about having respect. It's about engagement. It's about building up those elements of trust and friendship and camaraderie. If I was in a room with you, I wouldn't be checking my messages on my mobile.

Towards the end of the discussion, Dave highlighted another difficulty he faces from digital technologies.

> While I've been talking to you, I have five missed calls and three alerts for incoming emails. Therein lies the problem, isn't it? I'm trying to get this message off my screen. I'm being hounded. New technology means you're constantly available, people will know that I'm online and asking why I'm not responding to them. For example, I've got two phones: one for work, the other personal. I haven't even checked my works phone yet but I'm sure there's loads of stuff waiting for me. That is a further problem. There is only so much I can respond to. It means stress. And that's probably why people talk about stress levels going through the roof. It so happens that I'm a calm person. Many people often accuse me of not having a pulse because I don't let things get out stressed.

Conclusion

It is a cliché to say that in times of adversity communities show a passion for shared solidarity, the COVID-19 pandemic was and continues to be one of those moments. It created the need and space for people to respond to the societal problems initially ignored by more conventional safety nets. Indeed, the pandemic threw into sharp relief the inadequacy of those safety nets when people, especially the more vulnerable, were left stranded and isolated as the lockdowns were implemented. The stories in this chapter will resonate with the myriad of MAGs formed during Spring 2020.

This involved the creation of both personal relationships which people wanted to continue after the pandemic and distant relationships with persons who may never meet. The actions of the MAGs are a clear manifestation of the deep well of solidarity that exists across the range of localities and communities. The existence and work of the MAGs undermine many of the common-sense notions seemingly prevalent. Cooperation rather than competition was needed to effectively undertake the work of the MAGS showing, in Gramsci's formulation, a good new sense emerged. The basic premise of the MAGs was simple. People needed help, people can organise that help, and others will respond willing to that call for help. The emphasis was on the practical assistance that could be delivered and in doing so provided a stunning illustration challenging the dominant ideology that the market is the most effective mechanism for the efficient distribution of necessary goods.

Each stage of the pandemic threw up its own problems confronting MAGs and organisers looked to digital technologies to facilitate the collection and distribution of food and other essential items. This process shows the creative endeavour required to ensure the message, we can help you, was delivered across of a range of media. From turning to funding by the Fans for Foodbanks to taping flyers in apartment blocks for seniors, MAGs used a multitude of ingenious mechanisms linking old school methods and DTs. This activity also revealed that using DTs also generated the need for more, rather than less, involvement of people as well as problems associated with confidentiality and security, problems that had not been anticipated at the beginning.

A spirit of cooperation infused the discussions between MAG organisers wanting to share and improve upon the processes they were using. They saw competition as a significant barrier to effective mutual aid work and engaged in a wider re-evaluation about the priorities of and the possibilities for DTs. The widespread practical expressions of solidarity and cooperation, clearly evident in the work of MAGs, should encourage us to develop a critical view of the dominant ideologies, seemingly routed in common-sense, that focus on self-interest, competition, that those in power know best, and that movements from below are of little value. The truth is that if this so-called common-sense had been followed, there would have been much more suffering during the pandemic. The stories in this chapter are also stories of people changing through activity, of people beginning to see the world in a different light, of recognising the strengths and weaknesses of the much-lauded DTs and seeing the importance of traditional forms of communication. As I said at the beginning of this chapter, it is impossible to know just how many millions of people have been engaged in mutual aid work during the pandemic but the stories here show suggest that many will have experienced a shared understanding of the world that rejects common-sense for good sense. The next chapter covers the pandemic, DTs, and mental health.

References

Mao, G., Fernandes-Jesus, M., Ntonis, E., & Drury, J. (2021, July 28). What have we learned about COVID-19 volunteering in the UK? A rapid review of the literature. *BMC Public Health, 21*, 1470. https://doi.org/10.1186/s12 889-021-11390-8

Legal and General. (2020, May 26). *10 million Brits volunteering as the nation unites in the Isolation Economy, says Legal & General*. Retrieved September 20, 2021, from https://group.legalandgeneral.com/en/newsroom/press-rel eases/10-million-brits-volunteering-as-the-nation-unites-in-the-isolation-eco nomy-says-legal-general

4

COVID-19, Digital Technologies, and Coping with Mental Health

Introduction

Research focused on the value of digital health technologies during the pandemic has either ignored mental health (Negreiro, 2021) or has only outlined potential benefits. This chapter uses in-depth interviews with mental health professionals, those with a lived experience of mental health challenges, and/or as organisers/users of support groups, to explore their use of DTs during COVID-19.

COVID-19 news headlines invariably focused on deaths, the number of cases, numbers vaccinated, hospital admissions, and rates of infection. Yet, generally ignored by these headlines, another, silent COVID-19 crisis developed. Covid-Minds estimate that, globally, there were over 150 longitudinal studies seeking to understand the impact of COVID-19 pandemic on mental health (Covid-Minds, 2021). While the full results of these studies have yet to be publicised, already all the key mental health indicators, covering incidents of depression, anxiety disorders, schizophrenia, eating disorders, difficulty in sleeping, addictive behaviours such as alcohol consumption, and suicidal thoughts. have increased significantly (Panchal et al., 2021).

© The Author(s), under exclusive license to Springer Nature Singapore Pte Ltd. 2022
M. Healy, *Organising during the Coronavirus Crisis*,
https://doi.org/10.1007/978-981-19-1942-8_4

Before COVID-19, the WHO had already identified the link between pandemics and the increase in mental health challenges urging member states to develop the full range of comprehensive and integrated mental health services and psychosocial supports. The onset of the COVID-19 pandemic added extra urgency to this call (WHO, 2021) and highlighted the significant inequalities in expenditure on mental health compared to other areas of medicine (Cairney, 2021; Jia et al., 2020; McCartan et al., 2021). As with the pandemic in general, there are also variations and inequalities that influence the impact of COVID-19 on mental health, and access to remedial therapies (Proto & Quintana-Domeque, 2021). State funding support for mental health initiatives during the pandemic has been inconsistent and inadequate. In the Global South, where public health services were already under stress, COVID-19 has brought these services to near collapse. In areas such as the European Union and the United Kingdom, pre-COVID-19 austerity economics had a serious adverse impact on mental health provision (Barrera-Algarín et al., 2020). Consequently, while much has been written about what should be done to alleviate mental health challenges during the pandemic, the infrastructural support for such initiatives has been seriously eroded (Cummings, 2018).

The stories in this chapter show how ordinary people already coping with existing mental health issues, have responded to the challenges of COVID-19 with extraordinary courage, determination, and imagination. While governments have, at best, merely referred to the problems of mental health and COVID-19, those enduring mental health challenges have sought to find ways to resolve the difficulties they faced. The stories in this chapter will resonate with all of us who have either experienced, or know friends or family who have had, mental health challenges.

Fellowships During COVID-19

Sandra is a member of a local mental health well-being support group and is an activist in the local branch of her political party. She is also involved in a wide range of social movements and spoke of the direct personal impact of COVID-19- on her.

One of my dearest close friends nearly died, another friend had a cancer operation and caught the virus while recovering from the operation. So, I am aware that the virus is lethal, and I feel I'm right in the middle of it. I don't underestimate its impact and limit my social contact, observing all the rules before it was made law. Contemplating limited social contact was a problem and I had anticipated experiencing a lot of social isolation. But I've found there's much less social isolation because there's a lot more online interaction. I can now get to more events and meetings because they're online. I'm able to fully take part for instance, in my political party's regular local committee meetings.

While online connectivity offered a positive experience for Sandra, social isolation did have its problems.

Getting food was difficult for a while but now I get a regular organic grocery delivery and can make a weekly visit to a local mini supermarket. I was connected to a local mutual aid networks through WhatsApp.

Sandra described the range of digital technologies she used during the pandemic.

I'm using WhatsApp, Zoom conferencing, Google Hangouts, and Jitsi (a free conferencing app). Before, I occasionally used Zoom, but now I'm using it daily. My use of WhatsApp has increased three or four times. I have used Google Hangouts for my art therapy group.

Email has become a second-class method of communication and I don't always check for emails. Using WhatsApp or being on the Zoom means emails are not a priority. I use Facebook once every two days but not for interpersonal social stuff. It's more for sociopolitical activities. Sometimes I do like to share aspects of my life on there. But I've done less on Facebook recently.

I use Jitsi[1] weekly and recommend it because it's free. I organise meetings, like Stand up to LGBT Hate Crime, on Jitsi because I'm not paying a subscription. Someone in our support group used Jitsi and I decided to

---

[1] Free open source video conferencing software.

use it for other online activities. I could use my account to organised unlimited meeting rooms, which would be constantly available. I use it for a campaign group that meets once every two weeks. With Zoom, I attend things organized by other people.

When I realised how to do it, I helped others. A friend of mine emailed me saying she wishes her elderly parents had been on Skype before the lockdown. I told her that I use Jitsi and found it particularly good and it's a lot easier than Skype. So, I've offered it to other people such as our Stand Up to Racism group.

Sandra is describing the transfer of knowledge of digital technologies from one domain to another. She went on to talk about the impact of the pandemic on her mental health support group.

Before Covid, we had between five and ten local people at meetings. Our online meetings are now getting five or six, but the people have changed. For example, a group member who left to go back to Canada is now attending. I thought I'd never see her again and then suddenly, overnight, she's a regular part of my life again. We'd bought her a farewell cake. When I saw her again, I whooped with joy. She'd stayed on our WhatsApp organising group, which organises and plans meetings, and now is coming to meetings even though she's in Canada, she's a fully integrated member of the group again. She chaired the online meeting last week.

It was during this part of the discussion that Sandra began to explain the extent to which the pandemic and digital technologies had impacted on the life of her support group. Things had not developed as expected with contradictory currents emerging. Spatial and temporal constraints evaporated, and old relationships were renewed as new relationships formed.

Because its online, new people have joined because they're selecting meetings by convenient time rather than location. Members who used to attend our group are joining other groups at other times even though it's miles away say in West London. They would never have done that before when it was in real life, online makes it possible. They're meeting all new people in different areas in the support network that's also international.

The use of technologies during the pandemic has provided an enhanced experience concerning attendance at meetings, Sandra considers they have had a nuanced influence on the internal dynamic of the meetings.

Previously, meetings were structured around a reading and with people talking sequentially for about four or five minutes. Now it's mostly about the facts of the pandemic and its impact on them and how their week has been. People talk about how the meetings have changed and this is how I know some people have gone to online meetings in different areas.

Because people are in their own homes, we see another aspect of them and not everybody uses the app in the same way. Some might use it on speaker view, and others might use it on tile view. I like to use tile view because I like to see everyone's faces once. But you know, you can't control that.

Online meetings are more open and uninhibited because you're in an informal space. You're sitting in the front room of your home on a Friday night, it's dusk with low lighting, seeing people in their homes which wasn't possible before; this builds increased trust and intimacy. There's an element of a deeper understanding because it's about one's own personal experiences, feelings and so on. And people are more expressive and give more. We call it share, so they share more of themselves which increases intimacy. That's a weird thing. But. I think that is palpable.

I am not the only one who feels like this because I have discussed it with others. It's as if we have expressed and celebrated the sense of closeness. The intimacy and trust is there. Knowing that we're all in our own homes, which would normally be totally against one of our central principles of anonymity. The idea that you would now see people in their homes is quite a big step. It's a huge leap. But it works.

This insight counters the argument that technology is associated with pushing people away from each other and creating social isolation.

Sandra's deeper experience illustrates the profoundly positive effect technologies can have to promote social cohesion if under the direct control of the users. Sandra went on to talk about the developing sense of solidarity during this period of the pandemic.

> There is an enormous amount of gratitude and love expressed for us being there. And that togetherness is very sustaining. It is especially important as an integral part of our group's sense of being able to cope with life. I think there are quite a few people who sense this.

Sandra added a further insight into how the technology and the pandemic interacted to create a more favourable learning environment for students with a disability.

> A Shelter[2] support worker told me several of her disabled student clients are, at last, getting the online teaching they've been demanding for years. Suddenly, University managers were saying it's possible now whereas before it was impractical. Disability students are getting online teaching without struggling with transport. They have equal access like everyone else.

> Another interesting issue concerns sight. A blind member of our SWP[3] branch doesn't switch on his video during meetings because it helps him have more equality of access since people can't read his expressions and he cannot see theirs. He feels he's on a more level playing field.

However, there were problems linked to the security of Zoom meetings.

> Meetings are sometimes invaded by vandals posting inappropriate content and porn and other stuff. Group security and safety is something that's been taken on board. Now people must be at the beginning or 10 minutes after the start. Or they can text someone they know and ask to be allowed in. Previously in face-to face offline meetings, if someone came in after it began, they would still be welcome. But now because of these horrible pornographic invasions we had to put in these new rules.

---

[2] Shelter is a charity that helps people without a home.
[3] Socialist Workers Party in the United Kingdom.

The strong sense of solidarity within Sandra's mental health support group along with a relatively small number of participants, creates a supportive environment to help with technical issues. However, for other types of meetings she believes technical problems can create barriers to the effective use of DTs.

It's easy to see who wants to speak in offline meetings but I have been in online meetings with 60 people which makes it difficult to manage speakers even if they are concerned with mental health issues. People don't necessarily grasp how to show hands or know how to mute. Turning the video facility on and off can be a problem. This is especially a problem for people new to the technology. I know of online meetings with over 170 people which makes it difficult to share. It has meant longer Zoom session of over 90 minutes. It also requires breakout rooms with someone deciding where we should go.

Some feel uncomfortable with video while others want everyone to turn it on. In one meeting somebody insisted I put my video on, but I wasn't comfortable doing that because I wasn't feeling well, and my mother was in the room. This issue obviously needs much deeper discussion to make sure that it's safe for everybody. Other support networks encourage participants to have their video on, if possible but if people can't, they're still welcome to attend. Video is important because it's a face-to-face event because it's what's called a fellowship and a founding principle is that nobody will ever tell anyone outside that room that you were there or what you said. There've been debates about how to handle this issue, but the most important thing is to make the meetings as safe as possible for everybody. These discussions have been constructive.

As video meetings expanded, a consensus emerged within various groups that recognised the reluctance of some participants to use video and removed the requirement to show video. During a later interview, Sandra described an unforeseen but significant problem associated with online meetings connected with the ownership, control, and sustainability. Someone had created over 15 instant online Zoom groups with a link to a timetable meaning everyone could access the sessions.

These groups were a lifeline for many of us. Then suddenly, two months ago, the meetings were cancelled because the Zoom subscriptions were not renewed and the timetabled was deleted. It was shocking. Who knows how many groups stopped! It became too stressful for the organisers. Each group had to either decide to get its own Zoom account or find another group or stop.

Sandra further explained the problems ran deeper than subscriptions or organisational stress.

12 step fellowships are meant to be self-supporting, run by and account-able to people who use the group. Decisions are not made behind closed doors. So, setting Zoom groups may have seemed a good idea but was very much against the spirit of the fellowship. This isn't a technical problem.

Despite these problems, Sandra cites one example of good practise, when resources are available.

It's the fellowship for adult children of alcoholics and dysfunctional fami-lies called ACA Morning and it starts at 07h30 in America. So, US members are rubbing their eyes, in their dressing gowns and drinking coffee saying good morning, we reply, good afternoon, we all laugh. This daily meeting was organised since COVID-19 with its own website, social activities, creative workshop, email list. A password gives access to various sections to contact people. It's become an international community that doesn't look like stopping because they've got a solid group of organisers.

The following story concerns mental health work in Northwest England.

Mental Health Discrimination in Northwest England

Garrick works for organisations focused on ending mental health discrimination in Northwest England and has extensive experience working with English local authorities in developing race equality at all levels of education, including governors. He also established a local authority black staff forum, to aid staff wishing to challenge discrimination, and for 20 years, organised an annual diversity festival in partnership with local authority social and education services. The motivation for the Partnership for Racial Equality arose from the closure of the Merseyside Racial Equality Council, and the work of the Wirral Racial Equality group, founded by two foster mothers with black children and running weekly self-help sessions designed to educate people about Caribbean and African culture. Previously, Garrick had lived in South London.

> The Northwest was quite different from South London where I lived prior to 1989. My five children were the only black children in the new school and initially, we did not see another black family, and seeing another black person was a treat. That started me thinking about improving the situation.

> Within the partnership we did really good work around race relations, and initiated training packages for Merseyside police, developed policies covering local authority housing and social services and appointed a caseworker who would focus on cases concerning discrimination.

Garrick's work developed a focus on the discrimination experienced by those with mental health challenges.

> **Time to Change** was established when two organisations, **Rethink Mental Illness** and **Mind**, recognised that people who experience mental illness also suffer from stigma and discrimination. **Time for Change** developed into a social movement receiving funding from various sources and was able to develop an international presence in regions such as the Caribbean and South Asia.

> People are embarrassed to talk about their mental health because of discrimination. **Time for Change** developed partnerships with voluntary organisations and the public sectors using programmes like the Employers Pledge which commits employers, such as universities, trade unions, Student Unions, and voluntary housing sector employers, to actively help

employees with mental health difficulties. Our work expanded into York-shire and Southwest England using volunteers organised by 5 experienced workers.

The Pledge programme runs workshops and masterclasses on mental illness and workplace discrimination, monitors employers adopting its policies, with significant face-to-face workplace meetings, planning sessions and one-to-one discussions. All this effort came to a shuddering stop on 23 March 2020, the date of the first UK COVID-19 lockdown. Garrick and the others involved with this activity held several Zoom meetings to discuss communications options.

> People preferred Zoom and the 23 participants included nurses and doctors from St. George's and Tooting hospitals because they're part of the bigger picture, and community facilitators from Warrington, York-shire, and South London. We discussed maintaining our peer support work during isolation and the lockdown. It was clear people had differing experiences with social media, with some, for example, having never used video conferencing before and others needing extra training.

The discussions also revealed that technical competence was not the only barrier to employing digital technologies in this area.

> A bi-polar sufferer explained that going beyond 10-15 on Zoom had an adverse impact on his health. Others were extremely uncomfortable with video because they didn't want to be seen and we agreed that voice only was possible. There were serious concerns over security and confidentiality since we would be delivering a statutory service to individuals and proto-cols covering online meetings were required. Several participants were not comfortable with the process and the meetings revealed the different levels of digital skills and digital access people have and the challenges that needed overcoming.

> Despite this, we knew our peer support must continue because anxiety along with more severe mental health challenges would increase because of the lockdown and isolation. We planned online workshops accessible

to individuals and groups and considered alternative means of communication. Microsoft Teams was not considered as good as Zoom. Some asked: what's wrong with the good old-fashioned telephone?

> Our WhatsApp group works quite well but we are restricted in the work we can do across ICT platforms because some people don't want to use those means of communication. That poses challenges and we're trying to find what's best for each group and individuals. We continue to support individuals online and **Rethink Mental Illness** the charity site with special information for people isolating. There is also a dedicated site for adolescents and young adults since they face huge challenges arising from not being able to freely socialise.

Garrick talked of the specific difficulties facing seniors because they often find technologies problematic. Garrick's team decided to schedule regular fortnightly meetings to share experiences in dealing with COVID-19.

> We wanted to know if what worked successfully for one person/group could be used elsewhere and we knew this was going to be a long-term challenge. We must think about how we are going to deliver our services in a different way during lockdowns. We don't know what normal will be, so communication is still going to be a massive challenge.

The issues Garrick talked about covered administration and supporting those in need. The suspension of face-to-face work led to frustration within the team, many of whom also had a lived experience of mental health challenges. It was this personal experience allied to being able to help people in similar circumstances that had sustained the work of several groups for 12 years.

> We all have different levels of mental health challenges with some having more severe difficulties than others. I have colleagues with a bipolar condition, and this is where the peer support comes into its own. We try to care and support each other even when we're not able to see each other by using all forms of communication to maintain contact. While we don't know how effective all this work will be, we must avoid a situation where someone is not contacted for weeks or months.

Garrick also highlighted the communication problems medical professionals have while wearing protective clothing and the use of digital technologies. Nurses from King's College hospital now carry a badge with their face on it, encouraging patients to look at the badge rather than the facemask. However, this was still person-to-person in a shared physical space. The lack of this personal contact was on-going problem for Garrick's peer group.

> You can't substitute for that unique intimate contact. I don't know what impact this will have on mental health communities when we come out of this pandemic. How damaging will it be for individuals? We already know of someone who took their life. People are so frustrated with their own situation; they're restricted in their movement and they're suffering physical health and mental health. Even with the new technology peer-to-peer contact has declined. We can send text messages, but there can be a delay of 2 or 3 days before we get a response. If we don't get a reply, we just don't know what is happening.

> Before COVID-19, there was 53-year-old member who suffered from mental health, but he tried to hide its severity. People don't like to talk about these things. He died at home, and it was two weeks before the neighbours noticed. We are genuinely concerned about those living alone and encourage members to keep in contact and follow-up someone who hasn't responded. This is not easy because during lockdowns or partial confinements; we just can't jump in a car to visit them.

Garrick spoke of a Monday evening group established before COVID-19, in Liverpool's Lime Street station because of suicides on the rail network. Normally between 6 and 8 people attended the sessions and it has an online presence.

> We get many telephone and email inquiries. For example, a woman told us her son has stopped university and doesn't leave the house anymore. We try to support those individuals by telephone. Before the pandemic, some people found it difficult to come to meetings and express themselves; they don't have the confidence to do that. We tell them to come and share when they are ready; they're not compelled to disclose

information. We do whatever we can and signpost them to appropriate information, so they know how the process works.

The pandemic lockdown meant the Monday evening group could not meet and they used telephones and digital technologies to maintain contact with each other.

Some of our members will express the way they're feeling on Facebook if they're having a rotten day. We then can respond to that message and encourage them. We found that social media can help with existing contacts, but it is difficult for new people. When a new person comes into the group, we establish some sort of relationship with them before we invite them to the WhatsApp. We don't do that straight away because we must get to know each other. It's a process using landline phone numbers and email.

Garrick emphasised the reticence members have in speaking about their problems and highlighted the role digital technologies can have in this context. Speaking specifically about a yearly one-day event *Time to Talk*, where his team engaged with the community to discuss mental health, he mentioned that lived experience champions who feel uncomfortable with face-to face contact used social media to spread the message about *Time to Change* and *Rethink*. Sharing stories is a vital part of this process.

For these people, social media is especially important. I've just received two stories from Time to Change nationally, one of which explains the issues that one person went through, and she wanted to share to encourage other people. These stories are important because they help others identify their own problems and know they're not alone. They give others more confidence to talk about their experiences. Social media are an excellent way to circulate this information. We have podcasts where people record their stories, and we have a radio station that puts these stories together.

Our motto is: conversations change lives. and if you don't have a conversation, your life will not change, you've got to have the conversation.

During a later interview, Garrick re-emphasised the technical and social difficulties facing those with mental health challenges. He did however mention several important positive developments.

> During the confinements, we brought together many organisations on Zoom to develop some new approaches particularly around the peer support. After many weeks of discussion, we developed a toolkit which is now available online and it combines, in an organised way, all the ideas coming forward to try and deal with some of the issues such as confidentiality, online safety, and undertaking peer support including online.

The second positive development was the emergence of an international dimension to these discussions.

> We had more access to a wider audience, more communities, including international and we're able to tap into meetings in Australia, the United States, as well as different parts of the UK.

His work has fully embraced the potential DTs has to offer. Further initiatives included a free 24/7 emergency help telephone line provided by *Mersey Care*; a recognition that digital communications cannot fill all the needs. Yet, Garrick also underscored the major difficulties of accessing online services with those suffering domestic abuse.

> Victims may have one space in their house, but the abuser is also there making it extremely difficult to use Zoom or a telephone. Basically, those individuals weren't accessing support because of fear of the abuser. Many organisations have identified the massive issues for women who could not seek the help. And then, there is the increase of alcohol use in the home. These problems prompted a considerable conversation about the domestic violence agenda, the care for children and the involvement of social services. These are areas where the virtual couldn't help. Digital technologies just cannot fill this huge gap.

Garrick believes that while mental health organisations may include a virtual option for peer support, most are eager resume traditional forms of communication.

> People need to see someone, to see body language and eye contact.

Garrick's experience indicates that, digital technologies work well for meetings concerned with organisational issues enabling productive, positive discussions and facilitating shared stories. However, when it comes to work focused on peer support or on domestic abuse, DTs cannot effectively replace the one-to-one contact in a safe physical space. He was also keen to emphasise the adverse impact digital technologies can have people with severe mental health challenges such as bipolar disorder, psychosis, schizophrenia, and psychotic disorders. While Garrick highlighted the limitations of the technology, he believes access to DTs should be a human right.

> Governments have talked about delivering a better broadband service for 25 years but have yet to deliver. There should be digital policies to support individuals who are vulnerable and isolated. While some organisations offer free training courses and provide laptops, it's to help people to find employment. We need to go wider than that because of the poverty in the Northwest. How do we help those individuals? You cannot separate mental and physical health.

The next story concerns problems of organising and supervising psychotherapists during the pandemic.

Organising Psychotherapist Training During COVID-19

Joanne is a psychotherapist who undertakes supervision, organises, and participates in various training programmes, and does some teaching.

Before the pandemic, supervision was a mixture of face-to-face and telephone. I believe face-to-face is important. One of my supervisees is a former member of my team when I worked in the NHS,[4] so I know her enough to do telephone only supervision. Before the lockdowns, our meetings were both social and professional. I saw her when we had a local group analytic meeting on Zoom during the confinement.

Before Covid, these local group analysts met for an hour and a half every two months locally, then moved to Zoom in early March 2020 and now meet every six weeks for an hour. The meetings are mutually supportive, but different from before because we're not discussing or organising things nor are we planning the workshop we had hoped to hold in the autumn.

Joanne talked of the impact lockdowns had on different members of the group.

I'm retired, so my life is relatively straightforward. Among these local group analysts, there's another retiree who's had a difficult family time. Everybody works to some degree, some at home. One has been in Covid wards in full PPE and has talked about that. There is a huge range of experience within the group and while I feel tension and a lack of energy to do things, there's much more cohesion. Our previous priorities have been abandoned so we can support each other.

Joanne mentioned that attendance at online meetings had been good and initially considered that DTs did not significantly impair discussions.

I'm not sure that technology has made a huge amount of difference, but the pandemic has. We're all on the same river but on different boats on that river. It is different experience for someone living alone and shielding compared to someone living with a partner and child and working online.

She also considered the extent to which social distancing and the virtual aspects of the technology influence the content and feel of the meetings.

---

[4] British National Health Service.

It's difficult to separate the influence of the technology and the impact of the pandemic. Some people have found using Zoom a lot is tiring and eye strain can be a problem.

I supervise someone one-to-one by phone, but her work experience has changed. She self-isolated because the virus was in her household. Fortunately, she tested negative. She provided a therapeutic programme in a residential setting for very disturbed individuals but because there seemed little containment of participants, it didn't feel safe for my supervisee to simply move their therapy online. The residents would continue to receive some degree of support from the staff at the house and therapy would restart when more support and containment was provided.

We talk about risk assessment communication within her team, on how to enable others to understand why her work has changed. So that's a new piece of work that's related to the pandemic.

When the pandemic started, another phone supervisee also started working from home, but he's got major caring role. I've been giving significant support over the phone. His workplace managers needed to be aware of his situation and we got the union involved because he cannot do a full-time job at present and is being pressured to do more. The purpose of our phone calls has changed because of the pandemic. He has very slowly moved on to Zoom. So, both supervisees now use online video. One uses Microsoft Teams and the other Zoom. The Zoom user is extremely cautious about this. Partly because of his nature and partly his home circumstances; apart from anything else, he can't be sure of not being interrupted. So, this work has not really been influenced by the technologies.

As our discussion continued, Joanne described a range of technical difficulties.

The assessment panel interviews for my professional institute scheduled for late March were shifted online. I spent several days doing Zoom tutorials, getting a professional licence, doing trial runs, and then doing a final trial run with the two other panel members. I asked to do fewer interviews in one batch to allow more time for discussion. So instead of doing three, in a sort of extended session over about four and a half hours, we were doing two which left more time for discussion.

Things ran smoothly until I had a problem with the ethernet cabling which comes in from the street into my house and connects to the modem in my study. Somewhere along the line the cable was banging around during fierce winds, disrupting the fragile broadband connection. There were also interruptions with the people we were interviewing. Someone had her teenage son in an open plan house, sending her texts asking her for food! She'd had a clinical interview by Zoom a few days earlier, in the bathroom, the only part of the house with decent reception! The circumstances in which she was being interviewed were a minefield of distractions.

Joanne described a process in which DTs, while facilitating the continuation of work, involve significant distractions impeding their smooth working. She went on to talk about the nature of the panel Zoom interviews.

The interviewing panel meets before the interview to discuss the areas we want to cover. The interview takes some 90 minutes and can be quite intense; you can't be doing with too many distractions. It is possible to mute and unmute by pressing the spacebar. But there's some interruptions you must attend to. There was a moment when I thought my partner had fallen downstairs. I couldn't ignore that.

Interviews were followed by an assessment board meeting on Zoom. Zooming all day is exhausting and people can get used to multitasking on Zoom, reducing the screen and doing something else. I think one panel member, who does little Zooming, was finding it difficult. She felt she wasn't where she should be for the interview, it wasn't the normal setup. She wanted to have a more intimate conversation and considered Zoom too impersonal. Perhaps none of us like change but we handle it with varying degrees of reluctance or enthusiasm depending on our outlooks, our characters, our previous experience.

Joanne is also responsible for convening a panel of readers to assess end-of-course work submitted by trained therapists completing a supervision course. In 2020 they had 14 papers to review and used telephone conferencing provided by *Whypay*, a free telephone conferencing service.

> I convened a telephone conference for a marking panel – we've been doing this by telephone conference for years now. The experience was mixed. One person wasn't available, and another had a close bereavement and couldn't cope with the work. The lockdown affected the students work because it was clear that several couldn't access references or a library when they were writing the papers. We tried to make allowance for this and noted that some reports indicated the referencing wasn't complete. We appreciated this problem and took a generous approach when marking.

For the students, having an Internet connection was not enough if they were unable to access relevant texts for their assignments. This problem was exacerbated by the lack of contact with an academic librarian, a major problem, and the failure of the library's main server in March. For the administrative lead concerned with this work, the server failure meant a deluge of emails requiring her to work extra significant hours from home. For the markers, telephone conferencing, rather than video calls, was considered more effective.

Digital technologies were not able to overcome a further problem facing Joanne during lockdowns.

> Lack of library access created difficulties. I liaise with the part-time librarian who works for our Institute, but she cannot access books either, nor the technology to scan and digitize papers; she can only work with what's already digitised and available over the web.

> I was invited to write a word response to a paper, including some personal experience or opinion. I wanted to cite a paper; I had the paper copy. But I couldn't determine where the copy originated. Eventually, using Google, I tracked down the author who gave me the reference and I submitted my paper. But I was asked to submit electronically through a portal. I had to get myself a unique identifier. Then, the paper, now on Adobe Reader,

comes to me from the editor for further edits. This created several serious and frustrating technical difficulties resulting in the loss of my additional edits.

I go on the Adobe site; I'm already having problems with Adobe Photoshop. I suspect it's the interplay between Apple constantly upgrading my Mac and Adobe not being quite in sync because every time Apple updates its virus protection system, there's glitches with non-Apple applications. There have also been two major upgrades when they moved from Sierra to Mojave, and then from Mojave to Catalina. Consequently, lots of pay portals didn't work and including my copy of Adobe Photoshop which kept crashing. I had to buy a new version of Photoshop which had to be installed using the phone.

During this part of the discussion, Joanne listed software and hardware difficulties ranging from problems associated with programme upgrades, incompatible software, system failures, battery failures, putting programmes in the trash bin and then re-installing, time and trouble accessing online help, and Kernel crashing. Joanne was "frantic that these problems would happen in the middle of a Zoom interview". Ultimately, Joanne bought a new computer. She then went onto describe the experience of a meeting run on Zoom.

Normally this quarterly meeting of therapy professionals has 20-26 participants with plenary sessions bookending the day. In between there's a more formal, seminar like session. Because of the pandemic we've gone online for the first time; it was quite challenging and different. Firstly, attendance increased to 39, many from overseas. The feel of the group was also different. I was tasked with helping participants through the process which was quite difficult when switching screens from gallery to speaker view while trying to watch the event. I co-hosted the large meetings while somebody else did the admin and organised the breakout rooms. Technically, I found it very tiring, very demanding.

On the nature of the discussions, Joanne said:

It is difficult to separate the impact of the pandemic from the influence of the technology. The subjects discussed were different from previous events. People wanted to discuss the impact of Covid restrictions or to talk about loss, or their patients' loss. They also wanted to discuss women's experiences under the pandemic. The increased attendance meant that many who came for the first time didn't have a shared history of the group. Regular participants did not have the same sense of being in a safe space that existed before. These significantly influenced the nature of the discussion with technological implications over laid on these issues. Some participants were agreeably surprised at the intimate nature of the discussions. Several comments focused on Zoom backgrounds with many people simply showing their homes or using a photograph.

Joanne is highlighting an important aspect of online participatory video meetings. People become aware of the surroundings of others, colours, shapes, personal items, such as photographs, and the presence of domestic animals. These can enhance the intimate environment because it offers insights into someone else's life that is not possible in offline setting. Digital technologies enable greater social distancing but at the same time offer the potential for more intimate connections. Joanne uses a photo of the room in which they previously met as a mechanism for starting and finishing the online meetings. It is a method of setting boundaries.

Joanne regularly participates in several other online meetings some of which are new.

> I've participated in numerous professional large groups meetings. For example, I'm on a course that moved online. This has widened participation. I also attend a new regular Sunday lunchtime international Zoom meeting organised a professional Society for its members. It's an exciting initiative with a take up of between 120 to 140 people. Yet, there are problems. The online meetings developed out of an email forum which was dominated by a relatively small number of people. This has fed into the online video sessions with some people thinking they can interrupt others while others should not interrupt them. They go into lecture mode and deliver speeches.

> I do intermittent video sessions with a course that I've been a part of that meets in a block over a weekend. Participants come from Canada,

Finland, Germany, Austria, Denmark, Australia, and the UK. We met face-to-face in early March which included someone from Italy. But we met online in May and will be meeting online twice in July. I've also dipped into two other events, which are not automatically international.

I'm deeply disappointed that the international conference I was supposed to be going to in Spain, has moved online. I will be conducting a group in three languages with an uncertain number of people somewhere between 20 and 50. It was difficult enough when I did this in Berlin three years ago with a group of 65 in one large room. I don't know how it's going to work online.

Joanne believes the use of digital technologies during the pandemic will continue as the lockdowns are lifted.

Will we continue to meet virtually even though we could meet face-to-face? Or will we have a compromise? There's been much discussion of how we would do this, but there certainly is some momentum behind the idea that something virtual should continue. People are saying that online international meetings should continue. The technology offers so much potential. I've been in discussions where people have come from all over the world. For instance, I attended a seminar on lucid dreaming that was available for free with participants from different parts of the globe. But I have also heard about similar things using only audio via WhatsApp, Signal or Telegram. So, I don't think it's entirely just video technology. There are also possibilities with audio.

She recognises the possibilities technology has to offer and during our second interview Joanne said the lockdowns had provided the impetus and time needed to develop her technical skills. She now feels competent enough to provide a degree of training to family, friends, and colleagues. She believes people are generally more resilient about DTs. However, she outlined several new difficulties. The lack of skilled digital workers had created problems associated with accessing online help. The transition from lockdown to normal work patterns will mean a tremendous increase the pace of working and the time needed to organise activities. Uncertainties concerning the eventual mix of online and offline work linked to problems of access to appropriate physical spaces will also need to be addressed.

Peer-to-Peer Support During the Pandemic

For five years, Dorothy has been a coordinator with a peer-led mental health support group involving 20 volunteer coordinators with lived experience of mental health issues. Before the pandemic, the group held weekly informal all day walk-in sessions with breakfast, board games, chats, followed by an early evening meal, and a more structured discussion. The sessions provided a safe, non-judgemental space allowing people to leave their stresses and pressures outside making it easy for people to talk about their mental health. Members also organised twice weekly guitar sessions which were especially important for men because of their reluctance to open-up about their problems. Confidentiality is a critical element with the group. Two coordinators were always present to ensure that the relaxed environment adhered to basic rules.

> There are 50 regulars, about 200 who'll come occasionally, and some who come, get what they need, and then we might not see them again because they're doing well. I really like our group because it brings together people, who wouldn't normally share the same space. Our oldest member is 80 and our youngest is 20. Activities, like playing games, often lead to further discussion as people begin to realise there are others like them. For many, just finding out they are not on their own is powerful. We started working with one of the social prescribers locally which encouraged more people to come. This has been a real challenge.

Email, text messages, a phone tree, and Facebook had provided a basic but efficient one-way information system, but the Facebook presence had created problems.

> It required constant monitoring with some personal postings being seen by everyone. We were concerned about the impact on coordinators because it generated off-line calls from users at all hours, including holidays. We also got wellness check calls from the local police. It was a lot

of pressure on us, and we do have our own mental health issues. It was such a mess that in the end we reverted to a simple information page.

The coordinators closed the centre just before the lockdown.

It was a shock. We had problems contacting people who are homeless or don't have a phone, or Internet. We had to simply post a note on the door and the guitar sessions were suspended. It was difficult at the start and our online weekly video chats were challenging. I tried the first one via Facebook video, but realised it only allowed for eight people on a call. While we were on the call, I was also phoning someone to explain how it works. Then suddenly people were messaging saying they couldn't get on and asking what's happening.

Dorothy described the problems linked to shifting onto an online environment. The calm, ebb and flow informal relaxed chats spread over several hours were compressed into a rigid timeline dictated by the technology.

Normally, a larger group discussion develops into smaller groups, with people having more personal conversations. Offline it's possible to be conscious of situations where a coordinator is in a long intense conversation. I'll check on them and make sure that they're okay, particularly if it is difficult to disengage. Coordinators are now having these conversations via a phone call or video or message and there's no one to tap the brakes.

I speak to the guy who runs the guitar group by phone because he does not have the internet at home or a smartphone. A member of his group does not read or write, so we also talk to him by phone.

While the pandemic had a negative impact on attendance at Monday's sessions and the guitar group, going online enabled wider participation.

I've really enjoyed being able to connect with several people who wouldn't normally come to our sessions. We also get messages on Facebook, whether it's via a group chat or group video and people will post on the page saying, you know, here's a picture of my cat or garden. They ask, how's everyone? It's just nice to ask if everyone's doing OK.

One member, who used to be a coordinator but resigned has been able to call more often using Facebook. This has been helpful for her, particularly when she needed support. Someone else relied on his wife to bring him but now he Just switches on his laptop and off we go.

Dorothy found DTs particularly useful during the pandemic for straightforward simple tasks, like ordering prescription online and being able to connect via Facetime with a close friend who was in hospital.

I work for the NHS and so was offered counselling, but counselling over the phone is challenging. It is no substitute for being there in person and sudden technical difficulties can make it impossible to get in touch with anybody. Those with mental health challenges are already feeling fragile and often need to build up the courage to make that phone call or to try and ask for help through official channels. Waiting an hour to get through to the local surgery and then talking to an overworked overstressed receptionist, is not a pleasant experience. It's a nightmare.

The group also decided to use Zoom.

We also subscribed to Zoom to enable slightly longer meetings, because 40 minutes just wasn't quite enough. We figured out what people were comfortable with and stuck with it.

Discussions can end up being or feeling a lot more structured and managed, than before. I know it is a necessity, but it is not the same. Trying to explain that being online means changing things can be an issue and expectations can be different. Some people just wanted to have a chat, play a game and, you know, show dog or cat pics. A nice catch up, but that isn't really a support group. Others wanted more intense conversations about their situation. We are trying meet these different needs with people that don't normally see each other. It's complicated at times and we can't please everybody.

A real online support group session requires more structure and including everyone, without selecting people can be challenging. Some people just want to listen, that's fine provided we make sure they've got opportunity to speak. Sometimes we had to steer the conversation away from sensitive issues. That is difficult online. In our face-to-face sessions we could have breakout moments if someone was upset or wanted to talk about something. That's just not possible online. It's been a substitution and we've made do because we've had to, but it's not the same.

Going online also meant additional pressure associated with organising online meetings.

Before, Mondays were a firm day, and we used Facebook to decide who would get what for the session. Now we have long conversations about the best time to meet because everyone's busy and we're trying to constantly adapt and try and fit in with everyone; it does become quite difficult. It can be frustrating.

Dorothy described how the pandemic and the use of DTs had a more profound impact on the work of the support group.

The pandemic brought to a head problem bubbling away for years. Funding was an issue, but we also thought differently about how we should respond to the pandemic. How we should be offering support became a real concern. Some of us were worried about the legal consequences in continuing with face-to-face contact. I'm deeply concerned about everyone's mental health, but I'd also like to keep them physically safe as well. Others insisted mental health is the most important thing so we should continue with face-to-face at any cost.

The pressures arising from the pandemic allied to the group's precarious financial situation resulted in a serious internal discussion. Financial pressures meant the group decided to vacate the group's existing premises which was a wrench for everyone concerned. The pandemic meant these discussions took place online and Dorothy believes this adversely impacted on their tone and volume.

Our Facebook chat group, previously used to organise practical matters like who has volunteering on Monday, turned into big debate about what the future of the group should be, and how we should be reaching people. Before, this would have happened in person with everyone having time to take a minute or have a break if things were getting a bit heated, allowing time and reflection for sensitive matters. Online it ended with people sending long Facebook messages and it was impossible to judge the tone and the context. People were getting irate and upset.

It was also intrusive because someone could post at 9pm while others may be in bed or at work and so received the message at odd times of day. This caught people off guard with everyone posting at random times of day or maybe a week later. It was very confusing. A lot of people got upset about this and left the Facebook group causing more confusion. Others were blocked on Facebook, so we couldn't see their messages. It just became a nightmare and quite aggressive and unpleasant. Everyone's struggling and they didn't want to get dragged into unreasonable conversations. The technology also encouraged sub-conversations on say, a phone, to comment about someone who is talking, without that person knowing what is being said. Face-to-face, everyone's in the same space at the same time.

We were divided, with some keen to keep offering online support while others said that it was excluding many people and weren't comfortable with it. We split into two camps, the people that wanted to meet face-to-face regardless and the rest of us who thought it wasn't safe to do that. We said online support might not be perfect, but it's what we've got for now. It caused a rift within the group.

Then I had to take time off and the online service dwindled since we didn't have enough of us coordinating it. We then hoped everything we would be back to normal in April. Everyone's been waiting to back to face-to-face sessions. This meant it has been quite difficult to manage the online thing. It is a very intense activity when you're trying to support a group of people, virtually without any of that sort of physical interaction to see what's going on.

Dorothy recognises the benefits DTs can have in communications between peer support networks by significantly reducing travelling time, enlarging participation, enabling frequent catch-up chats, and making the meetings more productive. The pandemic also prompted the use of unfamiliar technologies, such as Google Hangouts, even if this created difficulties and confusions for those unfamiliar with these techniques. While going online offered some positive possibilities, it created several challenges for the Dorothy and her colleagues including the difficulty of keeping personal and work communications separate.

Looking to the future, Dorothy would like to keep the Facebook page going but there are problems because of insufficient resources.

> We are missing many people because not everyone was available during the day. Something virtual is needed even if we can't do a face-to-face weekly meeting. But this can be fragile. Previously, I've got enthusiastic about running an extra meeting once a week for six months but then it folded because I couldn't continue. There's enough who would like us to keep the Facebook page, but do we have the resources for that challenging responsibility?

Despite potential difficulties, Dorothy believes the use of DTs can have a positive impact provided their limitations are recognised.

> It will make us think differently about how we reach people. But while these technologies have increased possibilities for greater engagement, they are more suited to organisational meetings rather than peer-support.

> Video meetings are problematic because many people just won't do them. You just can't read people's reactions in a video meeting; it's hard to know when to speak. The conversation may flow but then there's pauses where everyone's waiting for someone else to reply, and suddenly everyone speaks at once.

> Someone I know refused remote counselling because she's living with a partner and kids and didn't feel she'd have the privacy. I think people who participate in our online groups either live in alone or have access to private space. But many people don't have that combination. It's one thing talking to the people in a room but online, somebody can be recording or video sharing. It makes another barrier for people to share.

Dorothy is confirming that for members of her group, especially those in family situations, online connections just cannot match the safe, confidential intimate experience of offline sessions. Dorothy's experience emphasises that while technology can help, it requires a great of input and organisation to make it work effectively. Further, if the people doing the organising are themselves fragile, for whatever reason, digital machines just cannot compensate for this problem. In this context, an online presence is a poor substitute for the face-to-face environment previously experienced by the group.

> It's been a very difficult year. I've lost three quite close people and if the group physically had been there, I would have felt a lot more comfortable turning up, knowing I could sit outside if it got too stressful. Whereas online feels strangely more intense and I know you can switch off at any point, but that became quite difficult. I didn't know who knew what during the online sessions. It just wasn't the same. I really missed having our Monday open sessions.

Conclusion

The pandemic and related confinements had serious negative impacts on those struggling with issues associated with mental health. The actions of the participants in this chapter indicate they recognised that it was impossible to simply wait out the pandemic. The key question: how to overcome separation in a moment calling for quarantine and isolation, required a solution. Their needs and the needs of others demanded real practical action based on collective effort and DTs were seen as critical elements in developing strategies to cope with these circumstances. While government websites (Centre for Disease Control & Prevention, 2021) posted lists of seemingly common-sense proposals, mental health activists recognised they had to move beyond platitudes and engage directly with their communities. In doing so, they confronted and attempted to resolve the multitude of the problems connected to DTs.

The stories in this chapter indicate that digital meetings/communications present possibilities for intimate experiences by building trust and undermining feelings of isolation during confinements. They also offer the potential for widening encounters with others; time and space can cease to be restricting parameters. Yet, these possibilities are constantly undermined because of more alienating encounters with digital invasions and disruption, resulting in diminished control of access, and generating a myriad of technical problems especially during sessions with large numbers of participants. Online meetings seem to work effectively in highly structured situations, especially with appropriate technical support but in more unstructured conditions lacking technical expertise, they add greater stress. The confinements and pandemic highlighted the unequal and precarious access to technology experienced by those living in the margins. Sections of society's marginalised groups were pushed further to the edge. Technologies supposedly designed to cultivate inclusiveness, simply added further to the divisions in our society.

Where video conferencing was used extensively, other, unanticipated, problems began to emerge. Group organisers experienced high levels of anxiety associated with maintaining and updating the online presence and providing a secure and confidential environment. End user skill levels also arose as a difficulty requiring organisers to become tutors in digital technologies further increasing stress levels. As the pandemic progressed, the alienating world of the video conference became apparent as mental health sufferers yearned for a return to the physical presence. Ultimately, for those experiencing mental health challenges, the digital meetings cannot replace those encounters in a shared spatial and temporal environment.

Social networking technologies such as Zoom, at first seemingly freely accessible, were revealed as commodities requiring purchase no matter how important they are in mental health support. Licences must be bought for access beyond a limited service, emphasising the control the owners of software have over users thus highlighting the alienated relation between the two. While Zoom has provided support for mental health activities (Shirkhoda, 2021), it did not offer its services either for free or at a reduced price to mental health support groups. Further, evidence is beginning to emerge showing that online video conferencing is itself contributing to a condition classified as Chronic Zoom (video meeting) Syndrome (CZS) (Anderson & Looi, 2020).

The pandemic lay bare the failure of governments to address the growing problem of mental health. The arrival of each new COVID-19 variant brings continued restrictions and fear. Yet, the stories in this chapter show that mental health activists struggled in conditions not of their choosing and, using technologies they came to recognise as limited, attempted to create open, shared environments within which they sought collectively to seek solutions to their problems. In doing so, they changed themselves. They became more proficient at using the technologies, developed a critical view of DTs, recognised that what binds them together is a shared experience not bounded by place, acknowledged that it was their actions that can provide the impetus for change. They have created networks that may well continue to exist. I believe these stories are indicative of the determination and courage of all grassroots mental health activists working during the pandemic. They contrast starkly with the lack of real care exhibited by official bodies and encourage us to ask what action should we take to force a change of priorities, to properly fund and support mental health work during the continuation of this pandemic and to prepare for the next. Perhaps we could start by creating campaigns demanding that organisations developing digital technologies, like Zoom, place support for people's mental health before profit. We can use the technology to do that. The next Chapter looks at the creative arts during the pandemic.

References

Anderson, K., & Looi, J. C. (2020). Chronic zoom syndrome: Emergence of an insidious and debilitating mental health disorder during COVID-19. *Australasian Psychiatry, 28*(6), 669–669. https://doi.org/10.1177/103 9856220960380

Barrera-Algarín, E., Estepa-Maest, F., Sarasola-Sánchez-Serrano, J. L., & Vallejo-Andrada, A. (2020). COVID-19, neoliberalismo y sistemas sanitarios en 30 países de Europa: Repercusiones en el número de fallecidos [COVID-19, neoliberalism and health systems in 30 european countries:

Relationship to deceases.]. *Revista espanola de salud publica*. Retrieved April 16, 2021, from https://pubmed.ncbi.nlm.nih.gov/33111713/

Cairney, P. (2021). The UK government's COVID-19 policy: Assessing evidence-informed policy analysis in real time. *British Politics, 16*, 90–116. https://doi.org/10.1057/s41293-020-00150-8

Centre for Disease Control and Prevention. (2021, July 22). *Coping with stress*. Retrieved September 24, 2021, from https://www.cdc.gov/mentalhealth/str ess-coping/cope-with-stress/index.html

Covid-Minds. (2021, July). *Covid-Minds longitudinal studies*. Retrieved July 10, 2021, from https://www.covidminds.org/longitudinal-studies

Cummings, I. (2018). The impact of austerity on mental health service provision: A UK perspective. *International Journal of Environmental Research and Public Health, 15*(6), 1145. https://doi.org/10.3390/ijerph15061145

Jia, R., Ayling, K., Chalde, T., Broadbent, E., Coupland, C., & Vedhara, K. (2020). Mental health in the UK during the COVID-19 pandemic: Cross-sectional analyses from a community cohort study. *British Medical Journal Open, 10*, e040620. https://doi.org/10.1136/bmjopen-2020-040620

McCartan, C., Adell, T., Cameron, J., Davidson, G., Knifton, L., McDaid, S., & Mulholland, C. (2021). A scoping review of international policy responses to mental health recovery during the COVID-19 pandemic. *Health Research Policy and Systems, 19*(58), 1–7. https://doi.org/10.1186/s12961-020-00652-3

Negreiro, M. (2021). *The rise of digital health technologies during the pandemic*. European Parliamentary Research Service. Retrieved May 20, 2021, from https://www.europarl.europa.eu/RegData/etudes/BRIE/2021/690548/EPRS_BRI(2021)690548_EN.pdf

Panchal, N., Kamal, R., Cox, C., & Garfield, R. (2021, February 10). *The implications of COVID-19 for mental health and substance use*. Retrieved April 12, 2021, from https://www.kff.org/coronavirus-covid-19/issue-brief/the-implications-of-covid-19-for-mental-health-and-substance-use/

Proto, E., & Quintana-Domeque, C. (2021). COVID-19 and mental health deterioration by ethnicity and gender in the UK. *PLoS One, 1*(16), e0244419. https://doi.org/10.1371/journal.pone.0244419

Shirkhoda, R. (2021, September 13). *Zoom cares: Supporting mental health & global connection*. Zoom Company News, Zoomtopia. Retrieved September 30, 2021, from https://blog.zoom.us/zoom-cares-mental-health-grants/

WHO. (2021, May 21). *World Health Assembly recommends reinforcement of measures to protect mental health during public health emergencies.* Retrieved June 10, 2021, from https://www.who.int/news/item/31-05-2021-world-health-assembly-recommends-reinforcement-of-measures-to-protect-mental

5

COVID-19, Digital Technologies, and the Creative Arts

Introduction

The Covid lockdowns had a devastating effect on the production of the creative arts. It is difficult to give an approximate figure of those employed in the creative and cultural industries (CCIs) worldwide and estimates tend to reply on registration on sites such as LinkedIn, which itself only accounts for 20% of global employment. Nevertheless, UNESCO estimates that over 10 million CCIs jobs were lost during 2020 not including those working in the tourist industry (UNESCO, 2021). This was a rapid and extensive decline in CCI employment, particularly in urban areas, where most of the work is concentrated, and the self-employed, the dominant from of employment in the sector. There has been some, albeit limited, support for the sector from local government sources and/or generated from within the industry through crowd funding schemes, but this could not prevent the closure of theatres, concert halls, literary events, music festivals, and other events as the virus spread across the globe (Mayor of London, 2020). The *Center for an Urban Future* provides a detailed description of what this devastation meant for the cultural and creative organisations of one city, New

© The Author(s), under exclusive license to Springer Nature Singapore Pte Ltd. 2022
M. Healy, *Organising during the Coronavirus Crisis*,
https://doi.org/10.1007/978-981-19-1942-8_5

York, but it is a story that could be replicated across all urban areas (Savitch-Lew et al., 2020). Each new wave of the pandemic further increased the precarious nature of the CCIs as rescheduled concerts, gallery openings, and other cultural events were hit by further cancellations (Nhat, 2021). The timing and severity of these closures may have varied from country to country, wave to wave, but the cultural and creative world has sought to adjust to the new conditions.

However, the lockdowns also created the time and space for a flourishing of creativity, encouraging and environment which opened possibilities previously denied. National orchestras, such as the Malmo Symphony Orchestra, streamed their concerts online reaching out to wider, multinational audiences (Malmo Symphony Orchestra, 2021). At the same time, individual musicians concentrated on producing their own online concerts, and/or developed video courses, often posted on YouTube, for those wishing to learn an instrument. DTs helped independent artists establish their own collectives with access to international audiences and UNESCO has argued that DTs could play a crucial role in the recovery of the CCIs (UNESCO, 2021). While MSM carried the headline stories, relatively little attention has been given to the impact of Covid on grass roots creative endeavour. From a research perspective, there is a growing body of work seeking to investigate the global, regional, and national impact of COVID-19 on the CCIs but much of this is from an economic viewpoint with frequent references to revised or digitised business models.

Away from the MSM, with its spotlight on mainstream arts or research focused on economic issues of CCIs, there is another extensive and inclusive world of artistic endeavour at the grass roots level. The work of community and specialist arts workshops and theatres, in various forms, is crucial in providing more than an entry point for those who later may make significant contributions to artistic life. It opens doors of access for diverse communities, engaging with traditional and innovative forms of delivery and imaginatively using artistic techniques to explore subjects such as those focusing on social and mental health concerns. It is work that has a long and rich history often embracing a radical perspective and incorporating social criticism in their activities; for many engaged with this work it is simply impossible to divide their creativity from their political perspectives (Craig, 1980). The chapter draws upon the experiences of grass roots artists during COVID-19 as they applied DTs in determined effort to continue their imaginative activities. It opens with the views of Rhoda, an activist poet based in South Wales and then goes on to engage with the work of Rubi, who was a final year student at an art school in Holland.

Creating and Presenting Poetry During COVID-19

After retiring as a university lecturer and therapist, Rhoda became an activist poet and prior to COVID-19 often performed poetry at open mic sessions and political events. She has published several books of poetry and has co-written a book on surviving difficult times. The pandemic confinement had a dramatic negative impact on her.

> Initially, I was shattered because much of my poetry engages with my politics and I would read a poem at a vigil for tragic events like Grenfell or Charlottesville for example, whether it was pouring rain, or the sun was shining. The surroundings affect the way people hear poems. Floodlit fountains, for example, can help transmute grief and anger as well as the words.

Rhoda was surprised at the impact the lockdown had on her. She felt frightened, upset, and coping became a significant issue. She had some therapy sessions using WhatsApp in her car which provided a safe, private space and created the sense of being in a therapy room or in a cocoon. Yet there were limitations. Rhoda's therapist focuses on the relationship between thought and body movement so non-verbal cues are crucial.

> In the car, she can only see above my shoulders. I'm saying the same number of words, but there's less information. Also, during the lockdown, I bothered less about getting fully dressed or using makeup, dragging myself around in the same old clothes. But she couldn't see this change.

However, as the lockdown progressed, Rhoda felt increasingly able to cope as she developed a greater appreciation of what the technology could offer.

> I realised I hadn't lost everything and could do many things online, such as poetic events, political meetings, and therapy sessions. I learned about Zoom, which was a lifeline because we've had Monday night sessions with poets from many different countries. I wasn't cut off from anybody which was a positive, fantastic feeling.

Engaging with the technology provided Rhoda with the impetus to develop her skills. She can organise online video breakout rooms, appreciates that "chat" facilitates positive feedback, host emotionally sensitive events, share poems, is more comfortable with the medium, encourage free-flowing conversations and feedback, and recognises the benefit of not trying to control everyone's input. She has also attended social events on Zoom where people can talk spontaneously and celebrate together online.

> I'm more positive about technology now and I have been able to meet and build relationships with people who are geographically distant. I've also been able to publish, distribute and sell online more copies of my latest poetry book than I did at live, local events. Book launches are easier, so it's become an international book.

Apart from building extensive networks with poets and activists nationally and internationally, she has had greater access to diverse political seminars and conferences, therapy videos, and online workshops, and courses. It has been possible to link with the international Black Lives Matter movement, the women's movement and with environmental activists holding online themed music and poetry events.

As online activity increased, she was participating in poetry events several nights a week, compared to 4 or 5 a month previously.

> I've seen poetry presentations with strong contextual material to create mood, light shows, film material, colour, photographs, props etc, and of course these can be more easily manipulated than in real situations.

We have an online friend, in Scotland, we've never met in real life, who organises big open mic sessions, getting us to make videos of our poems on a theme which he then edits into a film and submits to film festivals. People are fusing poetry with film. For me one of the fantastic things is being able to easily record, making permanent copies of events. I can replay other people's poems and use recordings to look at and improve my own performance. Previously, I have been shy about singing and playing the piano at a music event. Now I record beforehand and offer a video to play on the night. We could have more video-links at live events to include people from farther afield, to control presentation and to present more exciting content.

There's a political poet based in Bristol who went on a poetry cycling tour and she asked us to write and upload poems on various themes, such as recycling and conservation.

I organised an event with poems about death, an emotional subject, especially in the pandemic, and I didn't mute or schedule contributions which created an intimate environment by allowing people to feel free to contribute when the moment was right. It made the event more organic by enabling people to respond to each other's problems. People found this rewarding, and reducing my control created space for others to take responsibility and developed sensitivity to each other.

It raises questions about power relations within groups. I think of the power hosts have when organising meetings. They can mute, decide who speaks, and control the schedule of speakers and sometimes it's important to loosen up and share out power.

Previously a poetry or writing workshop/course would have been expensive because of travel and accommodation costs; courses in the UK can cost of several hundred pounds just for accommodation. Online courses have cut these costs dramatically,

I've just completed a four-week online course organised in Nashville, and I'm doing another 4 month online Canadian course, costing £300, and meeting even more people. I didn't know that we could do all this a year ago.

Support from qualified IT volunteers meant her Live Poets night events reached wider audiences and did not experience serious technical complications. However, there were several problems including increased stress on hosts, participants prevented from exchanging informal, spontaneous notes, and the absence of non-verbal cues which diminished the poets' sensitivity to audience reaction. Rhoda felt that Zoom breaks facilitate informal chats and sending private Zoom messages, but the sense of the tension in the audience was missing.

> You don't get that feeling of horror or delight or even laughter. It just doesn't compare to real life. And there are many people who can't join in with these meetings because they just they just can't cope with the technological challenges.

As our conversations developed, Rhoda articulated criticisms of the digital environment. Apart from technical problems such an intermittent or fragile connectivity affecting volume or unevenness of poem presentation, and low-level end-user skills, her short-sightedness has increased, and she has developed chronic back-pain from sitting at a computer. Extensive daily online activity means she is wound-up at the end of the day feeding into insomnia and burn out. These problems meant Rhoda reduced the number of meetings she attended to achieve greater equilibrium. Rhoda listed a series of non-technical but critical problems.

> There's something subliminal about sharing the same physical space and showing support for someone who's grieving by, for example, making a cup of tea. Saying, "I'm here, I'm sitting at the computer for you" is not the same because it can't capture the vibrations of another person or unexpected movements.

> We've some poets that need nurturing because technology frightens them especially if they've got weak unreliable connections. Poverty is also an issue, not being able to afford a computer or pay for broadband. Poetry appeals to many people with mental health challenges and in the creative arts, there's a higher proportion of people dealing explicitly with emotional challenges than, say, in more technical fields. People need training and support to engage with technology, others are frightened of

this media. The cost of connecting can be an issue. Sometimes these fears and problems about technology will be described as technical limitations when in fact underneath there are psychological barriers. But for people with disabilities, particularly where mobility is an issue, it's fantastic.

In developing this theme, Rhoda talked about her perceptions of herself in an online environment.

I've a deep sense of the visual aesthetic and conscious of my appearance to others while on stage or lecturing, in therapy or on Zoom. It's quite hard work and, unlike in real life, I see myself on camera during a video session. This is an extra, useful dimension but demands more of an interchange. Seeing the whole person lets me know they also engaged. Yet, people's settings can be distracting, depending on whether they're conscious of their background or just sit in a messy bedroom or kitchen regardless of what it looks like to others.

Rhoda explained that much of her work uses Facebook and she has noticed there has been a significant increase on platform censorship as the pandemic has developed.

It's not possible now to post hundreds of individual invites and promoting to a bigger audience means paying. Word surveillance seems greater with political poems suffering compared to those about flowers. Facebook has become more interventionist and increasingly decides who to mute. Not everything is plain sailing with technology and particularly for women, there is the ever-present concern about unwanted responses or persistent trolling.

Rhoda also spoke about the relationship between the pandemic and DTs as they emerged in her personal life.

I've been double vaccinated, but I constantly think about safety when I go out to avoid bringing the virus home. Maybe that's why I'm slowly experimenting with more flexibility on the media. I was never brilliant anyway, at the level of small talk and intimate, casual informal conversation and the pandemic has reduced those opportunities. Zooming is possible but it requires planning, people can be busy and it's just not the same as in real life where you can potter around a kitchen, talking while you're doing things, talk about whatever comes into your head, or what happened in the shop yesterday. So that is a whole level of relating that's not happening. I mean telephoning has just gone. In my world, nobody uses the telephone at all.

Rhoda feels safe and comfortable in her technological cocoon but also recognises the contradiction.

I feel free from threats. It's like a dream, like watching the television all the time. But having the Internet as my only source of information, means I cannot be a witness to events and my poetry may suffer, maybe become too abstract. I'm quite a chatty person and like spending a few hours browsing in a bookshop, searching online book sellers is just not the same. The unexpected event, the black swan moment, is missing. Online, life is much more pre-arranged and controlled.

We also discussed notions of authenticity and the concept of real life.

Ideas of authenticity online are interesting. Does distance make some-thing inauthentic? I've seen people presenting their most passionate and fantastic revelations feeling safer on a screen than they would in real life. It is possible that if someone delivers a sexual or an emotional vulnera-bility piece at a real event, they, particularly women, could be stopped in the carpark. Online, you just switch off and nobody knows where you are physically but of course there are the dangers of online stalking.

This comment also highlights the anonymity available from an online presence. Rhoda considers the pandemic a contradictory experience. It is a serious health crisis but is also a transformative process.

Overall, I think it's been a fantastic 18 months for technology, and it has opened a multitude of new opportunities to people. But we need to remember that many have felt unable to engage and becoming more marginalised. For some, the intensity of looking at static faces and having their own scrutinised at close quarters is too emotionally daunting. For some older people, the upheaval of installing technology and learning how to use it is problematic. We need to think about all of this. Building in support and training, developing very simple and inexpensive equipment, using the telephone and recording equipment more, and finding ways to be inclusive of these people is important.

While DT's have facilitated wider participation with poetry, they do not figure as a subject for poetry itself.

I haven't found technology interesting enough to write a poem about but there are numerous writers concerned with dystopian narratives, and I think poets have a role anticipating possible future scenarios, to warn against dangers, to witness events. Maybe we should hold the mantle in our poetry, for things that technology can't or shouldn't be allowed to take over, like human relationships and love and touch and even sexuality, which is very much technologised. Poets can say something about technology even if technology itself enables poets to reach wider audiences.

Rhoda's contradictory experience is indicative of many in the poetry community. The following story describes the COVID-19 experiences of Rubi who is closely concerned with constructing physical safe spaces.

COVID-19 and the Creative Arts: A Student's Story

Rubi was preparing to graduate from an arts academy in Holland when the lockdowns were imposed and describes the impact of COVID-19 on them as "monumental".

I am involved with planning and building atmospheres in physical spaces in my professional field, scenography and stage design. The final year is solely concerned with a self-determined project so there aren't any formal lessons. I've been involved in several projects including Student Radio Maastricht, which has a viewership of around 2000 each week, and large output of community shows.

In September 2019, Rubi decided to create an independent community Art Centre, that would also be a queer safe space, for their final year project. They were prompted to do this because of the lack of inclusive spaces in Maastricht following the closure of the Mandril Cultural and Political Centre in November 2019, and the eviction of two big squats. Consequently, only one remaining large community, Landbouwbelang, remained.

> We decided to start our own space because we have a different philosophy to Landbouwbelang. In January [2020] we approached the existing B32 squat to collaborated with them and convert a former art gallery into a music venue, with our first event on 14th February. Our events ranged from small very intimate affairs to those with between 50-100 people. We had six more events planned with local and international acts, focusing on creating inclusive safer spaces, environment where you can be yourself without fear or judgement from other people. There's much talk in the queer community about safe space but you can never create truly safe space because there's always going to be someone who feels excluded.

> The pandemic meant the cancellation of all our shows and since I was also using this space as the basis for my final year thesis on how to create inclusive spaces; everything became unclear. All the plans I had for creating a safe space in Maastricht suddenly became impossible to do. It also means I can't graduate in the way I was expecting. It's been very difficult to navigate this pandemic to complete my degree. Suddenly, my six-month plan and full agenda with long weeks of meetings ceased to exist. During April [2020], I didn't know what to do with my life, everything I had planned wasn't possible and there's no opportunity to get myself involved other things. So how do I move forward? How do I complete all the things I'd started but now don't exist? I then developed the plan to interview people about art and education.

Rubi's response to the lockdown was to engage with several online activities such as joining an online queer house party.

> But that felt odd for me because a static idea of communicating is not what I've in mind when I talk about running events. There's a lot of things making it extremely hard to navigate in a digital realm.

Rubi described the digital technologies, which included Zoom, YouTube Live, Twitch, and Facebook Live, used to enable the online events but highlighted the limited feedback during live events and the control the host has over the constrained interaction during Zoom sessions.

> During streaming you're listening to one music stream but seeing many faces, it's an odd experience. With streamed panel discussions there maybe four people discussing a topic with viewers making comments. It's not the same interaction as a live audience.

> Cyberspace with its own rules, its own ideas, its own way of behaving, is not the same as offline reality. You can contact anyone anywhere in the world at any time but not in a physical space. They're different worlds because what is possible in physical space cannot be found in digital space. I am not against digital technologies which I use in my daily life. I'm always editing videos and using sound engineering technology. Technologies are tools to do stuff and I also see them as exploratory media. And, in my teens, I talked a lot to people online which helped me discover discovering my own queer identity.

Rubi believes that existing attempts to create online safe digital spaces do not encourage inclusion in the way non-digital spaces can.

> In the non-digital, physical world, all sorts of cues confirm it's okay not to talk or be in a corner, allowing others to check on you. Being active online requires a level of self-confidence and privilege. You need a computer, have access to Internet, in a safe environment before you begin to be yourself online. Many in the trans community are in unsafe situations or negative domestic circumstances. How is someone meant to navigate safely when there're in negative or unsafe conditions?

Rubi explained how the creative response to the pandemic increasingly fused with their personal life and political perspective. Art, the personal and the political became explicitly entwined. After three years as a founding member and occasionally chairperson of the radio station's board, it became increasing problematic for Rubi as the station moved from a one concerned with the creation of community safe spaces to one focused on an online presence.

> Something happens when interest is focused online and where the value of content is determined by the social media presence of likes and shares, of wanting online attention. The absence of physical spaces has turned our attention toward the idea of branding; the more likes and shares the better the brand. I increasingly find this at odds with my own view of how these organisations should be functioning which should be to make people feel safe.

Rubi talked about how the pandemic crisis crystallised several strands of thought in this area.

> The current crisis brought into focus many thoughts I've had for a long time. It enabled me to form a more coherent idea of what it is that drives my own political views on how and why I want digital spaces to be and feel. That created the conditions for me to rethink everything. Maybe these ideas would've surface anyway, but more slowly.

From their perspective, Rubi considers it impossible to recreate online those critical elements existing within a physical space.

> The sensory input for the digital realm is visual and audio, with viewing from a static angle. I can move my computer around to give a wider context but it's camera's perspective not the 360-degree realm of being in a space. Even the audio input is limited, you can't hear what I can hear like birds, traffic, aeroplanes, or the cat running in and out. All these aspects create the environment, all sensory input is important. I'm not such a fan of in my own work if it means people sitting and looking at a theatre piece. I want to be involved in immersive projects.

The creation of safer spaces in Rubi's community had been a collective effort involving at least 20 people and forming part of a wider movement.

> Everyone who enters a space becomes involved in it and locally we just provide the stage for the space to happen. In Europe there's a history

of squatted safer spaces, and queer/anarchist spaces that are different to traditional community centres. But the pandemic has impacted on these spaces, and many have closed. This has created a huge mental health problem with increased substance abuse and people falling between the cracks in mental health services. That cannot be solved online.

Attempts have been made to create safer spaces online but generally, Rubi, along with many others, does not feel comfortable with them.

> There's one queer house party thing or quarantine club. It's like a Zoom meeting and you join it. There's another with a DJ and using individual screens, trying to be a party in your living room. But you're supposed to be happy, posing in front of the camera and drinking. It's based on what you can see via webcam with someone's blurry face over a poor Internet connection or in a Zoom call with 1500 other people. It lacks the personal touch and is missing the interaction possible in a real party setting where you can bump into someone, talk by the bar, or in the garden.

> There is something else, the vibe. Many people sharing the same space combine to create a positive atmosphere. I often attend live events, a concert, or a squat event to soak up the atmosphere or to lift my mood. But if you're stuck in the bedroom where you sleep, alone, feeling a bit depressed or in a low mood, interacting with the same square image, it's not good. It's hard to replicate the electric energy created in a room with other people surrounding you.

The spread of COVID-19 forced Rubi to use more traditional methods to undertake primary research for their final year thesis such as interviewing a range of practitioners concerned with art and education and who are also artists. The interviews were about the relationship between art, education, and the creation of political physical public spaces. Ultimately, however, Rubi decided to take a different route and produced a radio show and presented a thesis about utopia together with a web site containing all the documentation associated with the final year project. It was also possible to refer to the original plans they had for their final year.

I ended up taking a very different turn. The interviews were informative, but I wanted to research much more about community action and safer spaces and how we make spaces inclusive to all and removing barriers to access. To think about how different spaces can engage in a participatory way. For example, most people's conception of an art centre is either you've got workshops, or you've got an exhibition space, or concerts, and it's very little for the audience; more about the idea of the artist being elevated.

I am exploring different ways of thinking about how we use space and what does space mean. What does it mean when we can't touch each other and live in a world where we have to be distant to one another physically?

I consider arts education to be an intrinsically physical act. It's more than lectures or readings online, or essay writing. It's about relating to topics in space, time and context and other people. It is extremely hard to replicate these activities in a digital space and different professionals have their own relationships with the physical. For example, I'm in contact with a theatre maker in Berlin working with rituals of space and rituals of how people come into spaces and what they feel within it? How does me coming and shaking your hand and looking you in the eye, make you feel in a certain space? If something already exists in the physical realm, it's hard to digitise it but I appreciate that cyberspace can provide a safe space for queer people to explore their identities.

Rubi had concerns about matters such as security, censorship, access, and control, and in doing so raised more fundamental aspects linked to the options currently available to socialise online.

As well as issues such as digital space, I share my community's scepticism of the technology. We ask why we use Zoom, for example, when it has all these issues. We don't have much choice since no other platform matches its quality. I mean, for me, it needs a revolution in many ways because how these technologies develop is intrinsically tied to current priorities which are always about profit. Some services are free but only because they're making profit from our data. Technologies, particularly digital technologies could be made free and accessible.

Despite these general concerns, Rubi recognises that many professionals in their area of expertise, scenography and stage design, are embracing digital technologies, particularly virtual reality, to create new ways to experience theatre.

> I've experienced several fascinating virtual reality events such as the Prague Quadrennial 2019 theatre Festival. It was exciting because it was developing theatre for virtual reality settings. I think this will develop rapidly over the coming decade. Part of the fun of virtual reality is the prospect of imagining alternate reality. I wouldn't want to replicate our reality but it's intriguing to play with images, particularly self-image. Virtual reality can enable me to create a different self-image, like a multicoloured pony.

This remark prompted a discussion about technology and authenticity.

> I don't ask what does authentic mean because for me that's saying something is or isn't authentic. This conversation seems very authentic, but an online crowd experience makes it harder for me to be myself. And of course, what's authenticity anyway? I know that I don't feel comfortable using online technologies in a group context.

Looking to the future, Rubi considers video calling will be normalised as will remote working. The pandemic has pushed the boundaries of technology in the arts.

> Because we are confined, it encourages different ways of using technology in the arts. For example, there's been many interesting live events using video technology such as being in a theatre with dancers from 10 different countries, on different screens improvising with each other's movements. This is about combining physical space and digital space. And I think that combination is what's interesting for me.

Rubi's experience highlights the difficulties during COVI-19 in trying to create a safe community environment. The following section looks at the impact the pandemic had on the work of an existing community arts centre based in the UK.

Community Arts During COVID-19

Eleanor Shaw is an Artistic Director for a Community Arts and Health organisation in Wales, with a background in drama, the spoken word, and storytelling. She was able to move most of her equipment from her office to her home before the first confinement.

> My office is now the spare bedroom containing a printer, laptop, a table and chair and important files. I also moved some digital recording equipment which I use for filming, and I can link it to my mobile phone, my landline, and my computer. We now pay for accounting software, Dropbox storage, and Zoom because the 40 minutes free wasn't working. Going digital required training on digital safeguarding, so we've organised training sessions for this.

> We're a small organisation, not familiar with DTs and this was a massive problem for us when the pandemic broke. My laptop wasn't working properly for three weeks so my Zoom chats were with people I couldn't see. Initially, I was very stressed wondering if we could connect to those who needed us. For many, it is a real lifeline, especially older people who live isolation. I wanted to buy 10 iPads for several older people who want to Zoom with us but who haven't got the kit at home. We also had to create Google Hangout sessions with our younger users. We decided to take it day by day.

The lockdown affected the organisation's activities with, for example, a fortnightly story sharing workshop moving online using mixture of Zoom, WhatsApp video and telephones. These sessions were recorded and used to create a video of lockdown stories. Before COVID-19, the group also ran a monthly spoken word open mic event, with tea and cake, and a real mixture of ages. The lockdown required changes to this event.

> We were going to use Zoom but realised that many would miss out because they can't access Zoom etc. Instead, I asked our regulars to send me an audio, a video, a spoken word snippet, or a story. I phoned one of my older participants on her landline and recorded her on my

mobile. She's partially deaf which added to the challenge. We've also had some very sophisticated videos sent in. We created a mashup of this material which was shown on our YouTube channel. Because it was popular, we'll continue with this, and will have a monthly living, breathing documentary showing how people feel.

The group is now using a full spectrum of DTs including Zoom, WhatsApp chat, WhatsApp Video, Google Hangouts, Facebook messenger, Microsoft Teams, Twitter, and Instagram. Managing this technological "spaghetti junction" was a significant challenge.

Most young people Eleanor works with have several challenges such as low self-esteem, anxiety, problems with communication skills, and lack of aspiration. Normally they struggle with communication in daily life and the pandemic demands that they communicate with technologies which those with good communication skills find challenging. Eleanor believes there will be post-pandemic problems with the return to larger groups of 30 or so.

I thought our **Young People Speak Up** group would be the most successful. The participants are referred to us through Youth Services and not like your typical confident young person. They're familiar with the digital world using texting etc, but not confident speaking face-to-face offline. We've completed four sessions now and I've been surprised. For the first two sessions, hardly anybody would come to the camera. We suggested that instead of having one large group, we'd have smaller WhatsApp groups. Since doing that, the conversations made us realise they hate this form of communication; they really don't like seeing themselves online and they don't like participants seeing them in their homes because it shows another side of them. It raises anxiety levels. To be honest, I also really struggle with having to constantly look at myself on a video chat.

They're really struggling because their lives have been completely turned upside down. School and social groups gave structure, now they're stuck in their bedroom, possibly with other siblings and spending more time with mum and dad. They have smartphones, but it may have a cracked screen, or there's not enough data to connect with us. We're constantly

texting or ringing them after a video chat to see if they're okay and refer-
ring to the youth service so they can get extra support. Of all our groups,
this has been the most challenging.

She amplified her comments on young people using technologies like
WhatsApp.

One described the moment before lockdown started when media studies
students at her college were told that teaching would be delivered via
Google Hangouts or Google classroom. She said everybody melted saying
this is the worst day of their lives since they'll have to connect showing
their faces on a screen. It's difficult and a challenge for any 16/17 year
old dealing with anxiety concerns to see themselves on a screen, especially
if there are tensions within the group. Online, there's nowhere to hide.
They sometimes say they can't connect or there's a problem with the app.
I found that moving to smaller WhatsApp groups works better, it eases
the anxiety.

We were able to shift between bigger and smaller groups before the
pandemic because we were in one neutral space away from home and
the information these young people would share in real life was intimate.
They felt they could speak up because it was a space where they talk
without judgement. Now, they're being asked to continue with the same
conversation as before but at home in a space full of judgement. The
technology can't compensate for a non-neutral space.

Despite these caveats, Eleanor considers DTs are helpful in certain
instances and talks of one young person, from a very challenging family,
who is not a traditional poet nor good in school, who submitted an
"amazing poem" which will be turned into a film. DTs facilitated this
positive sharing process.

Eleanor explained that while participation of young persons had
marginally declined, the story sharing had increased because of links
with drama students at the University of Wales. YouTube videos of this
activity often receive over 130 views compared to the 40–50 who used
to participate in the live event.

We were also just starting five intergenerational projects with schools and care homes and youth groups. These will now go ahead online using digital technologies, but everything takes much more time. Imagine, I'm trying to speak to 20 different groups! More time means greater commitment with everyone working slower. Previously, if I'd planned a project, it'd be up and running. Now, I'll be lucky if this happens soon.

Eleanor's organisation has two types of senior audience. Those living in their own homes and others in care homes. While the first group has been involved with digital and offline connections, the latter need a modified approach.

We're testing the possibilities of using Facebook Messenger video with a small group of residents in a care home with a tablet on a dining room table. We'll have a story session and see how that goes. But this is based on trust between us and the home's activities co-ordinator whose working life has completely changed. For her it was one more task demanding her time. For the individual phone stories, we told her that if she can simply hand the phone to a resident, we'll do the rest.

People will accept a singer or an entertainer, but it takes time to appreciate the value of stories or story writing. It's difficult to speak, over the phone or online, to someone I've never met about an activity not known or understood. The technology does not necessarily help in building trusting relationships.

Eleanor's team has discussed issues associated with technical competence and she notes that while low skill levels can be offset by sophisticated equipment, not everyone feels safe using them. Many participants want equipment to be disinfected and are fearful of people coming into their homes.

Technology has enabled one story teller to collaborate internationally but we've also gone old school with stories over the phone. One of our story tellers will phone someone, ask them to put on the speaker phone, to relax and listen to a story over the phone. This is followed by a chat about the story. This is important for people living in isolation with just a landline.

While it is taking time for these initiatives to settle, we're all trying to cope with the mayhem of the pandemic. We've got one lady, 60, who joined one of our Zoom sessions although we couldn't see her because her camera wasn't working. She really wanted to be there, to be stretched rather than sitting back all day.

In considering whether the online video environment influences language structure, choice of words, or body movements of participants, Eleanor said:

Offline in real life, we don't normally film the workshops and when we do everybody changes straight away even if I say don't look at the camera. This is particularly for people with dementia. If they see a camera, they're looking at it straight away.

In Zoom it's different because everyone can already see themselves before recording so I've not found any change in people's behaviour during recording. We don't use Zoom with our young people, and you can't record in WhatsApp. There is one young person who's making a documentary film on this process by filming on her mobile. That will be edited, and everyone will have to give consent.

During our conversations, Eleanor's comments began to reveal contradictory experiences with the technology. It can enable a flowering of ideas and expression but can also inhibit communication and foster exclusivity if, for example, access is limited.

The lockdowns have revealed that many people, more than we think, don't have the technology at home, especially families. They may have a games box, but they don't have laptops or smartphones. A massive push is needed to make these technologies accessible and that requires thought and planning. The local council, which has lots of kit told me they've locked their offices and can't loan us their computers etc. I asked the local uni if we could borrow their iPads but they said they've got access issues; everything is so slow. That's the tip of the iceberg because there are many organisations that provide support networks which are unavailable now.

It's quite shocking how people have just been left isolated, their stories not covered in media are they? Here I am, in my bedroom, doing what I can trying to save the world, when it's a bigger problem. We need the right people to organise things.

DTs seemingly bring people together while creating a barrier to more intimate discussions and Eleanor described the problematic nature of online conversations.

Previously, I ran a performing arts department at a further education college, so I know that teaching these courses now is a real challenge personally and professionally. My online discussion with those teachers is missing all those important cues, such as, essential in first encounters. I can see myself on-screen which a distraction and I find myself unintentionally shouting and wanting to know more about their environments, their backgrounds. Today, I detected a feeling of sadness amongst the teachers.

Eleanor finds extensive online communication tiring. For example, a video meeting with a colleague followed by an online workshop with 16 participants, talking about intimate feelings and delving deep to create poems and stories, had left her exhausted.

I've got 16 faces in front of me on a screen and trying to measure if everybody is ok. All those things we'd normally do in a space together, in a circle are missing. What's the temperature, distractions, light, those things that I'd put into place for a workshop to make sure that it's going to be the right atmosphere. Now it's about me asking everybody to mute their mics when someone talks. It becomes all about me, my energy.

These additional difficulties online events demand the development of coping strategies.

I can't speak for my colleagues, but I try to be present in the moment and adapt those coping mechanisms I'd use in a real space. I'm learning now to be aware when my husband's at home, to ensure I'm upstairs, in a warm, comfy room with the door shut and can't be disturbed for a couple of hours.

Despite all the difficulties, Eleanor was determined to continue the work of the organisation and she contacted her team emphasising the need to continue their work and itemised the current projects. She asked for proposals about how the team could be involved during the pandemic and pledged her commitment to raise funding. She was determined the group would survive the crisis.

> I was quite conscious of this. I've a graduate colleague who joined us in September [2019] and while inexperienced she's massively talented. When the lockdown started, I asked her if she'd want to be involved since there'd be a cut in wages with sporadic payments because of the financial difficulties I mentioned earlier and problems with furlough payments. She continued because she loves the work and the people we work with. Luckily, some funds came through. But we also discussed the implications of revised work patterns that are not 9 to 5. I've asked her to create a log of conversations she has with participants to ensure safeguarding.

Eleanor also spoke of the pressure on her and her colleagues because of funding problems.

> We're all self-employed artists. I'm the director of our organisation but still self-employed because we don't have core funding. Before Covid, we submitted numerous applications for three-year core funding but every funder, including the lottery is now focused on emergency Covid funding. I'll still not on a salary for another year. It's very stressful for our free-lancers and their families because it's not clear what the self-employed will receive from the government.

While some grants were forthcoming, financial constraints meant the group had limited spending for necessary equipment and at one point, Eleanor took a wage cut of 50% to keep the organisation afloat. This situation highlights the precarious nature of creative artistic employment and the dedication of those determined to keep some degree of service going.

> Luckily, I will be able to pay myself for the next couple of months. It's hard but we're a lot better off than some organisations our size. Not

having core funding really hurt us and shown how vulnerable we can be in crisis situations.

Once we get back to face-to-face, we will continue with online work. But it won't replace the face-to-face work because that is so important; it must happen. Many people we work with, including myself, have been through traumatic moments in our lives, and face-to-face gatherings, being in a room with people you can connect to, where you can smell, taste, and touch everything, are essential to human wellbeing and development. I strongly believe it's crucial we still have these encounters.

Eleanor's experience illuminates the precarious nature of employment in the cultural and creative sector and the efforts grass roots organisers have made to continue working in the most difficult circumstances. It also shows that while DTs have the potential to partially ameliorate the adverse conditions they face, there are significant problems with the technology that undermine the quality of online interactions. The next section looks at the impact of COVID-19 on Brazilian artists.

COVID-19, Art, and Digital Technologies: A Brazilian Perspective

Pre COVID-19, estimates indicated that Brazilian CCIs employed almost 1.9 million people (3.7% of the employed), with 44% self-employed (de Jesus, 2020). Like many other countries, COVID-19 had a disastrous impact on this sector, but it was mediated and sharpened through President Bolsonaro's pandemic denial policies and his administration's hostile attitude towards creative arts in general which classified artists as part of the opposition (de Jesus, 2020). The following story reveals how the pandemic impacted on Brazilian artists.

Caio Ribeiro is a published poet, working in theatre and urban settings and living in Cuiabá, capital city of the Brazilian state of Mato Grosso. Currently he is engaged with hybrid art projects, funded by the local state, linking his poems to body movements to produce performance videos. Before the pandemic, Caio's collective focused on community interventions, including schools. The pandemic brought this work to a halt. While Brazilian President Bolsonaro was in COVID-19 denial, local politicians, like Mato Grosso governor, Mauro Mendes, a Bolsonaro supporter, recognised the urgency of the pandemic, imposed a partial lockdown in March 2020.

> The lockdown was like breaking our legs. The police closed us down just when we were about to release a play called Vida Provisória. I didn't know about the virus because we were rehearsing continuously in an artistic residence. It was also a nightmare not being able to go into schools.

> Students were using screens but there's no touch, no feeling, no passion, and no desire in the screen. And we work with desire because it moves kids. Imagine a class with 40 students, most of them using the cell phones because they don't have a computer in home, with poor connections and other problems. How can I motivate them with the arts on a small screen? The camera is just a picture for a character or photo. We kept working but it was hard. In the end I said 'Guys, I can't. It's impossible because I'm feeling it's a monologue'. Also, two of our group had to leave to find work.

> The pandemic also ended another school-based project, called the Fabric of the Poem. It involved creating poems with students by using scissors to cut out words from songs, stories and then put them together. We take a word and choose where to put it on the body. So, we have a word fire, put it on our forehead and ask what we can imagine from this. We create images and go back to the words to create a poem. It's the playfulness and sharing that creates the poem.

Caio helped the Movimento de Artes Cênicas de Mato Grosso to create a mutual aid group, Respiracena, to provide food and other necessities for struggling artists.

> We created this campaign, to enable artists to tell their stories and ask the community for donations to provide bags of basic food like rice, beans, soup, to survive for a month. We used Instagram and the Facebook to market the campaign, and Zoom was the central space to discuss and develop the ideas for the campaign.

To avoid fees, the campaign did not use crowdfunding platforms. A bank account was opened with people making direct online transfers with strict records of income and expenditure. The MAG eventually closed when artists began working again. Caio went on to outline his artistic work during this period.

> I'm a writer so also work with books and particularly in a special small, printed format called ZINE. Before Covid, I could sell Zine's at a street performance but lockdowns and limited physical contact prevented this. So, we created the MATAPACOS magazine (named after a black dog involved in Chilean protests) which was my first experience of a digital magazine for art, culture and politics. The first edition had only poems, another edition covered music and included QR codes linking to music groups. University teachers have written about Brazilian culture.

> We have a close partnership with a Portuguese platform called PLATAFORMA DO PANDEMONIO which enabled us to publish a special edition covering the pandemic in Portugal and Brazil. A traditional Portuguese theatre group, Bando, sent us a complete script of one of their plays which we included in the issue. The last edition appeared at the end of 2021 and was called the INDENCIÁRIA covering poems on different kinds of relationships in short and long narratives. The magazine has been a complete success because people shared and with editions having 2000+ downloads: a lot for our state.

Caio was already familiar with a range of DTs including Zoom and used various drawing and printing programmes to visualise his poems. Nevertheless, he found it difficult to transition to complete reliance on DTs during lockdowns.

> Virtual presentations generate problems. I'm on a small square screen, and I move in and out of the screen. I am here then not here. My preferred approach requires direct eye contact, which is difficult online, so I stopped and had to adapt, to create another experience and start using digital formats designed just for the viewer.

> I needed to understand new techniques such as including audio, changing my background, I decided to put current projects on hold and start

new ones, this led to more problems with filming. I needed to buy new equipment like a better camera, microphone, and good headphones.

At the same time, Caio could not pay the rent on his studio and moved his equipment into his home. All the boxes containing costumes, books, plays scripts were in his bedroom, living room, and kitchen. For Caio, this situation became more than a storage problem and it led to additional stress, turning his home into an oppressive workplace.

> Before, my home and workspace were separate spaces. Now it's in my living room, and I have had many crises of work because there is no separation between house and workplace, between rest and work. It is extremely confusing. I decided to lock everything in my son's room which means he sleeps in my room. Being in the workshop helped stimulate me, I'm there to work but now I wake up with everything around me. Everything is work.

> I became too aggressive because I was also reading about Covid, politics and Bolsonaro. I felt weak. I'm locked in my house with all this stuff, and I can't create anything, I can't see people. It was a moment of darkness. I began to have online therapy which helped even though it was not in a shared physical space. Two social networking sites, Mastodon and Discord also helped me. They are less aggressive than Twitter and I met other artists, to discuss politics. I was able to move away from mainstream social media concerned with covid deaths. I needed to get away from that.

By mid-2020, the Mato Grosso state instituted a system of grants for artists engaged in creating hybrid digital work accessible online and offline.

> CulturaEmCasa is a digital platform streaming cultural events into homes. Artists receive a grant to create digital plays, monologues, play songs, or short concerts to be streamed. I helped write the proposal submitted to the Secretary of Culture who agreed with the idea. Artists submit ideas or projects and receive grants to help pay the bills. It was a partnership between the State and artists' independent movements that led to more projects.

Cultural events in Mato Grosso must now be hybrid, both offline and digital. An activity can happen in real-time and place, such as theatre but then it must be digitised and streamed. This impacts on the event itself, requiring, for example, multiple cameras placed in certain spots within a theatre. Caio outlined the problem with this process.

> A play is designed for the theatre but with hybrid, the viewer experiences it through a camera. It's theatre but presented like cinema which doesn't work well. I learned how to work with cinema, how to shoot like cinema. Theatre actors must learn how to act in films. But digital products are not live events. Sensations are missing when a live theatre event is filmed. After filming we must add fade outs, make cuts. It's a three-stage process. We film an event, edit the film, digitise it, and then stream. The events and processes are complicated and apart from having to learn a whole new set of skills, acting with an audience and cameras present creates a problem of priorities. What is more important, the audience or the camera?

Caio, while appreciating the need for this kind of activity during the pandemic, believes it undermines theatre as an experience.

> I don't like this partnership with the audiovisual stuff in theatre because I don't believe that you can have the same experience if you watch me in your house. At home, you feel secure, surrounded by all the things that you love, it's your house. But when you go to the theatre, you are entering the unknown, when you sit there to watch, you're not secure anymore. You wait for something, everything to happen. So that's the magic of the theatre. If we normalize watching theatre, not films, not TV shows not video Arts Theater, at home, I think this will kill theatre, diminish actors' skills, kill the magic.

Caio is acknowledging that working digitally involves a compromise requiring degree of self-censorship, which he thinks will have to continue because of the virus. It has also had a permanent impact on how he works.

The virus is not going away and it's impossible to go back because my mind and body have changed. I don't do the physical preparation required as a performance actor since the video is relatively easier. Since so many things have altered, it will be hard to change back again. Only, I need my monologues without the hybrid stuff and when this pandemic crisis is over, I want to go back to the theatre because it's the art of the present. You watch me in the same place and time, I can concentrate on the audience.

Caio applies his criticisms of the digital environment to his series of virtual courses covering poetry writing that he developed as another income source. While courses were relatively successful, he believes they are not a long-term project.

I have problems when I shoot a course because I'm talking to the cameras. 'Hello, my name is Caio when we're going to learn how to do poems'. I can't watch this because I'm talking with an imaginary person. I find this hard. I did it to get some money but it's not for me.

For Caio, the impact of COVID-19 could not be mitigated using DTs. They created a further set of problems that he feels undermines his desire to engage in artistic endeavour. His experience indicates that DTs, rather than opening possibilities for wider social engagement, are inherently problematic if applied to activities that revolve around live events. His experience also shows that adapting, moulding artistic interventions to accommodate DTs can generate an environment where significant self-censorship and compromise is required to complete a project.

Conclusion

Initially frozen in the headlights of the virus, grassroots creative artists quickly recognised the urgency of practical action to ensure that lockdowns did not mean social isolation and the suspension of the creative process. In doing so they looked to greater use of DTs and began to appreciate that digitised spaces offered opportunities for greater audience participation and different arenas for creative possibilities. Options seemingly included greater freedom of expression, equality of access, and the potential for enhanced collaboration within the creative endeavour.

However, this activity was contradictory as a new set of problems began to emerge. Questions concerning the relationship between digital and physical spaces, the replication of offline power relations in online environments, the very real fragility of the digital experience, the covert levers of control including self-censorship to obtain funding (European Expert Network on Culture and Audiovisual, 2021, p. 114), or to protect oneself from online dangers, and the overt mechanisms of control and censorship. These issues raised questions concerning the way technology is designed, can be used and its limitations in the arts.

The activities described in this chapter also highlight several inconsistencies linked to the use of DTs which are often presented as offering quicker, more efficient ways of working. These stories show that using DTs frequently require greater organisational effort to make them effective. The seemingly smooth use of technology is, in fact, the opposite by generating additional stress, and, in certain situations, magnifying feelings of inadequacy and undermining confidence. Rather than presenting a level playing field, DTs can amplify, while also disguising, power relationship inequalities such as who, for example, controls informal Zoom sessions, who decides themes to be discussed, who determines the participants, and ultimately, who decides what actions need to be followed. Additionally, the narratives within this chapter also reveal the extensive inequalities linked to accessing and using DTs. For many, their technological infrastructure is limited and problematic.

With the closure of artistic venues along with a concomitant reduction in earnings, some creative workers were able to use DTs to augment their income by monetising their output through using channels such as YouTube. Similar possibilities became available for those seeking grants to continue working. The stories in this Chapter highlight the imaginative way a wide range of digital tools were employed in the creation and distribution of videos, via various social media, which became an increasingly crucial aspect of artistic endeavour during the pandemic. Yet, at the same time, this process strengthened the commoditisation of art. The value of an inventive video posted on YouTube is not determined by its relevance to or its illumination of the human condition, but by an algorithm analysing the number of views and subscribers it achieves. Hit the magic number, and the video will start generating income from advertising that can have nothing to do with the video itself and possibly undermine the theme of the video. The artistic video becomes just one more commodity. Once the video is posted, its creator can only sit and watch what, if any, affect it will have from a monetised perspective.

A positive experience related in several instances concerns the greater possibilities of collaboration enabled by DTS. A reworking of time and space created the potential for artists from different geographical, cultural and disciplines to work together in a way not previously considered viable. It can appear that DTs subvert divisions within the arts. The poem becomes a video, which is woven with others to form part of a wider social story. A video on dreams and place incorporates the partnership of musicians and the participation of viewers in its creation. However, activities such as these encourage an already underlying transformative process that deepens and widens the socialisation of artistic endeavour further intensifying the division of labour within the creative activity. By bringing together artists from differing specialisms to create an event or artifact, artists limit the potential possibilities of developing their own range of skills. As such, the creative environment increasingly takes the form of socialisation evident in other areas, such as manufacturing. On the surface, it can appear that the use of DTs during the pandemic has widened collaboration when the reality is that the underlying impulse has been to reinforce and expand the division of labour within the arts. Yet this process is itself contradictory because the pandemic and the use of DTs have also encouraged a greater sense of solidarity within the arts overcoming spatial constraints.

Precarious employment is the norm for most professionals in the artistic sector (Curtin & Sanson, 2016) and the confinements under COVID-19 have made the situation even more problematic. The pandemic has acerbated this alienated environment with grants hard to obtain, lost income not being guaranteed with furlough schemes, and the expansion of precarious employment models drawing upon DTs (European Expert Network on Culture and Audiovisual, 2021).

The conversations in this chapter show how artists have reflected on the impact of the pandemic and have searched for expressions of this moment in their work; they recognise that what is happening to them is happening to the rest of humanity. They exist in a shared collective social experience called COVID-19 and have looked for ways, in circumstances not of their choosing, to bind together their approach to their work with the practical experience of living under COVID-19. In doing so, they have had to grapple with notions such as authenticity, how real is the virtual, the idea of isolation, as well as the positive and negative impacts of DTs. The common-sense view of DTs as being the mechanism through which wider access to cultural and creative events is possible, is increasingly being replaced by a good sense understanding that sees DTs as a threat to the CCIs both in form and content. It will be interesting to see how successful experiments in developing hybrid artistic moments can be overcoming existent barriers. Perhaps DTs within the arts will encourage a return to Brechtian perspectives.

There is no benefit in speculating how creative activity will develop in the future because it is now clear that COVID-19 is not a passing phase. After six waves of the pandemic, we now know that it has become a permanent fixture which, together with the increasing use of DTs, will further deepen and widen precarious employment in the CCIs. Finally, these stories show that while DTs may present potential in innovative creative expression, ultimately, it is the face-to-face encounters during artistic endeavours that offer the possibility of providing a fulfilling experience.

References

Craig, S. (Ed.). (1980). *Dreams and deconstructions: Alternative theatre in Britain*. Amber Lane.

Curtin, M., & Sanson, K. (Eds.). (2016). *Precarious creativity: Global media, local labor*. University of California Press.

de Jesus, D. (2020). Necropolitics and necrocapitalism: The impact of COVID-19 on Brazilian creative economy. *Modern Economy, 11*, 1121–1140. https://doi.org/10.4236/me.2020.116082

European Expert Network on Culture and Audiovisual. (2021). *The status and working conditions of artists and cultural and creative professionals*. Retrieved

November 10, 2021, from https://www.fim-musicians.org/wp-content/upl oads/2020-eac-study-creative-sector.pdf

Malmo Symphony Orchestra. (2021, March 12). *Digital concert hall*. Retrieved October 21, 2021, from https://malmolive.se/en/digitalconcerthall

Mayor of London. (2020, September 21). *Mayor's culture fund helping to support 141 grassroots music venues*. Retrieved October 29, 2021, from https://www.london.gov.uk/press-releases/mayoral/mayors-culture-fund-helps-141-grassroots-venues

Nhat, M. (2021, May 14). *Artists suffer loss as Covid-19 resurgence prompts show cancellations*. Retrieved October 26, 2021, from https://e.vnexpress.net/ news/life/culture/artists-suffer-loss-as-covid-19-resurgence-prompts-show-cancellations-4277960.html

Savitch-Lew, A., Dvorkin, E., & Gallagher, L. (2020). *Art in the time of coronavirus: NYC's small arts organizations fighting for survival.* Center of an Urban Future. Retrieved October 21, 2021, from https://nycfuture.org/research/ art-in-the-time-of-coronavirus

UNESCO. (2021). *Cultural and creative industries in the face of COVID-19: an economic impact outloo*. UNESCO. Retrieved October 25, 2021, from https://unesdoc.unesco.org/ark:/48223/pf0000377863

6

Covid-19, Digital Technologies, and Protest Movements

Introduction

The pandemic lockdowns enforced a moment of isolation or rigorous social distancing but, as the previous chapters have shown, events also encouraged people to look outward. It was also the same for protests. After a brief pause, circumstances forced people to go onto the streets. A small minority protested government anti-covid measures, but most protests were a continuation of movements evident prior to COVID-19 or were a response to specific events. Health workers in Myanmar protested against the military dictatorship (Essex & Weldon, 2021), Columbians demonstrated against tax increases, poor social services, and police violence (Human Rights Watch, 2021), and the Lebanese October Movement (France24, 2021), are just three of a multitude of protests occurring since the pandemic began. COVID-19 did not mean the cessation of societal conflict. This chapter explores how DTs have been used by grassroots movements to organise the struggle against racism, sexual oppression, and oppressive government policies. It includes stories from those who have been involved in two of the largest protest movements ever recorded, the Black Lives Matter movement (BLM) and the Indian

© The Author(s), under exclusive license to Springer Nature
Singapore Pte Ltd. 2022
M. Healy, *Organising during the Coronavirus Crisis*,
https://doi.org/10.1007/978-981-19-1942-8_6

farmers' protest (IFP), as well as those mobilising over the death of Sarah Everard in the United Kingdom and resistance to government instigated attacks on street markets in Nigeria. The chapter opens by looking at BLM and then moves on to focus on Sisters Uncut in the UK.

Black Lives Matter

On 25 May 2020, George Floyd was murdered by Thomas Chauvin, a Minneapolis police officer. The last 7 minutes of George Floyd's life were captured on video by a passer-by, and it went viral across the internet. Within hours and days, a tsunami of protest followed, with street demonstrations in over 2,000 cities and towns in over 60 countries. It was an international protest movement leading to the creation of BLM groups across the globe. In the United States, BLM is a very broad movement involving activists from a wide variety of autonomous organisations, many of whom existed before the death of George Floyd. The genesis of the BLM resulted from the work of three female Black organisers: Alicia Garza, Patrisse Cullors, and Opal Tometi following the acquittal of the killer of Trayvon Martin in 2012. The movement grew rapidly as further unaccountable killings occurred and as people who had been organising separately recognised the need to form a national network but with autonomous local branches (Howard University Law Library, 2021). This section focuses specifically on three of these groups, the Atlanta Justice Alliance, BLM Minnesota, and BLM New Jersey. Organisers from several other local BLM groups expressed interest in participating in this discussion but, unfortunately, space has not allowed their stories to be included here.

The Atlanta Justice Alliance

The Atlanta Justice Alliance has been in protesting injustices for several years. These protests take the form of demonstrations and the provision of mutual aid for marginalised groups in and around the Atlanta area. Raven and Goat spoke about the use of DTs in their work.

Raven: Social media technologies help push back and bring attention to injustice by making things easier than before.

Goat: I'm a local leftist engineer and available to anybody wanting to protest against repression, racism, sexism. I'm not a digital technical expert but help with all sorts of practical measures. I'm also involved with the city's grassroots comms group which uses every available means, such as track cameras and live streams, to observe bad actors, whether the police, or local fascist groups, or whoever else. We don't hack public or private systems, but we do use our own methods.

Raven: For example, there may be a demonstration about to enter a street where there are police. By using live streaming, we can advise protesters to change route.

Goat: People on the ground will contact a unit close by, in a coffee house or at home, who will then disseminate latest developments to someone in the demonstration. We use private messenger apps like Telegram and Signal and run a live feed so that protesters can see what I'm seeing. Sometimes we'll just use old fashioned walkie talkies. We use the best means for a particular event to avoid direct confrontations with the police.

Raven: If someone is arrested, recording events can be useful in subsequent court hearings. We also use scanners to constantly monitor police radios and such like. We also use traditional media such as flyers, posters, and organise support for other events, such as vigils or pickets of police stations, and distribute these using Instagram or Facebook.

Goat spoke about the development of the comms group in Atlanta.

Goat: The small grassroots comms group consists of hardworking talented people covering a wide range of technical skills. They're amazing and inspiring and when the BLM protest movement blew up last year, they became involved. It's mutual technical aid supporting horizontal power structures. We spread the load so if someone gets sick or arrested, somebody else can continue; the core group has expanded recently. It's liberating information. I'm known and trusted in the local movement. They know I will be responsible if I use a camera, I'm not gonna be pulling pics of people's faces. Suspicion is high because Atlanta is one of the 10 most surveilled cities in the world right now outside of China.

Speaking of events after the summer of 2020, Raven indicated that protests, in the form of street demonstrations had diminished but that ongoing protests in the form of mutual aid had continued. In this context, mutual aid was not the same as COVID-19 mutual aid discussed in Chapter 2 .

> *Raven*: Mutual aid means speaking out against the injustices here and across the country. Local governments don't want houseless or shelter-less people existing in the public eye. After closing homeless shelters, the Atlanta city council placed huge boulders under overpass bridges to prevent people moving there. The homeless then moved to the city parks. Now the council wants to prevent the homeless from being fed; providing food is a protest action. The attacks on the houseless links to racism and mental health issues as well as substance abuse
>
> *Goat*: Mental health and substance abuse issues are not treated as illnesses; they're treated as personal moral failures. It's bullshit.
>
> *Raven*: Working together, several organisations help these people and others who are not your typical case. This pandemic means people out of work, losing their homes and then their cars. We also feed people that have homes and who are still working. We don't discriminate, if you need a meal, come see us. If you need a jacket, you will find one here.

They explained how the mutual aid work operates.

> *Goat*: We don't have enough volunteers to do one-to-one work and 20 can feed 200 people. We get cooked meals, tables, provide generators, make signs, do whatever is required, from all over the city. We'll go to some of the larger encampments in town. We bring food to them because they don't have cars and public transit is poor and expensive.
>
> *Raven*: Individuals also help, giving us information using apps such as Instagram and Twitter, and donating money using Cash and Venmo, meaning we can fill the gaps. We prepare soups, casseroles, and coffee, from different organisations coordinating through word and mouth.
>
> *Goat*: While there is little formal co-ordination between groups, it's exciting when we meet. It's the work of certain individuals and small groups, each with something to offer. There are local protest medics, and others, who'll treat infections, but since they're not doctors, they're

limited in what they can do since they can't prescribe medicines. They do what they can.

Raven: We don't target those self-isolating because of Covid, there's other groups focusing on that. But of course, we don't ignore helping someone when we can.

Goat: Recently, we had somebody who couldn't pay their traffic citations and so didn't have any transport. We got some money together to help pay their fees paid, getting them back on the road which meant they could help us cook and transport meals.

While Raven and Goat are describing a flexible degree of organisation, they also appreciate that ongoing discussions between activists are required.

Raven: There are several groups that have good working relationships and one or two people from each organisation participate in a larger chat group. This is where can post their actions and suchlike. But not an open chat space, it's for trusted people. We use various encrypted programmes.

They also talked about the pandemic's impact on protest actions.

Goat: Initially people were scared, staying at home. But later it played a significant role in mobilizing people on the street. Work takes up time, is exhausting and keeps us so goddam busy and when the pandemic hit, many people suddenly had more free time. They took their time and energy onto the streets.

Now it's different. Unemployment checks have stopped coming. People are going back to work or doing whatever they can, to make ends meet, to feed their children. Protesting has taken a backseat. Consequently, focus has turned towards city council meetings which are online because of Covid, but they are censored to blank out public comments and, because of the tedious nature of the meetings, the audience is small. That's torture for a small, dedicated group of activists.

Raven and Goat talked about how the activists have responded to the long-term nature of the pandemic.

Raven: While there are groups that host things like Zoom meetings, we don't. There's one, Fair Housing, very focused on the gentrification of specific parts of the city. I recently Zoomed with them to create a wider base of supporters.

Goat: I feel like there's a slow, gradual decline as our crumbling infrastructure continues to fail people and nobody does anything about it. So, we'll see when the next major disaster hits. On BLM, protests continue but charges are being dismissed against police officers

Goat: The government became afraid over the summer, but they're not anymore because people are not on the streets.

The discussion then covered the events leading to the killing of Vincent Truitt and the subsequent dismal of charges by a grand jury (Cobb County Courrier, 2021). Raven and Goat also talked about the increase in participation in protests during the pandemic.

Goat: During the last year, people's involvement has been exponential. Look at groups like the Socialist Rifle Association, which has almost tripled its membership over the past 18 months. Many people have been moving into this space of whether it's protests or mutual aid or wherever they fit in. Of course, there's wax and wane but protesting is more serious now, it's more than taking selfies on a demonstration for Instagram. The core participants have grown. People's eyes have become more open, people are woke now, more than a year ago.

The next section covers the activities of a BLM branch in Minnesota.

Black Lives Matter: Minnesota

BLM Minnesota, formed in 2016, is not directly connected with the main organisation which is common among BLM grassroots groups. Apart from several posts on a Facebook page, the group was quiet up to June 2020 when the events around the unlawful killing of George Floyd prompted an urgent need to increase the online profile of the group. The following interview was with Joli, one of the groups online administrators.

I've been involved with racial justice grass roots groups for 30 years. I crossed paths with Stephanie we connected and became friends. Stephanie is African American, and our many discussions resulted in us organising a Zoom group, meeting biweekly, called Let's talk racism. We advertised this on Facebook, and we've covered multiple topics. The group, of about 10, is very focused and committed to the discussions. Stephanie has her own her own stories and experience, and she's a life coach and work with empathy, compassion, and engagement. Our two niches just connected.

Our local BLM group gets most of its support from Minneapolis, St Paul, and a few of the larger suburbs, but our reach is also international because when there's a major event people want information or become involved, We're in a lull but with the trials of Chauvin and other police officers for the murder of George Floyd coming, we're expecting interest to rise.

Joli described the range of online activity connected with her BLM group.

We use Facebook to advertise, and learned about creating an invite, enabling people to show interest; we can issue reminders. We've also covered subjects like racism and the media, black voting and the election, parenting kids and racism, the psychological effects of racism on black and white communities. Attendance is at the Zoom meetings is normally between 5-7, and we have recently started film discussions. Stephanie and I are examining ways to automate emails to widen our audience. Since there's no money for commercial marketing, we're doing our own thing and that's hard.

I marched last summer, and the marches were larger than expected given the pandemic. Unfortunately, we couldn't produce a flier to host our own march and now things have gone quiet. But that's hasn't stopped us planning. We want to market differently. That's in addition to our Zoom discussions, I've also created PowerPoint presentation concerning allyship. We've connected with the Shakopee Diversity Alliance where I'll be presenting on how to be an ally, how white people accept that concept and start making change as white people. We're also exploring how digital technologies can promote these ideas. Overall, we're doing good.

It was trial and error through 2020 but now we've got our talons into it, we'll be working harder to reach more people because we have some excellent stuff. With Stephanie, as an African American and me, white and understanding how uncomfortable some discussions can be, I believe we have much to offer.

Joli emphasised the shared journey among the groups engaging with the issues arising from the BLM movement.

We're all trying to develop digital strategies to reach more people and there's some networking happening between groups especially concerning allyship and Black History month. Allyship networking will grow in 2021; we're even being contacted by law enforcement agencies. The technology has enabled this to happen because it broadens and deepens discussions about racism and how to fight it, facilitating more people being involved in this discussion.

George Floyd's murder has prompted many companies to implement unconscious bias, inclusion, and diversity training. There's a huge grassroots discussion concerning ways to change. As people become more knowledgeable of white privilege, white supremacy, 400 years of racist history, equality, and unconscious bias, they'll take these issues into their work, communities, and friends. It will no longer be just one person talking about these problems. Before, you could pack college auditoriums or get cultural centers together for a presentation. It was easier because calling one facility would mean about 50 to 100 participants. Now, we're posting on social media and if people don't catch the ad or they haven't been on Facebook, we miss people. Technology is not filling all the gaps.

When people think of grassroots action for change, they focus on marching. If they can't march, what happens then? Discussing issues is important and I'd like to know how other groups attract people to their online events. But I think people need to avoid seeing physical marching versus learning, education and understanding. This is a big problem for grassroots anywhere.

People ask: if I can't march, what do we do? We say, join our FB page and Zoom meetings, watch our videos, listen to discussions. Our work is centred around the idea that it's time for white people to start learning real history and begin to teach other white people about making change. Some people of colour are saying to us, "we've been doing this for way too long, we're tired, we're done, we've marched, you guys have the internet, Google, now go and learn it." Our group is brilliant because it brings black and white people together and because we have seen things differently, I learn from each session. Stephanie done many of educating, and she continues to support that.

Reflecting on my 30 years involvement in racial justice movements, I realise I was following people of colour, speaking on behalf of them. That's not what you do. Change involves difficult discussions, and this is what we're trying to do within the group, with allyship training. We will say the wrong thing, but we learn from that. Our group has a very tight base that wants to see change; we're not going to give up or shut down our site. With digital technologies we can access all kinds of resources. Since I've started using online more, I've noticed museums and colleges posting online events I can participate in. There are so many Zoom meetings about change. Maybe we've embraced our new normal, maybe we'll start to see a difference.

Joli outlined the latest developments in her area.

People have been regularly participating in events in George Floyd square and keeping it safe. We expect action to increase on March 8, when the trial starts, and we'll discuss that on our page.

Joli discussed changes in her attitude towards technology.

I was afraid of the technology, but I've grown technically more during the past 18 months than in the previous 30 years. I grew up in the 70's and 80's before the technology we see now and was still using a rotary phone in 1999 when I purchased my first cell phone. Now I schedule Zoom calls, can break down big meetings into the small groups, and bring them back all into the big meeting. Technology has helped me in my journey over issues like racism and allyship.

Using DTs has expanded the possibilities of reaching a wider audience but has also demanded more rigorous security measures.

> New members are on approval basis because of hate comments posted mainly at night-time, especially Saturdays. Since we can't be up all-night, checking posts, we'd wake up to a complete mess on the page. People didn't feel safe. We removed posts, blocked abusive members, and clarified our rules and then decided only to accept members on approval. We also check for scammers. Trust and making people feel safe are so important.

Joli's experience shows how developing technical skills is a critical part of participation and, just as importantly, challenging legacy ideas since technology is the mechanism allowing ideas to become practical action. It also influences reaction to technical problems.

> One Zoom call with the Shakopee Diversity Alliance developed an audio problem. Participants were relaxed, knowing we would eventually resolve the difficulty. We're learning something new, seeking solutions to problems, and realising it's about being patient and knowing we're all in this together, to support and learn from each other. We also learn to laugh about technical issues. Because of my involvement with BLM, I'm taking charge of some of the technical stuff at work, and even if it's not working right, I just say, "Be patient" and we have a little chuckle until we figure it out and move forward. We'll be Zooming until this pandemic is over and solidarity within the movement encourages a more patient attitude towards technology. It's the new normal.

The next contribution looks at the development of BLM in New Jersey, USA and draws upon an interview with Shevone, BLM, New Jersey.

Black Lives Matter: New Jersey

Prior to 2016, Shevone had been involved with race and environmental justice, and organising around food apartheid but had wanted to address other issues. The deaths of Trayvon Martin and Tamir Rice provided the impetus to build BLM locally.

It started with online meetings which then evolved slowly until the murder of George Floyd. Before Covid, we used social media like Facebook, Twitter, and Instagram to publicise our message because we could quickly and easily reach people, especially those of us living below the poverty line. That's something not mentioned often. BLM chapters are autonomous and Covid slowed everybody down allowing space for our voice to be heard. People see BLM as new, but its roots come from previous struggles, such as the Black Panthers, and it engages with current issues.

The technology makes us safe to be honest. In America, anyone who develops into a voice for people automatically has a bull's eye on the back. Leaders such as Medgar Evers, Malcolm X, Fred Hampton, end up assassinated. That's why there's a horizontal leadership in BLM which gives us a safety cushion enabling work to continue if someone is unavailable for any reason.

We're the network's floaters, if we get a call, Jersey BLM will show up. We've been to Standing Rock, Baton Rouge, Ferguson and Flint, Michigan, and Texas. Many of our actions you won't see in the media because we don't do it for the media attention. We appreciate the importance of media coverage, but it's a tool for change, not a channel for egos. We use the media to build the movement, to make other voices heard.

We use the word co-conspirators to describe those who are with us through thick and thin, and there's meetings about how to be better nonblack co-conspirators. We hold book bag drives for children, we feed the homeless. BLM is more than marching in the street about police brutality, it's about environment, socio economic equality, it's about even black joy.

Shevone, like many others connected with BLM, is directly involved in other direct-action and solidarity activities. During summer 2021, they distributed over 300 book bags to families that couldn't afford school supplies, at a giant Sunday cookout event that included children's face painting.

It was black joy Sunday organised using Zoom and email. Nurses gave COVID vaccines, provided immunisations for children, checked people for diabetes, and high blood pressure. Facebook, Twitter, Instagram are used to make people aware of what's going on. Emails are for intimate, private conversations, such as helping individual families who've suffered loss because of police action.

BLM is well known but there's other grassroots organisations doing great work without getting the recognition or funding they deserve. We publicise this work, so it gets the recognition and support it needs. Instead of it being just a BLM event, it will be their event which will be supported. I believe when something has a global presence, it must support other less well-known grass roots movements. We'll see a post or be contacted, and, after a full background check, we'll repost.

It's a quiet time now which happens in every movement. An event, such as the murder of George Floyd and the subsequent trial of Chauvin, will get much media attention leading to an uptick in interest. The other officers involved in George Floyd's murder are pleading not guilty and trials will create further waves of interest. The MSM didn't really care about the impact on George Floyd's family or the repercussions afterwards and the family tragedy that comes afterwards.

Shevone was highly critical of MSM's response to events such as the death of George Floyd which she calls "black trauma porn" and the "fascination of police violence on lack communities". However, she also sees social media as encouraging highly negative impressions.

Social media sometimes echoes this when videos showing police shooting a black man or some other type of trauma goes viral. Of course, the event gets the recognition as it should, yet many don't understand that for many black people social media is a double-edged sword because while it shows our oppression, but it also re-traumatises us every time we see another black body, it's like suffering from post-traumatic stress disorder. Toni Morrison[1] talks about post traumatic slave disorder which has generational consequences.

---

[1] An American novelist.

Imagine the impact on a community that constantly sees black bodies on the ground, they could be our sons, daughters, mothers, or fathers. Events should be publicised but in moderation because repeatedly watching people being murdered or brutalised takes its mental toll. That's why I said it's a double-edged sword. It's important to bring awareness to what's going on, yet we should be aware of the impact on a person and to a community. We're already brought up in our homes to handle the police a certain way, so we can make it home safely at night. I have panic attacks every time my two sons go out and worry until there're home again. We must talk about more these issues, and we promote self-care which involves stepping away from social media to decompress.

BLM is seen as either terrorists or good guys and it has reached a point where we stop being people and are just a resource. Journalists don't realise we have families, our own struggles with mental illness, and our own traumas. I cease being Shevone, instead I'm BLM New Jersey. There are times I close my smartphone because it is literally draining. But I also feel the pressure to be on social media all day just to make sure I don't miss something. That's burns you out. I realise I must decompress; racism is not going to end, and a three-day break is important. Some people overcompensate for this trauma by putting their value into what they do for others. It compels them to constantly stay on social media platforms leading to burn out. My grandmother told me, you can't pour from an empty cup and staying on these platforms, all day, every day, you're pouring and pouring, and not refilling. Decompressing and stepping back, spending time with your family or friends, watching TV, going to a restaurant, or a walk that's refills the cup. A lot of online organisers don't realise this.

From the moment I open my eyes in the morning to the moment I close them, I'm harassed online, being called a N*****, with hostile posts and phone calls saying they know where I live, where our children live. I've been doxxed.[2] This comes on top of the daily microaggressions and racism. Social media which should be mediated with trigger warnings

---

[2] Doxxing is to search for and publish private or identifying information about (a particular individual) on the internet, typically with malicious intent.

indicating what's going to be shown; it gives people the choice to watch or not. The technology sometimes cannot compensate for other pressures and online harassment can make organisers less effective. Poverty and homelessness can also be issues for many BLM organisers. I've got stable accommodation now, but I was homeless for a while during coordinating the BLM Jersey group.

There were and have been more deaths before and after George Floyd's murder and Covid did give people time to stop and think about these events, to witness what has happened, and to understand that what happened to George Floyd happens to black people every day.

Shevone recognises that while demonstrating is crucial, not everyone can march, but everyone with access can use social media to publicise events and can discuss issues online. She sees DTs as working in tandem with marching and considers them to be different ways to get to the same destination. However, she also appreciates there are problems.

Being online is also more dangerous because it can be infiltrated meaning trust is an issue. Now three people must now vouch for a person before s/he can come to our offline or online meetings. I know other BLM chapters have been infiltrated leading to the harassment of organisers. Look what happened to Malcolm X, Martin Luther King, and Medgar Evers. We're not paranoid, just very careful about security. Our general meetings can be open but planning sessions are closed. If white supremacists knew of our planned actions, it would put black people in harms way. We take precautions seriously because the safety of activists is so important.

These three stories are indicative of the way BLM activists have used DTs to organise and publicise BLM initiatives and to discuss those issues directly connected to the movement. They have also highlighted several series of concerns associated with DTs including fatigue and security. The next section covers the experience of a protest group based in London, UK.

Violence Against Women: Sisters Uncut

On 3 March 2021, Sarah Everard was kidnapped and murdered, in London. The police response, telling women to stay off the streets, caused outrage which was further fuelled when it became known that a serving officer in the Metropolitan Police, Wayne Couzens, had been charged with this brutal killing. Several organisations called for a vigil on 13 March 2021 at the Clapham Common bandstand, near where Sarah Everard had been last seen and despite a police ban, hundreds of people attended the vigil. The police responded by trampling on flowers and candles laid out in tribute and attempted to stop women from speaking. Sisters Uncut was involved in participating in the vigil and Aviah spoke about the work of the group and the action at Clapham Common bandstand.

I've been with Sisters Uncut since November 2014. We focus on domestic violence and opposing cuts to services for victims of domestic violence. We organised stunts, like occupying the roof of London Council offices and the red carpet at the film premiere of Suffragette, to highlight problems, getting media attention, force a particular narrative, and opposing cuts in benefits. After the red-carpet action, hundreds of people contacted us, looking to get involved. We went from relatively small London group, to establishing regional Sisters Uncut groups and three London groups.

Each group is different. Doncaster Sisters Uncut involves older women who've been active in the 1984 miner's strike. They're very feisty, many are pensioners and were determined to stop the closure of Doncaster Women's Aid. They were vocal at every local council meeting for six months and they won. The council reversed its decision.

In London, the groups are younger, taking different action. In East London, we occupied an empty council flat to highlight the 1000 empty council flats, saying these should be opened. We created a Women's Centre there during the summer months. North London Sisters occupied the closed Holloway Women's prison, turning that into a women's centre, demanding it be converted into social housing for women. So that's the kind of organising that we've been doing over the last few years.

Our initial focus was anti austerity, opposing funding cuts, but it became clear that successive governments were using domestic violence to increase police powers. We began critiquing this approach because survivors need independence with social benefits for housing and childcare, not a criminal justice response, We also saw that more domestic abuse survivors, more women, were being arrested and simply sending male perpetrators to prison for a bit longer was not going to solve the problem. It makes it worse. We developed an anti-carceral analysis arguing that prisons and policing were damaging us. During the past three or four years, our focus has towards criticising state funding priorities and organising alternatives to the justice system to deal with harm in our community.

Aviah described how DTs facilitate the work of the group which uses Facebook, Twitter, and Instagram to publicise meetings and posts statements and analysis of events on its website. Using DTs enable the group to rapidly reach a wide audience.

However, technology does also have its limitations because of its limited reach. An action like occupying Marian Court, East London highlights our campaigns, creates a useful space for women and reaches out to those not online. We organised a community centre with workshops and many people became volunteers and users. Having a stable, physical presence helped publicise the occupation in the local community. It meant we connected with people who don't use Facebook or Twitter. We had banners outside, a blackboard with a schedule of activities, we arranged a preschool breakfast club for kids, and organised kids' activities (which encouraged mums to pop in). We didn't simply rely on a Facebook or Twitter post. We distributed leaflets in the locality, including stores, held street stalls.

This use of traditional communications methods was extremely successful resulting in a broad range of people coming to the center. Aviah related that eventually, people began holding own meetings with many learning how to organise events such as workshops.

Not all groups use technology in the same way. Doncaster Sisters Uncut use it much less than we do in London. London. Their ways of organising and mobilising are quite old school and heavily predicated on developing quite personal relationships, perhaps based on the longevity of contacts built up since the miner's strike.

Aviah spoke about the impact of Covid on her life and work.

The pandemic has completely changed the challenging pace of London life, which can be difficult if you are an organiser, working and you've got caring responsibilities. Pre Covid, you had to go with the flow but this last year, things have taken a step back. Many people are not working and mutual aid groups, using technology, have begun to connect and reconnect those local people who need assistance with those offering help. Through this, longer-term relationships have started, that are hyper local. London is a big amorphous place that doesn't encourage community; this year, people used technology to find each other, even though they could already be next door, it's a non-linear process, it's community building.

We've suspended many actions during the lockdown but it opened-up space for more reflective political discussions through on online meetings. We tend to organise from action to action, which doesn't leave much space to reflect on how our politics at an individual and group basis influences the decisions we're making, the strategy we're taking. Space and time is needed to reflect on your politics and how your politics influences your decision to avoid problems later down the line. These online discussions can be difficult. Normally, we would meet and greet each other and socialise after a meeting even if there had been disagreements. In a difficult moment there would cues etc. We can reassure each other. It's harder to build those relationships online, it feels clunky doing that in a one-to-one Zoom meeting.

Aviah went on to describe the specific events at the Clapham Common bandstand.

We've been organising around the issues highlighted by Sarah Everard's murder and are used to taking actions like that at the Clapham Common Bandstand. What I wasn't expecting was the huge response to the video showing the police violence against our demonstration.

Reclaim the Streets initially called for the vigil because after Sarah Everard disappeared and her body had not been found, the police were telling women to stay off the streets. The vigil, which was also supported by the Lambeth Labour Party, was a response to police telling women to stay at home. There is a long tradition of police telling women to do that going way back to the Yorkshire Ripper in the 1970's. Women must go to work and live a full life.

Using Covid regulations, the police refused to authorise the vigil. This decision was challenged in court, where it was given back to the police; it is unclear whether political pressure was put on the police to ban the vigil. Ultimately, Reclaim the Streets called off the vigil, but we decided to go since many people were already going regardless of court and police decisions. We thought it important for freedom of assembly. We publicised our decision online and circulated safety information, about COVID and being safe around the police. It was extremely important to disseminate information very quickly so people can assemble safely.

None of us expected it to go the way it did. Photos, videos, and reports of the violent police attack on women at the vigil spread like wildfire through the MSM and social media. It triggered a massive national online conversation about the role of the police. People were angry because of the police's role in Sarah Everard's death, that police were telling women stay at home, and the murderer had previously been reported for indecent exposure. The police did nothing.

I don't take my phone to demos etc. so I didn't know until quite a few hours later about how the photos and videos had gone viral, and the developing political crisis. I had no idea there was that much mainstream or social media attention with calls for Cressida Dick, Met Police Commissioner, and Priti Patel, Home Secretary, to resign. It was stunning and probably the highest profile protest I've been involved in. The images circulating were striking. For me there's one stunning image of everyone with their phone's torch light on pointing at the bandstand revealing the violent actions of the police. It was dark when the police attacked the vigil and those at the back couldn't see what was happening so someone had the great idea to turn on everyone's phone torch to floodlight the scene. It was a moving and spectacular image. It was a genius idea and every time I see that image I'm amazed.

Technology was also extremely important in mobilising quickly to protest outside the Metropolitan Police HQ the following day. The events at the bandstand made us realise the connection between the government's police and crime Bill, and police violence against women. Since Clapham there's much work going on behind the scenes to build a broad-based coalition against the Police Bill. It involves activist groups, people and groups of people marginalised, such as travellers, who will be criminalized by the Bill. It's like four bills in one, it's scary and authoritarian. Opposition has forced people who wouldn't ordinarily share a common aim to show solidarity. It's been nonstop organising, things moving fast paced but I've been trying to make space for reflection, which is also needed, by scheduling time for discussion. This is a change from previously.

For Aviah, DTs provide critical mechanisms for quickly mobilising and communicating both within and between activists' groups. However, she was also aware of their limitations, arguing that they should be combined with in-person organising and one-to-one offline conversations. Security is also a concern.

While state surveillance and data sharing are massive issues, but we must take certain risks to organise, to get the word out. This is a contradiction. A Zoom meeting can be surveyed in one form or another and we cannot be certain everyone in that meeting supports the group.

Aviah had some comments about online accessibility.

Sometimes we've used sign language interpreters in our Zoom meetings, which can have up to 2000 viewers. People who ordinarily wouldn't have been able to participate have given us positive feedback on our attempts to make online events more accessible. Increasing accessibility also encourages people to get involved and organise something locally. The pandemic has also helped because it encouraged international online meetings.

Accessibility is more than planning for people with a disability. It also means adopting methods that connect with people who wouldn't be familiar with or respect our ways of organising, who wouldn't engage with our structures. It means knowing how they use technology.

Aviah developed this theme to talk about the way events and DTs had impacted on some of the fundamental organising principles of her group.

We've built up the group's trust and experience from years of organising, then suddenly we're catapulted into different ways of organising. People look to us for leadership when internally our group tries to be non-hierarchical. We've responded saying that people and groups can take positions of leadership at certain moments, but that leadership must be dispersed. We encourage groups to develop skills at taking the lead when necessary. It's a fluid, rather than a concentrated form of leadership. We're trying to learn from the struggles of the mid-20th century where power tended to be concentrated in a handful of leaders making it easy to undermine a group by removing the leadership. I think it is critically important that fluid forms of leadership require political education linked to experience.

Technology can help with this because it can democratise the infrastructure. For example, previously to put on the SWP Marxism[3] festival would have meant forward planning, booking rooms etc. with significant costs. After the events at Clapham, we realised we needed to bring together people who had been mobilising with those who hadn't. That's where the technology became critical because we could quickly organise an online public meeting that had 3000 people. Previously, only organisations with money could hold such large public events. Now we can do that and distribute an online form for people to complete so they can become involved. It's more democratic.

For Sisters Uncut, DTs provided the mechanisms enabling a swift and widely broadcast response to the circumstances surrounding the death

---

[3] Socialist Workers Party, a UK based revolutionary socialist organisation affiliated to the International Socialist Tendency. The Marxism festival is an annual event held in London, UK.

of Sarah Everard. However, they also generated problems for the group by potentially undermining its organisational principles and creating the possibility of an increased security threat. The next section looks at a protest movement in Nigeria.

Street Protests and the Federation of Informal Workers Organisation of Nigeria (FIWON)

FIWON was formed in 2010 in Abuja, Nigeria's capital city, and has sought to unite various bodies representing Nigeria's informal workers, who compromise 80% of Nigeria's workforce, under one national umbrella and currently has over 700 community-based associations from 27 Nigerian states. It represents millions of workers. FIWON's General Secretary, Gbenga Komolafe spoke about COVID-19 and the work of FIWON

> 10 years ago, I started organising informal workers, traders, the street vendors, market vendors, the artisans, carpenters, mechanics, cobblers, garment makers, farmers, and food processors and so forth that constitute most working people in Nigeria. They work on the streets, little workshops and at home. We also cover waste pickers and domestic service workers. There are more women workers than men in our Federation. In Nigeria, historically men dominate the formal sectors of the economy, while women run market stalls and operate as street vendors, food processors, garment makers, hairdressers, etc.

> These categories of working people are not unionised with no insurance and can't access social security or social protection programmes. They're extremely vulnerable especially where basic social and health services are very weak. We try to organise them into cooperatives to raise their concerns through advocacy and work with several state governments to improve basic facilities such as toilets and bathrooms. We've a cooperative society enabling workers to borrow money on better terms than the financial institutions. We have a very active Facebook page, website and use other social media such as Twitter. We are also train members on how

to protect themselves because there's substantial external pressure coming from the police environmental sanitation task force.

The Nigerian government has been pushing ahead with the closure of local markets as part of its modernisation policies to create what they call smart, modern cities with trams and shopping malls. In doing so it has undermined the informal sector and has encouraged collusion between developers and national and regional governments. Nigeria's informal markets occupy public land, and the redevelopment process involves the privatisation of these areas. Corruption is a prominent feature of Nigeria's economic life (PwC, 2016).

> They have forced the closure of markets in big cities meaning evictions is a big issue. Over 70 markets have been demolished resulting in hundreds of 1000s of woman traders being unable to trade. Our work also includes fighting these closures.

> We resist these closures by going to court but often the result goes against us. Other times we try to stop the closures by action but then the developers will call on the police and the army to get the job done. Recently to pre-empt resistance, little notice of closure is given. There's also been instances of mysterious fire outbreaks and then traders are moved for so-called safety reasons. Suddenly, the police cordon off areas and they are closed for months. Sometimes soldiers are used. Since we have challenged the police's right to undertake these operations, they are now using use armed gangs who are often policemen out of uniform. This makes it difficult to identify people because there's no name tags.

Gbenga talked about the problems of using digital technologies to defend informal workers.

> We use social media, and our Twitter and Facebook pages hold many stories about companies' misconduct. Unfortunately, many of our members are either too poor to be connected to or unaware of social media and are simply not attuned to campaigns run on social media. This means the message we make through digital media must be amplified by other traditional methods.

At the federation level, we have state chapters across the 27 of the 36 states in Nigeria. They have meetings where issues are discussed with elected delegates making contributions. We make good use of WhatsApp and other social media. At this level of organisation, use of social media is prevalent.

WHO figures seem to indicate that while COVID-19 in Nigeria has not had the same impact as in the Global north, it has followed the same spikes and waves. There have been several lockdowns that Gbenga believes had more of an adverse impact on the informal sector than the virus itself.

There wasn't any preparation by the government and no support for the poor people. Formal sector jobs were lost especially during the lockdowns, but some people received reduced pay. Informal sector workers have little or no savings to fall back on. Everyone in our cooperative took back their money during the lockdown simply to buy the most basic supplies.

Consequently, there was anger which led to riots against the lockdowns because of suffering with hunger and disease, with no access to basic health care services. We argued that the lockdowns were necessary, but more importantly it was crucial to educate the people about COVID and the need for basic precautions while going about daily life. There have been no further generalized lockdowns because the government doesn't want to risk further political problems. Instead, it emphasizes the need to use face masks and frequent hand washing with sanitizers. For many in the informal sector this can be a problem.

Nigeria has one export, crude oil, and the government increased the price of domestic fuel when the exports fell. This had a terrible impact since Nigeria depends on hydrocarbon for electricity; power from the national grid is unreliable and people use generators. Oil is also used as a solvent in all kinds of economic activity. The price increase also impacted on transportation and many industries have closed. At the same time, electricity companies increased tariffs by up to 300%. This further aggravated the employment problem because it meant industries had no access to energy. It was devastating for the informal sector.

The Nigerian Labour Congress was slow to respond to the crisis and its headquarters were picketed by younger members to protest over its refusal to react against government attacks. This forced the unions to make public statements concerning strike action, and they called, a short notice, for a general strike but then ended it without making any gains.

> There was an outburst of massive protests across the country on Independence Day, 1st October 2020 because billions were being spent on celebration while people suffered. These protests grew and 5th October youth groups and organisations sprung up all over the country calling for many demands, the most important demanded the government scrap of a notorious police unit; Special Anti-Robbery Squad (SARS). SARS is notorious for profiling and targeting young people, especially those with mobile phones. Sometimes these units tried to extort money from young people and there were instances of people getting killed or tortured. This led to many groups of young middle class young people demonstrating against SARS and our organisation, along with others, joined these protests. The protests lasted for two weeks, ending only after brutal repressions including massive killings, especially in Lagos where hundreds of protesters were killed.

> But it didn't end there. The protests were hijacked by street gangs, what the MSM calls hoodlums. They are unemployed with poor education, and very angry, with some being used by the police to attack people protesting market closures or evictions. They started attacking government buildings, courts, and police stations, over 100 police stations burnt. The protesters also started targeting politicians' homes, and warehouses holding massive amounts of food materials donated by corporate organisations to the government as bribes. They also looted warehouses containing food that should have been distributed during Covid lockdowns and was beginning to spoil.

> The interesting thing is that the so-called "hoodlums" had also been used to attack the protesters between 3rd and 14th October, but they switched and focused on politicians, the courts, the police stations, and food warehouses. After 15th October, the protests became massive springing up in every locality. Their demands became politicised because they were no

longer about closing the SARS but asking questions like why members of parliament are earning over $474,000 a year when prices of basic staples are increasing, and people are dying of hunger. I think this politicisation frightened the government leading to the brutal suppression of the peaceful protests. The initial protests started spontaneously over the SARS but the actions of the government, particularly concerning undistributed food at a time of hunger, inflamed people.

For the 1st October march, we made good use of Twitter and Facebook to mobilise mostly young people. But then the young protesters, most middle class, began to use social media to initiate actions. Some of them professionals, others were musicians. It included those who described themselves as social media influencers, with large followings on Twitter. During the initial phases, popular musicians entertained people on protest grounds which encouraged more young people to participate because they wanted to listen to music. These street extravaganzas were streamed online. Which meant it became a 24 protest with some people going home while others were just arriving. The protest sites were always filled with people.

Social media and events on the streets were feeding off one another but it wasn't social media that created the conditions leading to the protests.

Despite the use of social media, we still use traditional, offline modes of communication and we used flyers extensively to mobilise for October. We also had megaphones in cars touring the neighbourhoods and having a physical presence means we can sensitise people and encourage them to resist the vicious attack from the government. So traditional modes of mobilisation are still important even if we can have some limited access to mainstream media. We also organised small street meetings and neighbourhood meetings to discuss resistance to continued police attacks.

Now the mobilisations are not as big as last October, but they are continuing, and we have broadcasted podcasts of protests especially in Lagos, Abuja, and other cities. The police disrupt protests by arresting people, even those peacefully filming events. There's the case recently of a young man live streaming a scene where police were beating a woman and unfortunately for him, the police caught him, and he was detained for four days and was terribly brutalised.

Gbenga described the role of women in these protests.

Mostly young women have been at the forefront of the protests with one the most visible leaders being a diaspora group called Femco, Feminist Coalition, led by Nigerian women based in the US who raised almost 400 million US dollars to help those injured in the protests. So, women were leading the protests and helping with the injured. They also helped some protesters who had to go into exile. It's important to acknowledge the leadership role of women.

Now the situation is very tense. The government is discredited and trying to defend itself, particularly about the killings on 20th October. They tried to deny anything had happened and we still don't know how many were killed. The government continues with damaging policies including increasing electricity prices. Food is becoming more expensive and the war against Boko Haram in the north has spread to the northwest, huge swathes of which are now controlled by bandits. In the southern part of the country there is the so-called armed Fulani herdsmen, who have been destroying farmlands, killing people, and kidnapping.

Speaking 15 months later, Gbenga described the continuing protesting of informal workers referencing the Government closures of mechanic villages mechanic, which are clusters of motor mechanic workshops, and evicting mechanics to provide space for property development. He also mentioned the Government's Twitter ban in June 2021 because Twitter had supported the protests against police violence in October 2020 and had removed a Government tweet. The pressures arising from COVID-19 linked to ongoing struggles over police brutality and the closure of informal working spaces have ultimately politicised DTs in Nigeria. The policies of Nigeria's central and regional governments mean these protests are likely to continue into the future. The next section looks at the farmers' protests in India.

Indian Farmers' Protest

In September 2020, the Indian Government passed three neoliberal farming Acts designed to open up the Indian sector to large-scale, multinational agri-business. The passing of these Acts triggered the largest protest movement ever seen involving millions of farmers and their supporters. The protests contesting the farming Acts had been preceded by a movement opposing the Government's restrictive citizenship laws. However, as the protest developed and the determination of the farmers became stronger, it also became a struggle for the right to access the Internet (Horwitz & Purnell, 2021). This section opens with Anindito, an independent journalist who has regularly reported on the Indian farmers' protest.

Reporting the Farmers' Protest: Anindito's Story

This protest movement is huge encompassing millions of people. Each village has an elected council called a Gram Panchayat supporting the protests. Each village elects representatives for a regional body meaning there are local support groups for the protests, and they have been instrumental in organising the protests; you don't get 50,000 tractors in the same place on the same day by accident, it doesn't happen overnight.

WhatsApp had been the main tool for mobilising the demonstrations. The Government recognised this and attempted to stop it. The farmers began using Twitter and became familiar with hashtags etc. and recognised the value of multiple distributions. On 26th January 2021, India's Republic day, thousands of farmers and 50,000 tractors entered Delhi and occupied an area called The Red Fort. The government implemented measures to block off and online communications within a 3 kilometre area by closing off cell phone towers to isolate the protest site. There are several roadblocks as well. I had to leave the protest site and drive, using a taxi service, for 500 meters or more to file stories and upload pictures. The police also beat journalists as well as protestors.

Instagram and Twitter are widely used but the digital works with tandem with word and mouth. Each village will have a youth leader who often passes on information about news and meetings etc. The spokesperson of the Bharatiya Kisan Union (BKU), Rakesh Singh Tikait, has been to many village meetings organised locally prior to the 26th January. Using traditional word and mouth allied to social media means hundreds of people will come to each of these local meetings. Sometimes MSM is also approached. YouTube posting of these meetings means those who cannot be there on the day can access the meeting. This work was going on before January.

Now, cultural events happen at the Red Fort occupation with popular singers giving concerts although these have reduced because of police and government pressure. Song continues to play an important role in the protests with YouTube videos of popular singers being widely circulated. The YouTube Kisaan Anthem has over 48 million views. The most popular hashtag is #indianfarmers which during a 7-day period reached over 2.8 million people.

Anindito said that anti-protest fake news, often generated by official and quasi-governmental bodies, is a significant problem. He believes that despite the huge difficulties in fact-checking posts in a country with a population of 1.3 billion, 80% of people are aware of real events, because of social media, and don't accept fake news. He also described the widespread support the protests have received.

I have also met people called red eyes. These are family and friends of farmers living in New Zealand, Canada and elsewhere, who have come to support the farmers. Many are professionals, like doctors, some had elderly parents who couldn't participate, or had lost their parents but felt they must be here. Sometimes there's a carnival atmosphere at the occupation. Lots of colour, meetings, discussions. Some of the farmers have been at the Red Fort since November 2020. There are several community kitchens offering food to everyone, protesters, media people, supporters, who is there. Doctors have also established medical centres with a blood bank and there's a gym and spa. Some of the meetings can attract 1000's and there are many, daily smaller meetings. Women are deeply involved with the protest. In many cases, the whole family is protesting but interestingly, I have more images of men cooking at the communal kitchens.

Supporting the Farmers' Protest: Samita's Story

Samita's family has long been part of the farming tradition in India.

My family has a farming history and the Punjab, for various historical reasons linked to education etc., has a strong social identity. The Government favours large scale corporate farming at the expense of the smaller farmers and before these farming laws were implemented, the Government has been trying to undermine traditional farming. These laws will remove those mechanisms, such as appealing in the court, used by farmers if they feel they've been treated unfairly regarding pricing. Farmers fear multinationals will manipulate wheat markets without any checks and small farmers will be no match for multinationals backed by a battery of lawyers. The laws will also destroy practices that enable farmers to continue when crops are lost because of poor weather conditions. Farming is crucial in India where unemployment is high. It enables people to feed themselves. These laws will undermine this and are unconstitutional because they were passed when parliament was not in session. The Government did not consult the opposition parties nor the farmers and imposed a national policy on all local states despite India's constitution stipulating that agriculture is a local state responsibility.

These fears meant farmers have united behind their unions to resist the laws; they are demanding to be heard. The social structure of the farming communities has helped build support for the protests. Daughters, sons, grandchildren of farmers have joined the protests saying while we are not farmers, we do not forget our past. Many people see this a struggle for the democratic future of India, for their children's future.

The farmers' protest is the largest ever, yet the Indian MSM hardly covers it or publishes misinformation, so we get our information direct from the protest using digital media. The government has tried to seal-off the protest sites by digging up roads and using barbed wire, destroying important infrastructure.

Samita said that India's prime minister Modi had tried, unsuccessfully, to use DTs to undermine the protest but now they are being used effectively by the protesters. She mentioned the multiple YouTube channels organised by skilled volunteers with citizen journalists reporting using DTs to relay events from the ground. Farmers watch these videos on their shared phones.

> Protesters regularly contact their villages because whole families are protesting, and the children continue schooling using online classes. There's a constant rotation between the protests and the villages with trolleys, the Indian name for tractor trailers, carrying 10 or more people with supplies from each village going to the protest. After every 10 days, they rotate, with another 10 from the village. Using digital media, journalists on sites such as Navneet Chahal, alerted people to police attacks and the erection of barricades and barbed wire. Local shop keepers close to the occupation sites help the protesters by sharing their Wi-Fi passwords as an act of solidarity. The Indian farmers unions have formed a common platform and their meetings are organised through Facebook Live. India is geographically, linguistically, and culturally diverse, so protest YouTube channels are broadcast in English and Hindi.

Samita went on to describe the role of women, who make up 75% of those working on Indian farms, in the protests.

> The matriarch is a powerful and respected person in the farmer family, and everybody listens to her. Similarly, it was the elderly who first decided first to join the movement because to enable harvesting. The Government asked why women are in the camps and demanded they be sent back to the villages. The women responded by saying they were staying because it is an equal fight. It encouraged more women to come to the occupations. Women are targeted by the Government, for example, the Indian Constitution says you can marry whosoever you like but the Government focuses on marriages between Muslim women and Hindu men, calling these the love jihad. This is another reason why women are fully involved with the farmers' protest.

The government wanted to malign and divide the movement saying it's religious but there's no religion for farming, it's a global activity and each farming community feels oppressed because of the way they've been treated. When the Government called the farmers Andolanjivis (parasites), it backfired because the right to protest is a basic freedom, and this protest is peaceful. We've seen the emergence of many leaders who hadn't voiced their opinions earlier. It's amazing how everybody is speaking up in solidarity, there's newfound unity, which was lacking before. Unity among people has come out of this protest. For many people this movement is preserving the Indian Constitution and democracy. Solidarity comes from all areas including urban professionals with no direct connections to farming communities because they know this is also about basic freedoms. A Pandora's box has been opened by the farmers' movement allowing so many previously crushed voices to be heard.

The Government is also trying to curb freedom of expression authorizing the arrest and jailing of environmentalist Disha Ravi, 21, for circulating the farmers toolkit which suggests ways to help the farmers. All she did was to Tweet the document. Is that an offence? The Government wants to scare people, to prevent young people becoming involved in the protest. It's about stopping people from voicing their opinions. Hinduism is an open religion and women have always been at the helm of affairs. Now the Government wants to force women into the home, away from work or protests and this is a new concept. This is painful, it's hurtful. We don't want our progress halted. Each generation of women wants the next generation to progress.

There was a dispute in a factory close to the farmers protest site and the workers came to the site. The police targeted and arrested one young worker, Shiv Kumar, and brutalised him. His nails were taken out, he had multiple fractures, had plenty of injuries, and consequently developed a depression. The farmers lawyers got involved securing bail for him. He hadn't committed any crime, but his torture was illegal. The Government wanted to send a message: this will happen to you if you support the farmers, but his case was publicised on all the social network sites.

Building the Farmers' Protest: The Trolley Times

Mukesh is a member of the All India Student's Association and was the first person from his hometown to study at a prestigious international university. He has been politically active for several years starting including campaigns against the privatisation of higher education. He sees the Indian farmers protest as part of the general campaign against the globalisation of farming and privatisation in general.

> The farmers know they're fighting against the government and corporate interests because they fear losing their land and the destruction of common collective cultural traditions. They're also concerned about the devastating consequences on farming communities from increased drug and alcohol abuse and the health implications, such as cancers, associated with the long-term use of pesticides and other toxic chemical agents. Over 10,000 farmers committed suicide in 2019. They fear perpetual rootlessness or becoming refugees and understand the reasons for the Government's policies. They are linking their own personal experience within globalisation. Previously, agricultural matters had been decided at a state level, but now the federal Government is pushing its policies meaning farmers in all states will suffer.

> These protests are the latest in a long line of protests over debt and hunger going back several years. 2017 saw the farmer protests in Madhya Pradesh, Rajasthan, and Tamil Nadu. Six farmers were killed Madhya Pradesh. Farmers realised that small scale disparate regional protests weren't winning but they were the building blocks upon which the latest protests were built, and 250 farmers' unions decided at an All India Kisan Sangarsh Coordination Committee in 2017 to unite around a minimum of demands linked to freedom from debt, fair prices, access to grains and, latterly, resistance to the farming laws. This work was coordinated by an all-India coordinating committee. Consequently, they've delivered on the numbers participating, successfully organised the logistics, and organised visits to and from the protest sites. It has involved a lot of hard work to come to this moment. 2018 witnessed a huge farmers protest in Maharashtra with the Long March involving several thousand people walking to Mumbai. Tamil Nadu farmers also camped in Delhi for six months.

These protests were met with apathy or ignored by the politicians and MSM.

The farmers' protest started in Punjab in late summer 2019 when farmers' representatives organised village meetings to mobilise local small-scale protests, such as blocking highways, protesting outside retail outlets, and picketing offices of lawyers of multinational and corporate companies. Digital technologies, such as WhatsApp, facilitated this action and provided lots of information and content about how the protests were developing.

On 26th November 2019, farmers marched to Delhi and the MSM didn't cover the protest, but the social media did. Activists or small independent news portals provided information by being there on the ground. The authorities blocked roads, so independent journalists reached the march by biking over fields at night, risking their lives and possibly being arrested. Using WhatsApp, YouTube channels, Titter and Facebook, they published videos of police baton charging farmers and using water cannon, of authorities digging up roads or placing huge cement blocks, trailers, or trucks in the middle of roads. The videos also showed the police brutally beating older farmers. When those videos came out on social media there was a huge outrage in the villages. You don't forget videos like those; they showed how dangerous the situation was. Social media distributed these images enabling people to see the protest and the government imposed an Internet blackout at the protest sites on Delhi's borders to stop farmers building their own narrative to counter the propaganda. So independent journalists go where there's Internet tourism to publish images etc.

There are hundreds of thousands of farmers protesting and having brought their tractors and trolleys to the protest sites, they are not leaving. At the same time MSM and Government politicians spread misinformation about the protests. A major challenge was mobilising widespread support for the farmers during the first weeks of the protest, but there's also a huge communication gap within the protest sites because many farmers don't have smartphones or don't know how to use them.

We recognised that paper copy is important for an older generation and our team came up with the idea of the **Trolley Times**, a free newsletter, for the farmers. The trolley (trailer) has become an important symbol for the protest because it's part of popular culture for farmers to decorate their tractors and trolleys. There is a core publication team of 4 supported by a fluctuating number of volunteers, including translators, to produce the paper. We printed 2000 copies of our first edition, in Punjabi and Hindi, on18th December and distributed one copy for 5 or 6 trolleys. We asked people to read it, pass it on, to read out loud so everyone, literate or not, would be the audience, and to hold conversations around the topics in the bulletin.

The next afternoon after finishing distributing the bulletin, we realised that a national TV channel had reported about the **Trolley Times** because we had also published in social media photos of us delivering the bulletin. This started a wide-ranging discussion about the role of citizen journalism resulting in documentaries concerning the farmers' dispute. We decided to publish an online English version to communicate across the globe. This amazing response encouraged us to publish the **Trolley Times** weekly.

None of us are trained journalists, it just happened. We uploaded a basic website and asked people to download and distribute the **Trolley Times** PDFs on condition the content remains unchanged. Villages began to do so followed by urban areas across the country. Someone in Canada translated the paper into English which was widely read because there's a huge Indian diaspora. Editions have been translated into Bangla and Marathi showing people felt it was their publication. It usually has six to eight pages and it's always divided with equal distribution of content in Hindi and Punjabi, and it has a Punjabi front but on reverse, there is a Hindi front.

Initially we tried to report like ordinary newspapers, news of events etc., but we realised we needed to cover why farmers were protesting and the politics of protesting, linking protesting to a healthy democratic state. We make sure the health of the protesters is also covered because many have died. We cover the history of farm prices, the emergence of the Farming unions, profiles of younger protesters, especially women. We're trying to give a comprehensive understanding of the social composition of the protests by covering people across caste, class, gender, race, religion, food habits and everything.

We're trying to explain complex ideas using simple language which is not easy since many young contributors are writing for the first time. We also reached out to scholar activists knowledgeable about farm prices and asking them to explain their work in everyday language. This enabled us to publish an article on the history of farmers movement in Telangana, in Maharashtra, in Rajasthan, in 1940s 50s 60s, even 1907. We're showing how recent protest are part of a long history of protest. People share their stories via photos, videos, songs, poems and we've noticed that young people have come to appreciate the struggles and protests of the older generation farmers.

Farmers' meetings are crucial with farmer's leading crisscrossing the country to attend meeting. They also use Zoom, and it's common to see people in their 50s and 60s and even 70s, attending the Zoom meetings, and addressing webinars on a global scale organised by universities or trade unions. They have become familiar with the technology and to speaking late at night across different time zones. Previously, many of these speakers will not have used social media before and now recognise it's possible to remain within the protest sites while speaking to audiences across the globe. That is a big change.

One concern is updating on social media. Our paper is weekly, but the age of social media means constant updating almost every minute cross our various platforms. So then, after a week or so we started consolidating all social media as well. We have 57,700 followers on Instagram, 11,500 on Twitter, and there lots of YouTube channels showing videos about the dispute. We see the hardcopy newspaper and the social media presence as complementing to each other. Social media allows us to provide updates, while the newspaper enables a deeper analysis.

I've noticed that smartphone use has increased along with Facebook live and recording. Social media use feeds itself, the more people see their stuff online, the more they use it. Mobile connectivity is high in India and access is relatively inexpensive. Smartphones can be expensive but there is a large market for used phones and their use amongst farmers has increased. There will be 5 or 6 people in a trolley sharing a smartphone to watch a film, TV or get the latest news. Audio features such as Google Voice search also makes it easier for farmers to access content, it overcomes literacy problems. Farmers also use online translation captions so videos in one language can be understood in another.

Mukesh wanted to make one final but important point about the protest.

The farmers' protest is being led by an older generation who recognize it may be a long struggle and who have the experience of the issues. It is the older generation leading the younger. This is relatively unique. Young people are involved and learning about protesting; understanding the intricacy of it, the need to engage with many people, to listen, and keep a calm head.

Conclusion

The stories in the chapter are microcosms of protest movements in motion during the pandemic. They will resonate with many of those who have continued to confront and oppose racism and oppression despite the presence of COVID-19 and its variants. There is an implicit theme within each story, that of mobilising from below, of building upon a tradition of grassroots action to expand and build networks of protest. While official common-sense policies called for restricting social contact during the pandemic, in several instances, the lockdowns' provided the time and space for mass presence on the streets. In other cases, ongoing grievances fuelled the continuation of protests as governments sought to use the pandemic to undermine the opposition. COVID-19 did not mean an end to the awareness of these issues.

They also show the determination of activists to resolve the multitude of problems they encountered and their experiences of using DTs while doing so. The pandemic created the space and motivation for activists to develop their technical skills across the spectrum of DTS. Zoom meetings attracted audience participation in numbers not considered possible before the pandemic, it also enabled smaller discussions.

YouTube videos using instantaneous translation cut across language and cultural barriers, facilitating the reporting by non-professional journalists thus giving protesters a louder voice. Activists could see how DTs can help in encouraging democratic accountability by allowing for distributed decision-making and dispersed leadership roles. They also recognised the value of DTs in continuing the development of networks during periods when street protests were reduced.

However, as their interaction with DTs increased so did their appreciation of technology's contradictory nature. Zoom meetings can open up a wider audience, but they also provide a gateway for disruptive and threatening voices forcing activists to employ a range of measures to ensure the safety of participants. A successful online presence creates the conditions where site organisers or administrators become overwhelmed with extra activity, much of which includes moderating sites to screen out hostile interventions. In this specific context offline and online security meld into one. Fake news and official censorship have also been problems protest movements have needed to address. DTs provide the conduits for the speedy and widespread diffusion of fake news. Fake news can be both general and/or directed at specific groups. While fact-checking websites can offer some help, often it is group site administrators who are required to post clarifications adding further burdens to the task of maintaining the integrity of a site.

While online censorship has been prevalent for many years, a recent development is the frequency of governments to overtly block news websites and social media domains (Raman & Ensafi, 2020). The IFP and the Nigerian market protesters have also been subject to denial of access to the Internet, the former in specific locations and the latter have to cope with blocks on social media platforms such as Twitter. Shutdowns such as these have also become a common feature of Internet life as governments increasing used them to block access to information and communication. It has been estimated that between January and May 2021, there were at least 50 documented Internet shutdowns in 21 countries (Access Now, 2021). Further, policy initiatives, such as the UK's Online Safety Bill, will see the increased politicisation of Internet regulation (Dickson, 2021). Protest movements will increasingly face these problems and will need to adapt and develop techniques that may require a demised reliance on the use of DTs.

DTs have also impacted on the existing culture of movements in several ways. A group's guiding principles which were worked out and maintained within a relatively small community, are suddenly under stress because of new circumstances. Developing a wider audience creates greater levels of responsibility as others seek advice and guidance on becoming involved and have expectations of a group. The pressure builds as demands are made to, for example, update Facebook pages and YouTube sites, to constantly monitor online traffic to provide recent news, and to keep track of new and existing group members resulting in increased stress. The influx of new and welcomed supporters creates a dual problem. How to respond, which requires an internal discussion within a group's founding members, and to what extent can initial principles be maintained? DTs can undermine group cohesion while expanding its audience. As one interviewee said, space for reflection is critical in such a moment and DTs are not always well suited for such a discussion,

The Indian farmers' protest succeeded in forcing the Indian government to drop the controversial farm laws (Varghese, 2021). It shows that protesting repressive legislation can win but it also reveals how DTs can be extremely effective when working in tandem with but subservient to more traditional means of action. The farmers were united in their demands that the Indian government withdraw the farm laws and were extremely well prepared with significant support both at home and abroad. Some may argue that if DTs had been more widely available within the Indian farming communities, perhaps the protest may have had a different tone and volume on the streets. That is speculation but I believe the IFP has provided a template for future protest movements seeking to use DTs. Sharing the technology linked to a unified purpose seeking to achieve a set of specific demands creates an environment where wider questions, such as the role of women in society and the consequences of neoliberal economic policies, come to the fore. While time and space did not allow for an extensive detailed examination of how, for example, online meetings using Facebook and YouTube, were conducted during the IFP, I do know that frequently they were experienced in a collective setting enabling vibrant discussion within the audience. There is much to learn from the IFP.

References

Access Now. (2021, June 7). *#KeepItOn update: Who is shutting down the Internet in 2021*. Retrieved November 30, 2021, from https://www.access now.org/keepiton/

Cobb County Courier. (2021, May 5). *Vincent Truitt's family continues to push for prosecution of Cobb officer*. Retrieved November 10, 2021, from https://cobbcountycourier.com/2021/05/vincent-truitts-family-contin ues-to-push-for-prosecution-of-cobb-officer/

Dickson, A. (2021, June 9). *New UK internet law raises free speech concerns, say civil liberties campaigners*. Retrieved December 1, 2021, from https://www.politico.eu/article/uk-concerns-over-internet-free-speech-tech-regulation-power-grab/

Essex, R., & Weldon, S. M. (2021). Health care worker strikes and the Covid pandemic. *The New England Journal of Medicine*. https://doi.org/10.1056/NEJMp2103327

France24. (2021, October 17). *Two years after October 17 protests, Lebanon's economic crisis worse than ever*. Retrieved October 30, 2021, from https://www.france24.com/en/middle-east/20211017-two-years-after-october-17-protests-lebanon-s-economic-crisis-worse-than-ever

Horwitz, J., & Purnell, N. (2021, March 5). India threatens jail for Facebook, WhatsApp and Twitter employees. *Wall Street Journal*. Retrieved November 10, 2021, from https://www.wsj.com/articles/india-threatens-jail-for-fac ebook-whatsapp-and-twitter-employees-11614964542?mod=business_minor_pos4

Howard University Law Library. (2021). *Black lives matter movement*. Retrieved November 12, 2021, from https://library.law.howard.edu/civilrigh tshistory/BLM

Human Rights Watch. (2021, June 9). *Colombia: Egregious police abuses against protesters*. Retrieved October 1, 2021, from https://www.hrw.org/news/2021/06/09/colombia-egregious-police-abuses-against-protesters

PwC. (2016). *Impact of corruption on Nigeria's economy.* PwC. Retrieved October 21, 2021, from https://www.pwc.com/ng/en/assets/pdf/impact-of-corruption-on-nigerias-economy.pdf

Raman, R. S., & Ensafi, R. (2020). *Censored planet: An internet-wide, longitudinal censorship observatory.* University of Michigan. Retrieved November 30, 2021, from https://censoredplanet.org/censoredplanet

Varghese, S. (2021, December 8). *After a year-long strike, Indian farmers score a big win.* Retrieved December 9, 2021, from https://inequality.org/research/indian-farmers-victory/

7

Conclusion

Introduction

This has been a difficult book to write. It started as a research project focused on what I, along with many others, thought would be a relatively short moment in time linked to the first lockdown. Two years later, despite vaccine development, we know that COVID-19 and its evolving variants will be with us for a long time. It has progressed from a pandemic to become endemic. At one point, it became difficult to keep track of the cases and deaths registered; constantly looking at rising body counts is hard. This conclusion is being written in the middle of the fifth COVID-19 wave, driven by the highly contagious Omicron variant and with other variants rapidly emerging (Corum & Zimmer, 2022). It is likely that we will need multiple booster jabs to control the impact of the virus.

If the development of the virus has been challenging, so has having to witness politicians, who should regard our welfare as a number one priority, ignoring the reality of the virus or prioritising economic considerations over health concerns. Few national governments will emerge from this moment in history with a credible record. The spectacle, for

© The Author(s), under exclusive license to Springer Nature
Singapore Pte Ltd. 2022
M. Healy, *Organising during the Coronavirus Crisis*,
https://doi.org/10.1007/978-981-19-1942-8_7

example, of the UK Prime Minister, Boris Johnson, being fined by the police and offering absurd apologies for breaking his own lockdown rules and partying in his official residence in London, will live long in our memories. So too will the hypocrisy of Indian Prime Minister, Narendra Modi, who, while expressing gratitude to health workers, refused to consider further lockdowns in case they stalled economic momentum (The Tribune News Service, 2022). The virus has also exposed the frailties of a perspective that benefits the few over the many, with countries and companies competing against each other to obtain financial gain from developing and distributing vaccines. The pandemic has also exacerbated already existing inequalities (The Conversation, 2022), increased mental health problems (BLM, 2022), and created new ones linked to COVID-19 infection rates and deaths (Dwivedi, 2021).

This is one side of the COVID-19 narrative. The other side is encapsulated in the stories contained within this book. They show how the void generated by the failure of official policies was filled by an enormous collective effort and how people engaged in a critical examination of official policies to develop their coping strategies based on an emerging good sense. In the middle of a deadly pandemic, life went on, tasks needed to be undertaken, people needed help, and protests had to be made. In this process, grassroots activists looked to digital technologies to aid their work, technologies that are often lauded as offering a whole range of solutions to a myriad of problems enabling connectivity across a diffuse range of boundaries. They seem to offer the possibility of undermining spatial and temporal constraints, facilitating the possibility of enhanced, inclusive collective activity. However, as the previous chapters show, this was a deeply contradictory experience with DTs creating a whole new set of problems.

Since the conclusions of each chapter have already been discussed in some detail, a limited number of themes are reprised here. One key theme emerging from all chapters concerns the significant difficulties linked to access. In some instances, access to digital equipment such as smartphones or computers was a dilemma. For others the lack of Internet availability was the barrier linked to acquiring appropriate skill levels. This should not be a surprise since over 40% of the world's population has yet to connect to the Internet. Yet, there are other, perhaps surprising and often hidden reasons for people not connecting online. For many of those with mental health challenges, the digital experience is fraught with difficulties. Young vulnerable adults can fear the loss of anonymity associated with participating in online meetings. Homeworking, a much-vaunted option for work during pandemic and post-pandemic periods, is beset with a range of complexities including the transition from work to non-work activities, the availability of space, the pressure to continue working in unfavourable conditions, and adversely impacting on caring responsibilities. The widespread practice of remote working using video conferencing and other social media platforms has also encouraged online sexual harassment, a theme not covered in this book but one worthy of more research (Rights of Women, 2021).

The pandemic has led to increased online shopping, driving the boom in warehouse expansion, generating employment but also facilitating the spread of COVID-19. For those involved with protest movements, concerns over online security could result in offline physical security problems. Protesting Indian farmers and their supporters had access to online communications cut by state agencies. For those involved MAGs available software needed modification to assist in matching. With Sisters Uncut, DTs required a significant and rapid reworking of their preferred methods of organising developed over several years. Poets had to address issues concerned with control of Zoom sessions. Rather than being inclusive, the technologies have encouraged an exclusive environment. For artists, self-imposed censorship, the relationship between technology and artistic control, the impact of the digital sphere on authenticity, the problematic associated with the virtual versus the real, and the adverse impact on the division of labour within the arts, are just a few of the questions they confronted.

Issues such as these force us to confront the common-sense views we hold about the value of DTs encouraging us to develop a more critical appreciation of the way technology impacts on our lives. Taken individually, it might be considered that each problem could be resolved with specific solutions such as better training, greater accessibility and optimisation, machines with greater processing power, or cheaper Internet connections. However, the stories in this book will resonate with activists across the globe indicating that the problems outlined here are not accidental nor are they unique. The repetition of the same challenges linked to DTs, while taking different forms, across the chapters indicates that there is something fundamentally problematic about our interaction with DTs. In all the stories, there was an expectation that technology, in one form or another, would provide a resolution to specific problems, be they unionising Amazon workers or facilitating participation in international conferences. It became clear to participants that these expectations would not be satisfied. This failure flows from the inherent nature of the technology itself because it is, just like another commodity, a means to make money which depends on the labour–capital relation. While tech companies seek to manipulate data to "line their pockets" (Khanna, 2022, p. 284), they are simply doing what all capitalist enterprises strive to attain: increase profits.

Concentration of Research, Development, and Production

The concentration of research, development, and production in a limited number of companies has been a feature in the history of computing. Just five firms control 81% of computer manufacture and sales, with three taking 60% of market share (Statista, 2021). In the software sector, three companies dominate the market with the lion's share going to Microsoft (Statista, 2020) while the online digital sector is controlled by companies such as Amazon and Meta. On the very afternoon I wrote this paragraph, news came through that Microsoft had purchased video games giant, Activision Blizzard, for $69 billion to advance access to the lucrative gaming market which has audiences of 3 billion. It will make Microsoft the third biggest gaming producer (Microsoft, 2022). This was quickly followed by a report a few days later that employee in Activision Blizzard had formed the Game Workers Alliance Union, the first trade union of its kind in the industry (Paul, 2022) in a move that underscores the increasing labour unrest in the sector.

The pandemic has spurred the growth projections of all sectors of digital technology and as the sectors grow, so will the dominance of an increasingly limited number of companies. This process is evident in the mobile apps sector with Facebook, WhatsApp and Instagram owned by Meta. Video conferencing use, which has become so crucial during pandemic, is controlled by three products, Zoom, Microsoft Teams, and Google Meet. It has been estimated there are over 300 million Zoom calls each day covering 50% of the market in at least 44 countries (Dean, 2022).

Marx and Alienation

These statistics matter because they indicate that whenever and wherever we engage with digital technologies, we generally experience the same process which is dominated and determined by relatively few enterprises.[1] In short, billions of people share the same problems across similar platforms. In this sense our problematic engagement with DTs is an abstract challenge which, because of mediation through specific instances, may be expressed in a myriad of different ways and Marx's theory of alienation has much to offer in analysing our profoundly unsettling interaction with DTs.

Marx (1970) argues that the labour–capital relation involves loss of control over the things we make and our own labour as well as the processes employed in their creation, that in crucial aspects of capitalist production, we experience alienation. It is a condition that is both abstract, since it happens to us all, but is manifested in specific circumstances. The commodities and the processes used to create DTs are determined by the need to generate profits. A digital commodity, like many others, may have some usefulness, but we do not have any voice in how the commodity will be designed, made, distributed, and used. Companies producing DTs disavow any responsibility for societal problems arising from their use, such online gaming addiction or the implications for health and safety. Video calls could be a valuable tool in overcoming isolation and fostering social interaction, but they

---

[1] China is developing its own range of digital products but these exhibit the same tendencies (The China Daily, 2020).

are limited by time and participation unless we pay. The Zoom app was designed primarily as a business communications tool to compete with Microsoft's Skype and Google's Meet. Its merit will not be assessed on how valuable it will be to enhance or expand our social relationships but on the performance of the owning company on the stock market which will, ultimately, be contingent on its inroads into commercial markets.

A further aspect of Marx's theory of alienation is its reference to the way commoditised labour leads to self-alienation and one of the recurring themes in many of the stories in this book revolves around negative self-images on screens. Research indicates that this is a widespread phenomenon leading some researchers to refer to the emergence of Zoom dysmorphia (Rice et al., 2020). These images result from distortions by computer and frontfacing smartphone cameras but are assumed to be a real portrayal of our image and are creating a potential mental health challenge (Silence et al., 2021). This echoes some of the comments made by several participants about being self-conscious of their online screen presence.

Interaction with technologies demands that we modify our behaviours to adapt to DTs, and it can seem the machine acquires control over us. However, this would be a mistake since this is appearance only because the technologies are designed and developed elsewhere. The digital device is in effect a proxy for our normally hidden alienated relations with multinational hardware and software companies. Further, these devices, because of the pandemic, have rapidly expanded to mediate our alienated relationships with other people as exampled by the huge increase in online pornography (Zamboni et al., 2021), which is causing the emergence of a further mental health crisis (Marchi et al., 2021). The greater the number of people sucked into using digital devices, the wider and deeper the alienated experience. Furthermore, this process entails self-alienation since we look to satisfy our lives in ways removed from the process of work and the products of our labour. As one of the contributors to this book noted, online actions are increasingly considered an important aspect of our interaction with others. Our posts increasingly come to define who we are, and the number of likes, downloads, or subscribers determines the worthiness of our digital lives.

Significant problems were encountered by just using the technologies. A recurring sentiment expressed in the previous chapters concerns the amount of extra effort generated by the application of DTs. Whether, for example, it was a MAG, a protest movement, or a mental health organisation, the application of DTs required additional self-taught training, the application of enhanced security measures, extra hardware or software, and, in some instances, increased staff. This is not surprising since usability has long been a major problem which is further exacerbated by the constant churn in innovation of new technologies. The rapid, urgent need to apply them to social interventions also imported usability problems into the non-work environment. The increasing digital mesh between our work and non-working lives has further illuminated what Harvey calls universal alienation, a condition where the labour–capital relation spills over into the non-working environment (Harvey, 2018).

Apart from the impact of the virus, people have had to deal with multiple contradictory experiences during the pandemic including poor political leadership across a range of countries, confusing messages from the scientific community, inconsistent and conflicting rules governing social distancing, the need for, but the lack of, personal protection equipment, and the availability, but poor distribution, of vaccines. In the swirl of these difficulties, we turned to DTs which, as the stories in this book have shown, created further contradictions. If Marx's theory of alienation can allow us to theorise our alienated experiences with DTs, Gramsci's concepts outlined in Chapter 1 can enable us to comprehend how many people, but not everyone, responded, to the pandemic.

Gramsci

It is possible to discern the fracture both within and between the health scientists and politicians which, even as late as February 2022, was evident in the discussions concerned with lifting of COVID-19 restrictions. The UK Minister of Health, along with several other governments, advocated a rush to ending almost all measures designed to curb the Omicron virus, asking people to follow "common sense" actions, while health and educational professionals advised caution. The stories in this book reveal an interweaving of a rejection of the conflicting assortment of common-sense ideas, the emergence of a good sense, and a growing challenge to the dominant set of ideas articulated by government bodies. Resolving real practical problems required a dual confrontation of the common-sense policies being pursued by official institutions and the common-sense myths associated with DTs. This process saw the emergence of good sense in both areas. The problems associated with trying to make effective use of DTs fostered a critical assessment of their usefulness. Technologies which had been touted as being easy to use, were found to be complex. Developing an online presence that moved beyond an intimate circle, created problems of security. The creation of online events involved significant compromises such as accepting self-censorship, accommodating to the capabilities of the technology, and changing organisational structures. It is noticeable that in many of the stories, reference was made to the need to provide information in more traditional forms of hard copy such as flyers and newspapers. Those of us who have used wax stencils running on a Roneo duplicator, as I did in my bedroom for a period, fully appreciate the facility to create and print documents using digital machines. Nonetheless, the notion that virtual documents will replace hard copies is not supported by the evidence here. Quite the opposite it seems because DTs also create the need for hard copy. These are some of the examples showing that difficulties resulting from people engaging with real problems challenge a range of hegemonic ideas associated with digital machines.

There is a further important element of change that must be highlighted. A constant refrain across almost all the stories is how by engaging in activity, people also changed themselves. On one level, this can be seen in the urgent need to rapidly develop their digital skills. Tasks using DTs that once seemed difficult to undertake became routine, skill levels rapidly and significantly increased. However, the motivation to acquire knowledge and skills was rooted urgent need to cope with COVID-19. It seems that the virus has provided the greatest incentive to develop our digital abilities. COVID-19 has been both a problem and a catalyst for change.

Another element of change has been the emergence of multiple intellectual leaders developing organically at grassroots levels because they actively participated in "practical life, as constructor, organiser, permanent persuader" (Gramsci, Selections from the prison notebooks, 1971, p. 10) While many, such as those involved in the Sisters Uncut collective or BLM, may feel modestly uncomfortable with this description, the stories in this book show how they simply adopted this role unconsciously and provided guidance in both coping with the pandemic and using DTs. In doing so, they embraced an accountable style of leadership uncluttered by the problematic dichotomy that poses our well-being against economic imperatives and rejecting a leadership based merely on oratory.

Using Marx's theory of alienation and Gramsci's concepts to undertake and complete the research covered in this book, indicates they offer significant potential for examining the contradictions of our digital lives, contradictions that will deepen and widen as DTs slowly begin to cover the remaining 3 billion people currently offline. The technology itself will also intensify the process with the emergence of the so-called metaverse, a digital collective universe, running parallel to the real universe, that requires extensive use of artificial intelligence and demands intensive use of big data facilities. Advances in metaverse technology will also strengthen the tendency to the concentration and centralisation of digital research, development, and production.

However, the research potential available through using Marx and Gramsci must be constantly validated and reaffirmed by continuous research and analysis, and there are many other domains where this could happen. These could include environmental movements, animal welfare, consumer groups, civil rights organisations, those concerned with domestic violence, organisations focused on alcohol and drug dependency, international institutions such as Médecins Sans Frontiers, organisations concerned with addiction to digital gaming or substance dependence, the problematic linked to crypto-currencies, and the bias built into artificial intelligence computing. The use of DTs to mobilise opposition to Russia's invasion of Ukraine will surely feature as a research project in the immediate future. I believe that we should be cautious of all attempts to draw definitive and final conclusions from any single piece of given research and results must always be considered as fallible until they have been buttressed by additional evidence. I would also argue that while I advocate using Marx and Gramsci, it would be unwise to disregard the significant research concerned with the societal implications of DTs undertaken without embracing the perspective promoted here. As Wright remarks:

> The Marxist tradition is a valuable body of ideas because it successfully identifies real mechanisms that matter for a wide range of important problems, but this does not mean it has a monopoly on the capacity to identify such mechanisms. (Wright, 2009)

Having said that, I am also convinced that the perspectives advanced within the Marxist tradition, in this case those associated with Marx's approach to alienation and Gramsci's concepts, offer the most effective route for understanding and theorising the contradictions of our digital lives.

Every research project of this nature has a problem: it just cannot cover all areas. There have been, for example, many events and protests that could have been covered by this book: the work of Resistance committees in Sudan, MAGs in Africa and Asia, community organisations such as the Centre for Rights Education and Awareness (CREAW) in Nairobi's Kibera, Kenya, that could have been included. An awareness of these absences encourages me to continue this research for future publication. I have not researched those groups who have, for whatever reason, opposed COVID-19 vaccination programmes or the use of masks, nor those who believe the pandemic is a conspiracy. These groups also challenged the overarching common-sense approach, but they do so by ignoring the growing scientific evidence about the nature of COVID-19 and its adverse impact on our health. For some, like those I have met in the French Yellow Vest movement, these are genuinely held views based on a profound scepticism of governments and government policies. For others, like the neo-Nazis organising anti-vax strolls in Chemnitz, Germany, it is simply a crude attempt to further their divisive agenda.

Concluding Remarks

COVID-19 will not be the last global pandemic or catastrophe we will face. The bubbling economic crisis, the ongoing environmental catastrophe, and the concomitant social and political crises (I am writing this chapter as Russian tanks roll into Ukraine), are growing in severity. Our pandemic experience has thrown into immediate sharp relief the struggle about priorities focused on well-being versus profit and the contradictions associated with DTs. It has also shown that during the pandemic, while politicians dithered, many rose to the challenge, questioning existing ideas and being prepared to provide leadership, but to paraphrase Spock, it is leadership but not as we know it. It was, and continues to be, built on collective efforts designed to satisfy a real material need. This was an intricate process involving the use of DTs to create innumerable networks, many of which will continue as the pandemic morphs into an endemic. These networks will also carry a history of this period that is separate from the official story, a history encompassing the work of grassroots activists. It will be a history that will show that what we do matters and that linking relevant theory to our actions enables us to grasp the fundamental impulses driving the confused and contradictory ideas and institutions that dominate society. There are many more stories of the pandemic that need to be recorded. I have been fortunate that the ones I have encountered will become permanently available through the publication of this book.

This book argues that our individual experiences during the pandemic can be generalised thus revealing the systemic problems inherent in existing social, economic, and political structures and identifying those responsible for failing to adequately deal with a crisis of international proportions. The pandemic has also enabled us to see who our allies will be in a precarious future as we attempt to assert our long-term needs over short-term policies designed to buttress profits. If future crises will not be of our making, the stories in this book show that collectively we can begin to create the solutions. To paraphrase Gramsci, the challenge of our contradictory digital world is to live without illusions but without becoming disillusioned.

References

BLM. (2022, January 13). *COVID-19 and the impact on carers*. Retrieved January 17, 2022, from https://blmhealthandcareblog.com/2022/01/13/covid-19-and-the-impact-on-carers/

Corum, J., & Zimmer, C. (2022, January 11). Tracking Omicron and other Coronavirus variants. *The New York Times*. Retrieved January 16, 2022, from https://www.nytimes.com/interactive/2021/health/coronavirus-variant-tracker.html

Dean, B. (2022, January 7). *Zoom user stats: How many people use zoom in 2022?* Zoom User Stats: How Many People Use Zoom in 2022. Retrieved January 14, 2022.

Dwivedi, R. (2021, November 26). *The study showed that the age-adjusted COVID-19 deaths rates were five times higher in the working class vs. college graduate adults aged 25–64 years old*. News Medical Life Sciences. Retrieved January 10, 2022, from https://www.news-medical.net/news/20211126/Effects-of-social-class-ethnicity-and-gender-on-burden-of-COVID-19-mortality.aspx

Gramsci, A. (1971). *Selections from the prison notebooks* (1978 ed.) (Q. Hoare, G. N. Smith, Eds., Hoare, Q. Hoare, & G. N. Smith, Trans.). International.

Harvey, D. (2018). Universal alienation. *Journal for Cultural Research, 22*(2), 137–150.

Khanna, R. (2022). *Dignity in a digital age: Making tech work for all of us*. Simon & Schuster.

Marchi, N. C., Fara, L., Gross, L., Ornell, F., Diehl, A., & Kessler, F. H. (2021). Problematic consumption of online pornography during the COVID-19 pandemic: Clinical recommendations. *Trends in Psychiatry and Psychotherapy*. Retrieved from https://www.scielo.br/j/trends/a/Fn3x7HcQYX5XWkcJjhzpQWD/abstract/?lang=en

Marx, K. (1970). *Economic and philosophic manuscripts of 1844* (D. J. Struik, Ed., & M. Milligan, Trans.). Lawrence and Wishart.

Microsoft. (2022, January 18). *Microsoft to acquire Activision Blizzard to bring the joy and community of gaming to everyone, across every device*. Retrieved January 18, 2022, from https://news.microsoft.com/2022/01/18/microsoft-to-acquire-activision-blizzard-to-bring-the-joy-and-community-of-gaming-to-everyone-across-every-device/

Paul, K. (2022, January 21). Activision Blizzard employees form first of its kind Game Workers Alliance Union. *The Guardiian*. Retrieved January

22, 2022, from https://www.theguardian.com/technology/2022/jan/21/act ivision-blizzard-employees-union

Rice, S. M., Graber, E., & Kou, A. S. (2020, November). A pandemic of dysmorphia: "Zooming" into the perception of our appearance. *Facial Plastic Surgery & Aesthetic Medicine, 22*(6). https://doi.org/10.1089/fpsam.2020. 0454

Rights of Women. (2021, January 11). *Rights of women survey reveals online sexual harassment has increased, as women continue to suffer sexual harassment whilst working through the Covid-19 pandemic.* Retrieved January 5, 2021, from https://rightsofwomen.org.uk/news/rights-of-women-survey-reveals-online-sexual-harassment-has-increased-as-women-continue-to-suffer-sex ual-harassment-whilst-working-through-the-covid-19-pandemic/#survey-exposes-an-upsurge-in-online-sexual-harassme

Silence, C., Rice, S. M., Pollock, S., Lubov, J. E., Oyesiku, L. O., Ganeshram, S., Mendez, A., Feeney, F., & Kourosh, A. S. (2021, December). Life after lockdown: Zooming out on perceptions in the post-videoconferencing era. *International Journal of Women's Dermatology, 7*(5), 774–779. https://doi. org/10.1016/j.ijwd.2021.08.009

Statista. (2020). *Software.* Retrieved October 23, 2021, from https://www.sta tista.com/markets/418/topic/484/software/#statistic4

Statista. (2021, November 23). *Personal computer (PC) vendor shipment share worldwide from 2011 to 2021, by quarter.* Retrieved December 10, 2021, from https://www.statista.com/statistics/269703/global-market-share-held-by-pc-vendors-since-the-1st-quarter-2009/

The China Daily. (2020, March 23). *Chinese software company founded to develop domestic operating system.* Retrieved October 16, 2021, from http:// www.chinadaily.com.cn/a/202003/23/WS5e78273aa310128217281382. html

The Conversation. (2022, January 7). *New data shows COVID will continue to have a negative financial impact on many UK households.* Retrieved January 14, 2022, from https://theconversation.com/new-data-shows-covid-will-con tinue-to-have-a-negative-financial-impact-on-many-uk-households-174214

The Tribune News Service. (2022, January 12). *Economic momentum must continue: PM at Covid review with states, rules out lockdown.* Retrieved January 15, 2022, from https://www.tribuneindia.com/news/nation/pm-modi-holds-virtual-meeting-with-cms-amid-covid-surge-360957

Zamboni, L., Carli, S., Marika Belleri, B., Giordano, R., Giulia , S., & Lugobo, F. (2021). COVID-19 lockdown: Impact on online gambling, online shopping, web navigation and online pornography. *Journal of Public Health Research, 10*(1). Retrieved from https://www.ncbi.nlm.nih.gov/pmc/articles/PMC7893314

References

Access Now. (2021, June 7). *#KeepItOn update: Who is shutting down the internet in 2021.* Retrieved November 30, 2021, from https://www.access now.org/keepiton/

Anderson, K., & Looi, J. C. (2020). Chronic zoom syndrome: Emergence of an insidious and debilitating mental health disorder during COVID-19. *Australasian Psychiatry, 28*(6), 669–669. https://doi.org/10.1177/103 9856220960380

Andrae, A. (2017). Total consumer power consumption forecast. *Conference: Nordic Digital Business Summit.* Retrieved January 14, 2021, from https://www.researchgate.net/publication/320225452_Total_Consumer_Power_Consumption_Forecast

Avelar, L. (2021, July 21). *How can technology help combat climate change.* World Economic Forum. Retrieved January 12, 2022, from https://www.weforum.org/agenda/2021/07/fight-climate-change-with-technology/

Barrera-Algarín, E., Estepa-Maest, F., Sarasola-Sánchez-Serrano, J. L., & Vallejo-Andrada, A. (2020). COVID-19, neoliberalismo y sistemas sanitarios en 30 países de Europa: Repercusiones en el número de fallecidos [COVID-19, neoliberalism and health systems in 30 european countries: Relationship to deceases.]. *Revista espanola de salud publica.* Retrieved April 16, 2021, from https://pubmed.ncbi.nlm.nih.gov/33111713/

© The Editor(s) (if applicable) and The Author(s), under exclusive license to Springer Nature Singapore Pte Ltd. 2022
M. Healy, *Organising during the Coronavirus Crisis,*
https://doi.org/10.1007/978-981-19-1942-8

Basu, K. (2020). *COVID and common sense*. China Global Television Network. Retrieved October 22, 2020, from https://news.cgtn.com/news/2020-08-05/COVID-and-common-sense-SGzOohGlBS/index.html

Bhaskar, R., & Callinicos, A. (2003). Marxism and critical realism. *Journal of Critical Realism, 1*(2), 89–114.

BLM. (2022, January 13). *COVID-19 and the impact on carers*. Retrieved January 17, 2022, from https://blmhealthandcareblog.com/2022/01/13/covid-19-and-the-impact-on-carers/

BMJ. (2020, November). Covid-19: Politicisation, "corruption," and suppression of science. *British Medical Journal*. Retrieved November 18, 2020, from https://www.bmj.com/content/371/bmj.m4425

Bollyky, T. J., & Bown, C. P. (2020). The tragedy of vaccine nationalism: Only cooperation can end the pandemic. *Foreign Affairs*. Retrieved November 30, 2020, from https://www.foreignaffairs.com/articles/united-states/2020-07-27/vaccine-nationalism-pandemic

Braun, E. (2020). *In France, controversial doctor stirs coronavirus debate*. Retrieved November 10, 2020, from https://www.politico.eu/article/how-a-french-doctor-is-turning-into-a-pr-headache-for-macron/

Bustad, J. J., & Andrews, D. L. (2020). Remaking recreation: Neoliberal urbanism and public recreation in Baltimore. *Cities, 103*, 102757. https://doi.org/10.1016/j.cities.2020.102757

Cairney, P. (2021). The UK government's COVID-19 policy: Assessing evidence-informed policy analysis in real time. *British Politics, 16*, 90–116. https://doi.org/10.1057/s41293-020-00150-8

Cameron-Chileshe, J., & Payne, S. (2020). *Johnson tells UK to live 'fearlessly but with common sense'*. Fiancial es. Retrieved October 22, 2020, from https://www.ft.com/content/df14c89b-6cab-464b-ad15-fe9c45fb0f42

Carchedi, G., & Roberts, M. (2018). *World in crisis: A global analysis of Marx's law of profitability*. Haymarket Books.

Centre for Disease Control and Prevention. (2021, July 22). *Coping with stress*. Retrieved September 24, 2021, from https://www.cdc.gov/mentalhealth/stress-coping/cope-with-stress/index.html

Cobb County Courier. (2021, May 5). *Vincent Truitt's family continues to push for prosecution of Cobb officer*. Retrieved November 10, 2021, from https://cobbcountycourier.com/2021/05/vincent-truitts-family-continues-to-push-for-prosecution-of-cobb-officer/

Corum, J., & Zimmer, C. (2022, January 11). Tracking Omicron and other Coronavirus variants. *The New York Times*. Retrieved January 16,

2022, from https://www.nytimes.com/interactive/2021/health/coronavirus-variant-tracker.html

Covid-Minds. (2021, July). *Covid-Minds longitudinal studies*. Retrieved July 10, 2021, from https://www.covidminds.org/longitudinal-studies

Cox, J. (1998). An introduction to Marx's theory of alienation. *International Socialism, 2*(79). Retrieved May 20, 2020, from https://www.marxists.org/history/etol/newspape/isj2/1998/isj2-079/cox.htm

Craig, S. (Ed.). (1980). *Dreams and deconstructions: Alternative theatre in Britain*. Amber Lane.

Crehan, K. (2016). *Gramsci's common sense inequality and its narratives*. Duke University Press.

Cressey, D. (2020). UK universities left in limbo as schools and colleges told to close. *Research Professional News*. Retrieved April, 2022, from https://www.researchprofessionalnews.com/rr-news-uk-universities-2020-3-uk-universities-left-in-limbo-as-schools-and-colleges-told-to-close

Cummings, I. (2018). The impact of austerity on mental health service provision: A UK perspective. *International Journal of Environmental Research and Public Health, 15*(6), 1145. https://doi.org/10.3390/ijerph15061145

Curtin, M., & Sanson, K. (Eds.). (2016). *Precarious creativity: Global media, local labor*. University of California Press.

Davis, M. (2020). *California's apocalyptic 'second nature'*. Retrieved October 17, 2020, from https://rosaluxnycblog.org/california-fires/

de Jesus, D. (2020). Necropolitics and necrocapitalism: The impact of COVID-19 on Brazilian creative economy. *Modern Economy, 11*, 1121–1140. https://doi.org/10.4236/me.2020.116082

Dean, B. (2022, January 7). *Zoom user stats: How many people use zoom in 2022?* Zoom User Stats: How Many People Use Zoom in 2022. Retrieved January 14, 2022.

Department of Work and Pensions. (2021). *DWP COVID-19 employer pulse survey: Interim report*. DWP. Retrieved September 12, 2021, from https://assets.publishing.service.gov.uk/government/uploads/system/uploads/attachment_data/file/1003633/covid-19-employer-pulse-survey-interim-report-final.pdf

Dickson, A. (2021, June 9). *New UK internet law raises free speech concerns, say civil liberties campaigners*. Retrieved December 1, 2021, from https://www.politico.eu/article/uk-concerns-over-internet-free-speech-tech-regulation-power-grab/

Dwivedi, R. (2021, November 26). *The study showed that the age-adjusted COVID-19 deaths rates were five times higher in the working class vs. college graduate adults aged 25–64 years old*. News Medical Life Sciences. Retrieved January 10, 2022, from https://www.news-medical.net/news/20211126/Eff ects-of-social-class-ethnicity-and-gender-on-burden-of-COVID-19-mortal ity.aspx

Essex, R., & Weldon, S. M. (2021). Health care worker strikes and the Covid pandemic. *The New England Journal of Medicine*. https://doi.org/10.1056/ NEJMp2103327

European Environment Agency. (2021). *COVID-19 and Europe's environment: Impacts of a global pandemic*. European Environment Agency. Retrieved December 28, 2021, from https://www.eea.europa.eu/publications/covid-19-and-europe-s/covid-19-and-europes-environment

European Expert Network on Culture and Audiovisual. (2021). *The status and working conditions of artists and cultural and creative professionals*. Retrieved November 10, 2021, from https://www.fim-musicians.org/wp-content/upl oads/2020-eac-study-creative-sector.pdf

Evanega, S., Lynas, M., Adams, J., & Smolenyak, K. (2020). *CORONAVIRUS MISINFORMATION: Quantifying sources and themes in the COVID-19 'infodemic'*. Cornell University, Cornell Alliance for Science. Retrieved November 28, 2020, from https://allianceforscience.cornell.edu/wp-con tent/uploads/2020/09/Evanega-et-al-Coronavirus-misinformationFINAL. pdf

Ferguson, I., & Lavalette, M. (2004). Beyond power discourse: Alienation and social work. *British Journal of Social Work 34(3)*, 297–312. Retrieved from https://doi.org/10.1093/bjsw/bch039

Financial Times. (2020). *The Financial Times*. Retrieved from https://ig.ft.com/ coronavirus-lockdowns/

Flick, U. (2018). *An introduction to qualitative research*. Sage.

France24. (2021, October 17). *Two years after October 17 protests, Lebanon's economic crisis worse than ever*. Retrieved October 30, 2021, from https://www.france24.com/en/middle-east/20211017-two-years-after-october-17-protests-lebanon-s-economic-crisis-worse-than-ever

Georgieva, K. (2020). *Finding solid footing for the global economy*. IMF. Retrieved October 27, 2020, from https://blogs.imf.org/2020/02/19/fin ding-solid-footing-for-the-global-economy/?utm_medium=email&utm_sou rce=govdelivery&fbclid=IwAR3LnpvE_ZkejPqIyRTbbsxuHWhQDXjLeo UVGOG-omddY0AoMPNX_yZ48UQ

Gramsci, A. (1916). *Men or machines?* Marxist Internet Archive. Retrieved May 1, 2020, from https://www.marxists.org/archive/gramsci/1916/12/men_or_ machines.htm

Gramsci, A. (1917). *The revolution against 'capital'*. Marxist.org. Retrieved September 13, 2020, from https://www.marxists.org/archive/gramsci/1917/12/revolution-against-capital.htm

Gramsci, A. (1928). *Letter to Tania Schucht*. Retrieved April 17, 2021, from https://www.marxists.org/, https://www.marxists.org/archive/gramsci/1928/new-year-letter.htm

Gramsci, A. (1971). *Selections from the prison notebooks* (1978 ed.) (Q. Hoare, G. N. Smith, Eds., Hoare, Q. Hoare, & G. N. Smith, Trans.). International.

Gramsci, A. (2000). *The Antonio Gramsci reader: Selected writings 1916–1935* (Forgacs, Ed.). New York University Press.

Gray, E., & Merzdorf, J. (2019). *Earth's freshwater future: Extremes of flood and drought*. NASA Global Climate Change. Retrieved October 28, 2020, from https://climate.nasa.gov/news/2881/earths-freshwater-future-extremes-of-flood-and-drought/

Gutierrez, G., & Gonzalez, C. (2020). 'We are broken': Montana health care workers battle growing Covid outbreak. *NBC News*. Retrieved November 03, 2020, from https://www.nbcnews.com/news/us-news/we-are-broken-montana-health-care-workers-battle-growing-covid-n1245526

Hampton, H., Fayer, S., & Flynn, S. (1995). *Voices of freedom: An oral history of the civil rights movement from the 1950s through to the 1980s*. Vintage.

Harvey, D. (2018). Universal alienation. *Journal for Cultural Research, 22*(2), 137–150.

Healy, M. (2020). *Marx and digital machines: Alienation, technology, capitalism*. University of Westminster Press.

Healy, M., & Wilkowska, I. (2017). In M. Pirson & M. Kostera (Eds.), *Dignity and the organization* (pp. 99–124). Palgrave Macmillan.

Henley, J., & McIntyre, N. (2020, October 26). Survey uncovers widespread belief in 'dangerous' Covid conspiracy theories. *The Guardian*. Retrieved November 18, 2020, from https://www.theguardian.com/world/2020/oct/26/survey-uncovers-widespread-belief-dangerous-covid-conspiracy-theories

Horwitz, J., & Purnell, N. (2021, March 5). *India threatens jail for Facebook, WhatsApp and Twitter employees*. Wall Street Journal. Retrieved November 10, 2021, from https://www.wsj.com/articles/india-threatens-jail-for-facebook-whatsapp-and-twitter-employees-11614964542?mod=business_minor_pos4

Howard University Law Library. (2021). *Black lives matter movement*. Retrieved November 12, 2021, from https://library.law.howard.edu/civilrightshistory/BLM

Human Rights Watch. (2021, June 9). *Colombia: Egregious police abuses against protesters.* Retrieved October 1, 2021, from https://www.hrw.org/news/2021/06/09/colombia-egregious-police-abuses-against-protesters

Iley, B. T., & Bickley, S. L. (2021). *Looking to the post-pandemic landscape.* BlankRome. Retrieved September 20, 2021, from https://www.blankrome.com/siteFiles/COVID-19-Employer-Workplace-Survey-Summer-2021.pdf

ILO Monitor. (2021). *Covid and the world of work: Seventh edition.* International Labour Organisaton (ILO). Retrieved September 16, 2021, from https://www.ilo.org/wcmsp5/groups/public/---dgreports/---dcomm/documents/briefingnote/wcms_767028.pdf

IMF. (2020a). *World Economic Outlook Reports: A long and difficult ascent.* International Monetary Fund. Retrieved October 27, 2020a, from https://www.imf.org/en/Publications/WEO/Issues/2020a/09/30/world-economic-outlook-october-2020a#Chapter%203

IMF. (2020b). *Policy responses to Covid-19.* International Monetary Fund. Retrieved November 04, 2020b, from https://www.imf.org/en/Topics/imf-and-covid19/Policy-Responses-to-COVID-19

International Monetary Fund. (2021, December). *Safeguarding the world's health and wellbeing.* Retrieved December 31, 2021, from https://www.imf.org/external/pubs/ft/fandd/2021/12/pdf/fd1221.pdf

Jia, R., Ayling, K., Chalde, T., Broadbent, E., Coupland, C., & Vedhara, K. (2020). Mental health in the UK during the COVID-19 pandemic: Cross-sectional analyses from a community cohort study. *British Medical Journal Open, 10*, e040620. https://doi.org/10.1136/bmjopen-2020-040620

Johnson, B. (2020). *Prime Minister's statement on coronavirus (COVID-19).* Gov. UK. Retrieved November 04, 2020, from https://www.gov.uk/government/speeches/pm-statement-at-coronavirus-press-conference-3-march-2020

Katz, I., Weintraub, R., Bekker, L.-G., & Brandt, A. M. (2021, April 8). From vaccine nationalism to vaccine equity—Finding a path forward. *New England Journal of Medicine, 384*(14), 1281–1283. Retrieved December 29, 2021, from https://www.nejm.org/doi/full/10.1056/NEJMp2103614

Khanna, R. (2022). *Dignity in a digital age: Making tech work for all of us.* Simon & Schuster.

Kinnunen, A., & Gustafsson, A.-K. (2021, April 6). *Relative calm on the industrial action front in 2020.* Eurofound. Retrieved September 18, 2021, from https://www.eurofound.europa.eu/publications/article/2021/relative-calm-on-the-industrial-action-front-in-2020

Kovaceic, R. (2021, February 21). *World Bank Blog: Mental health: Lessons learned in 2020 for 2021 and forward.* Retrieved March 29, 2021, from https://blogs.worldbank.org/health/mental-health-lessons-learned-2020-2021-and-forward

Landler, M., & Mueller, B. (2020, October 6). In U.K.'s test and trace: Now you see'em, now you don't. *The New York Times.* Retrieved October 12, 2020, from https://www.nytimes.com/2020/10/05/world/europe/uk-testing-johnson-hancock.html

Legal and General. (2020, May 26). *10 million Brits volunteering as the nation unites in the Isolation Economy, says Legal & General.* Retrieved September 20, 2021, from https://group.legalandgeneral.com/en/newsroom/press-releases/10-million-brits-volunteering-as-the-nation-unites-in-the-isolation-economy-says-legal-general

Leon, C. A., & Elk, M. (2021, July 13). *The Bureau of Labor Statistics counted only eight strikes in 2020, payday report counted 1,200.* Institute for New Economic Thinking. Retrieved September 21, 2021, from https://www.ineteconomics.org/perspectives/blog/the-bureau-of-labor-statistics-counted-only-eight-strikes-in-2020-payday-report-counted-1-200

Levy, R. B., Kuretzky, B., & Vassos, G. (2021, July 14). *Ontario, Canada arbitrator upholds employer's compulsory rapid COVID-19 testing policy.* Littler. Retrieved September 12, 2021, from https://www.littler.com/publication-press/publication/ontario-canada-arbitrator-upholds-employers-compulsory-rapid-covid-19

Liguori, G. (2015). *Gramsci's pathways* (D. Broder, Trans.). Haymarket Books.

London School of Economics and Political Science. (2020). *Mutual aid groups and community responses to COVID-19.* Centre for Analysis of Social Exclusion. Retrieved November 11, 2020, from https://sticerd.lse.ac.uk/lsehousing/research/Mutual-Aid-Groups/

Malmo Symphony Orchestra. (2021, March 12). *Digital concert hall.* Retrieved October 21, 2021, from https://malmolive.se/en/digitalconcerthall

Mao, G., Fernandes-Jesus, M., Ntonis, E., & Drury, J. (2021, July 28). What have we learned about COVID-19 volunteering in the UK? A rapid review of the literature. *BMC Public Health, 21,* 1470. https://doi.org/10.1186/s12889-021-11390-8

Marchi, N. C., Fara, L., Gross, L., Ornell, F., Diehl, A., & Kessler, F. H. (2021). Problematic consumption of online pornography during the COVID-19 pandemic: Clinical recommendations. *Trends in Psychiatry and Psychotherapy.* Retrieved from https://www.scielo.br/j/trends/a/Fn3x7HcQYX5XWkcJjhzpQWD/abstract/?lang=en

Marx, K. (1970). *Economic and philosophic manuscripts of 1844* (D. J. Struik, Ed., & M. Milligan, Trans.). Lawrence and Wishart.

Marx, K., & Engels, F. (1970). *The German Ideology* (C. J. Arthur, Ed.) Lawrence and Wishart.

Mayor of London. (2020, September 21). *Mayor's culture fund helping to support 141 grassroots music venues.* Retrieved October 29, 2021, from https://www.london.gov.uk/press-releases/mayoral/mayors-culture-fund-helps-141-grassroots-venues

McCartan, C., Adell, T., Cameron, J., Davidson, G., Knifton, L., McDaid, S., & Mulholland, C. (2021). A scoping review of international policy responses to mental health recovery during the COVID-19 pandemic. *Health Research Policy and Systems, 19*(58), 1–7. https://doi.org/10.1186/s12961-020-00652-3

McCarty, R. (2020). *Opinion: Common sense best medicine against COVID-19.* The Missouri Times. Retrieved October 22, 2020.

Microsoft. (2022, January 18). *Microsoft to acquire Activision Blizzard to bring the joy and community of gaming to everyone, across every device.* Retrieved January 18, 2022, from https://news.microsoft.com/2022/01/18/microsoft-to-acquire-activision-blizzard-to-bring-the-joy-and-community-of-gaming-to-everyone-across-every-device/

Naimul, K. (2020, October 16). *Fashion brands accused of exploiting workers at risk of layoffs.* Reuters. Retrieved October 10, 2021, from https://www.reuters.com/article/us-bangladesh-workers-rights-trfn-idUSKBN27100B

Negreiro, M. (2021). *The rise of digital health technologies during the pandemic.* European Parliamentary Research Service. Retrieved May 20, 2021, from https://www.europarl.europa.eu/RegData/etudes/BRIE/2021/690548/EPRS_BRI(2021)690548_EN.pdf

Ng, K. (2020, October 26). Queues of people wait to leave empty plates in office garden of Tory MP who voted against free school meals. *Independent.* Retrieved November 24, 2020, from https://www.independent.co.uk/news/uk/politics/free-school-meals-conservative-mp-david-amess-empty-plates-protest-b1338075.html

Nhat, M. (2021, May 14). *Artists suffer loss as Covid-19 resurgence prompts show cancellations.* Retrieved October 26, 2021, from https://e.vnexpress.net/news/life/culture/artists-suffer-loss-as-covid-19-resurgence-prompts-show-cancellations-4277960.html

OECD. (2020). *Covid-19 focus on the economy.* OECD.org. Retrieved October 27, 2020, from https://www.oecd.org/coronavirus/en/themes/global-economy

Panchal, N., Kamal, R., Cox, C., & Garfield, R. (2021, February 10). *The implications of COVID-19 for mental health and substance use*. Retrieved April 12, 2021, from https://www.kff.org/coronavirus-covid-19/issue-brief/the-implications-of-covid-19-for-mental-health-and-substance-use/

Paul, K. (2022, January 21). Activision Blizzard employees form first of its kind Game Workers Alliance Union. *The Guardiian*. Retrieved January 22, 2022, from https://www.theguardian.com/technology/2022/jan/21/activision-blizzard-employees-union

Pavone, A. (2021, September 24). *Italy makes Green Pass mandatory for all workers*. Global Workplace Insider. Retrieved October 10, 2021, from https://www.globalworkplaceinsider.com/2021/09/italy-makes-green-pass-mandatory-for-all-workers/

Policy Link. (2020, April). *COVID-19 & race: Principles for a common-sense, street-smart recovery*. Retrieved December 10, 2021, from https://www.policylink.org/sites/default/files/Covid-19-race-compilation_final.pdf

Press, A. N. (2021, December 7). Amazon and Jeff Bezos's worst enemy is Chris Smalls. *Jacobin*. Retrieved December 12, 2021, from 2021 https://www.jacobinmag.com/2021/07/amazon-staten-island-jfk8-chris-smalls-jeff-bezos-union-organizing-working-class

Proto, E., & Quintana-Domeque, C. (2021). COVID-19 and mental health deterioration by ethnicity and gender in the UK. *PLoS One, 1*(16), e0244419. https://doi.org/10.1371/journal.pone.0244419

Public and Commercial Services Union. (2021, August 3). *Strong support for DVLA strike as month-long action underway*. Retrieved September 21, 2021, from https://www.pcs.org.uk/news-events/news/strong-support-dvla-strike-month-long-action-underway

PwC. (2016). *Impact of corruption on Nigeria's economy*. PwC. Retrieved October 21, 2021, from https://www.pwc.com/ng/en/assets/pdf/impact-of-corruption-on-nigerias-economy.pdf

Rajkumar, R. P. (2020, August). COVID-19 and mental health: A review of the existing literature. *Asian Journal of Psychiatry, 52*, 102066. https://doi.org/10.1016/j.ajp.2020.102066

Raman, R. S., & Ensafi, R. (2020). *Censored planet: An internet-wide, longitudinal censorship observatory*. University of Michigan. Retrieved November 30, 2021, from https://censoredplanet.org/censoredplanet

Rice, S. M., Graber, E., & Kou, A. S. (2020, November). A pandemic of dysmorphia: "Zooming" into the perception of our appearance. *Facial Plastic Surgery & Aesthetic Medicine, 22*(6). https://doi.org/10.1089/fpsam.2020.0454

Rights of Women. (2021, January 11). *Rights of women survey reveals online sexual harassment has increased, as women continue to suffer sexual harassment whilst working through the Covid-19 pandemic.* Retrieved January 5, 2021, from https://rightsofwomen.org.uk/news/rights-of-women-survey-reveals-online-sexual-harassment-has-increased-as-women-continue-to-suffer-sexual-harassment-whilst-working-through-the-covid-19-pandemic/#survey-exposes-an-upsurge-in-online-sexual-harassme

Roberts, M. (2022, January 1). *Michael Roberts' Blog: Forecast for 2022.* Retrieved January 2, 2022, from https://thenextrecession.wordpress.com/2022/01/01/forecast-for-2022/

Romer, D., & Jamieson, K. (2020). Conspiracy theories as barriers to controlling the spread of COVID-19 in the US. *Social Science & Medicine, 263,* 113356. Retrieved November 18, 2020, from https://doi.org/10.1016/j.socscimed.2020.113356

Sanchez-Paramo, C., Hill, R., Mahler, D. G., Narayan, A., & Yonzan, N. (2021, October 7). *COVID-19 leaves a legacy of rising poverty and widening inequality.* World Bank Blogs. Retrieved December 29, 2021, from https://blogs.worldbank.org/developmenttalk/covid-19-leaves-legacy-rising-poverty-and-widening-inequality

Savitch-Lew, A., Dvorkin, E., & Gallagher, L. (2020). *Art in the time of Coronavirus: NYC's small arts organizations fighting for survival.* Center of an Urban Future. Retrieved October 21, 2021, from https://nycfuture.org/research/art-in-the-time-of-coronavirus

Shirkhoda, R. (2021, September 13). *Zoom cares: Supporting mental health & global connection.* Zoom COMPANY NEWS, ZOOMTOPIA. Retrieved September 30, 2021, from https://blog.zoom.us/zoom-cares-mental-health-grants/

Silence, C., Rice, S. M., Pollock, S., Lubov, J. E., Oyesiku, L. O., Ganeshram, S., Mendez, A., Feeney, F., & Kourosh, A. S. (2021, December). Life after lockdown: Zooming out on perceptions in the post-videoconferencing era. *International Journal of Women's Dermatology, 7*(5), 774–779. https://doi.org/10.1016/j.ijwd.2021.08.009

Sitrin, M., & Sembrar, C. (Eds.). (2020). *Pandemic solidarity.* Pluto Press.

Statista. (2020). *Software.* Retrieved October 23, 2021, from https://www.statista.com/markets/418/topic/484/software/#statistic4

Statista. (2021, November 23). *Personal computer (PC) vendor shipment share worldwide from 2011 to 2021, by quarter.* Retrieved December 10, 2021, from https://www.statista.com/statistics/269703/global-market-share-held-by-pc-vendors-since-the-1st-quarter-2009/

Statista Research Department. (2020, September 14). *Number of fake or distorted statements on COVID-19 made by Brazilian president Jair Bolsonaro from January to August 2020, by month.* Retrieved November 19, 2020, from https://www.statista.com/statistics/1118867/bolsonaro-fake-statements-coronavirus/

Terkel, S. (2005). *Hard times: An oral history of the great depression.* New Press.

The China Daily. (2020, March 23). *Chinese software company founded to develop domestic operating system.* Retrieved October 16, 2021, from http://www.chinadaily.com.cn/a/202003/23/WS5e78273aa310128217281382.html

The Conversation. (2020). *Three major scientific controversies about coronavirus.* Retrieved November 10, 2020, from https://theconversation.com/three-major-scientific-controversies-about-coronavirus-144021

The Conversation. (2022, January 7). *New data shows COVID will continue to have a negative financial impact on many UK households.* Retrieved January 14, 2022, from https://theconversation.com/new-data-shows-covid-will-continue-to-have-a-negative-financial-impact-on-many-uk-households-174214

The Tribune News Service. (2022, January 12). *Economic momentum must continue: PM at Covid review with states, rules out lockdown.* Retrieved January 15, 2022, from https://www.tribuneindia.com/news/nation/pm-modi-holds-virtual-meeting-with-cms-amid-covid-surge-360957

Torry, H., & Harrison, D. (2021, December 27). *Omicron variant is expected to dent global economy in early 2022.* The Wall Street Journal. Retrieved December 28, 2021, from https://www.wsj.com/articles/omicron-variant-is-expected-to-dent-global-economy-in-early-2022-11640631554

Tracy, S. J. (2010). Qualitative quality: Eight "big-tent" criteria for excellent qualitative research. *Qualitative Enquiry, 16*(10), 837–851.

UNESCO. (2021). *Cultural and creative industries in the face of COVID-19: An economic impact outloo.* UNESCO. Retrieved October 25, 2021, from https://unesdoc.unesco.org/ark:/48223/pf0000377863

United Nations Environment Programme. (2021). *Greening the Blue Report 2021 The UN system's environmental footprint and efforts to reduce it.* UNEP. Retrieved December 28, 2021, from https://www.greeningtheblue.org/reports/greening-blue-report-2021

Varghese, S. (2021, December 08). *After a year-long strike, Indian farmers score a big win.* Retrieved December 09, 2021, from https://inequality.org/research/indian-farmers-victory/

WHO. (2018*). Climate change and health.* World Health Organisation. Retrieved October 28, 2020, from https://www.who.int/news-room/fact-she ets/detail/climate-change-and-health

WHO. (2020). *Nantes Entraide—Citizen mutual aid project.* Retrieved November 11, 2020, from https://www.who.int/news-room/feature-stories/ detail/nantes-entraide-citizen-mutual-aid-project

WHO. (2021, May 21). *World Health Assembly recommends reinforcement of measures to protect mental health during public health emergencies.* Retrieved June 10, 2021, from https://www.who.int/news/item/31-05-2021-world-health-assembly-recommends-reinforcement-of-measures-to-protect-mental-

WHO. (2022a, February). *Coronavirus disease (COVID-19) pandemic.* Retrieved December 28, 2021, from https://covid19.who.int/

WHO. (2022b). *World Health Organisation Global.* Retrieved January 14, 2022b, from https://covid19.who.int/region/amro/country/us

World Bank. (2021). *The World Bank group's response to the COVID-19 (coronavirus) pandemic.* Retrieved December 29, 2021, from https://www.worldb ank.org/en/who-we-are/news/coronavirus-covid19

World Health Organisation. (2020, October 17). *Public health services.* Retrieved from https://www.euro.who.int/en/health-topics/Health-systems/ public-health-services

World Healh Organisation. (2021, December 31). *WHO Coronavirus (COVID-19) dashboard.* Retrieved Decemer 31, 2021, from https://covid19.who.int/ table

Wright, E. O. (2009). Understanding class: Towards an integrated analytical approach. *New Left Review, 60*, 101–116.

Yuill, C. (2018). Social workers and alienation: The compassionate self and the disappointed juggler. *Critical and Radical Social Work, 6*(3), 275–289.

Zamboni, L., Carli, S., Marika Belleri, B., Giordano, R., Giulia , S., & Lugobo, F. (2021). COVID-19 lockdown: Impact on online gambling, online shopping, web navigation and online pornography. *Journal of Public Health Research, 10*(1). Retrieved from https://www.ncbi.nlm.nih.gov/pmc/articles/ PMC7893314

Index

Printed by Printforce, the Netherlands